Praise for

Such a Pretty Fat

. . . .

"Screamingly funny—I lost ten pounds just from laughing! Jen Lancaster says everything you wish you could but wouldn't dare. Exhilarating!"   —Beth Harbison, author of *Shoe Addicts Anonymous* and *Secrets of a Shoe Addict*

"Lancaster has tackled body image, health, and weight loss with honesty, humor, and a sharp sense of self-awareness that has become her hallmark. For anyone who has ever choked down a teensy portion of flavorless prepackaged food in joyless despair . . . Jen has been there, and is here to show the silly side and the empowering. You will cheer for her successes, commiserate with her setbacks, and split your sides laughing at both. Whether you cozy up to this book with a bowl of air-popped corn and a diet Coke, or a box of Oreos and a vanilla shake, one thing is certain: It is a delicious and guilt-free delight from start to finish."   —Stacey Ballis, author of *Room for Improvement* and *The Spinster Sisters*

"A surprisingly charming weight-loss odyssey. . . . Anyone struggling with weight issues while trying to maintain a sense of humor will find much inspiration, and plenty of laughs."   —*Publishers Weekly*

"Lancaster reminds us to laugh during laps and while counting food points on the way to a healthier size and lifestyle."
—*Chicago Sun-Times*

continued...

"Jen Lancaster may be one of the few authors around capable of writing her own sitcom; she's smart, wry, and never afraid to point out her own shortcomings while letting us into her uniquely funny world."

—Melanie Lynne Hauser, author of *Super Mom Saves the World*

"Jen Lancaster is the Holy Trinity of funny."

—Nicole Del Sesto, author of *All Encompassing Trip*

"After reading *Bright Lights, Big Ass*, I'm convinced Jen Lancaster is the illegitimate love child of Nora Ephron and David Sedaris. She's simply that great—a genetic hybrid of two of America's most-loved writers. In *Bright Lights, Big Ass*, Jen Lancaster gives the proverbial finger to the Carrie Bradshaw lifestyle, trading Barneys, Manolo Blahnik, and Bergdorf for her very own shopping Holy Trinity: Target, Trader Joe's, and Ikea; allowing women everywhere to rejoice in their sixty-dollar Isaac Mizrahi Target coats."

—Robert Rave, author of *Conversations & Cosmopolitans: How to Give Your Mother a Hangover*

"Jen Lancaster is like David Sedaris with pearls and a supercute handbag." —Jennifer Coburn, author of *The Queen Gene*

"Part *Seinfeld*, part antidote to *Sex and the City*, *Bright Lights, Big Ass* is the must-read for anyone who has ever suffered through a regretfully torturous workout with her trainer, a run-in with irrational, perhaps psychotic neighbors, a long-winded, insipid telemarketer, or the black hole known as Ikea. (And really, isn't this everyone?) Nothing and no one is spared from Jen Lancaster's acerbically sharp wit, as she gives voice to all of the things we wish we could say but don't. I defy you not to laugh out loud on nearly every page. Someone give this girl her own show already! *That* would be must-see TV."

—Allison Winn Scotch, author of *The Department of Lost and Found*

Praise for

Bitter Is the New Black

. . . .

"The woman is nothing if not spunky, and she does have her funny moments, particularly when sticking it to The Man."

—*The Washington Post*

"Carrie Bradshaw meets Barbara Ehrenreich in this memoir about white-collar unemployment after the dot-com bubble burst."

—*Kirkus Reviews*

"She's bitchy and sometimes plain old mean, but she's absolutely hilarious."　　　　　　　　　　　　　　　　—*Chicago Sun-Times*

"Jen Lancaster's confessions should be mandatory reading for the absurdly salaried young smart-arses around town…An honest, insightful, and ultimately feel-good handbook for what to do when ruin beckons."

—Deborah Hope of *The Australian*

"A classic story of comeuppance, written from real-life experience by the funniest new author from the blogosphere. A strong debut and a must-read for any American princess."

—Jessica Cutler, author of *The Washingtonienne*

Such a Pretty Fat

One Narcissist's Quest to Discover
If Her Life Makes Her Ass Look Big,

or

Why Pie Is Not the Answer

Jen Lancaster

NEW AMERICAN LIBRARY

New American Library
Published by New American Library,
a division of Penguin Group (USA) Inc.,
375 Hudson Street, New York, New York 10014, USA
Penguin Group (Canada), 90 Eglinton Avenue East, Suite 700, Toronto,
Ontario M4P 2Y3, Canada (a division of Pearson Penguin Canada Inc.)
Penguin Books Ltd., 80 Strand, London WC2R 0RL, England
Penguin Ireland, 25 St. Stephen's Green, Dublin 2,
Ireland (a division of Penguin Books Ltd.)
Penguin Group (Australia), 250 Camberwell Road, Camberwell, Victoria 3124,
Australia (a division of Pearson Australia Group Pty. Ltd.)
Penguin Books India Pvt. Ltd., 11 Community Centre,
Panchsheel Park, New Delhi–110 017, India
Penguin Group (NZ), 67 Apollo Drive, Rosedale, North Shore 0632,
New Zealand (a division of Pearson New Zealand Ltd.)
Penguin Books (South Africa) (Pty.) Ltd., 24 Sturdee Avenue,
Rosebank, Johannesburg 2196, South Africa

Penguin Books Ltd., Registered Offices:
80 Strand, London WC2R 0RL, England

First published by New American Library,
a division of Penguin Group (USA) Inc.

First Printing, May 2008
9 10 8

LIBRARY OF CONGRESS CATALOGING-IN-PUBLICATION DATA
Lancaster, Jen, 1967–
Such a pretty fat : one narcissist's quest to discover if her life makes her ass look big,
or why pie is not the answer / Jen Lancaster.
p. cm.
ISBN: 978-0-451-22389-0
1. Lancaster, Jen, 1967– 2. Authors, American—21st century—Biography. I. Title.
PS3612.A54748Z46 2008
813'.6—dc22
[B]   2007049710

Set in Bulmer MT • Designed by Elke Sigal

Printed in the United States of America

For Jennifer Coburn,
the queen (gene) of the good idea.

For Barbie, who opened the door
and shoved me through it.

And for everyone who
ever lived with a person on a diet . . .
I am deeply sorry.

C·O·N·T·E·N·T·S

C·O·N·T·E·N·T·S

*T*his is the true story of a fat, mean girl on a diet. For the sole purpose of relating this story, I had to compress a few time lines and alter some names and characteristics. But in case you're wondering, yes, I was that fat, I was that mean, and I did eat that much cheese. (And I thank you for not mentioning it.)

Nothing tastes as good as being thin feels.

—A Weight Watchers axiom

. . . .

Weight Watchers can kiss the fattest part of my ass.

—A Jen Lancaster axiom

Such a Pretty Fat

P·R·O·L·O·G·U·E

TO: jen@jenlancaster.com
FROM: jennifer_coburn@home
SUBJECT: Bright Lights, Big Ass Idea

Dear Jen,

After having just finished writing my fifth novel, I'm fresh out of ideas, but I have one for you.

I don't know if you've ever dieted before, but I have and I'm pissed off—a lot, especially when I see the size zero Desperate Housewives inhaling ice cream or when I see Dove fat ass cream saying, hey, it's okay to have a fat ass (but still buy the fat ass cream, please). When Paris Hilton washed that car eating a Carl's Jr. burger, I wanted to shove the hose down that skinny bitch's throat and turn the pressure on full blast.

Every dieting story out there is so damned upbeat and inspiring, but the reality is that when we're losing weight, we're not in the mood for all the smiley-faced gurus telling us how easy it is. No, we need YOU chronicling your journey and making people laugh at your witty observations about our culture, weight, dieting, and skinny whores in magazines. That's my pitch. Love it, hate it, or indifferent, it's all fine with me.

What do you think?

Jen Coburn

P.S. Anyone who says nothing tastes as good as being thin feels has obviously never had Korean barbecue.

TO: jennifer_coburn@home
FROM: jen@jenlancaster.com
SUBJECT: RE: Bright Lights, Big Ass Idea

Hey, JC,

What's shakin'? It's great to hear from you! Workwise, I'm fooling around with fiction that I can't quite call young adult because my protagonist is in college. (I'm hoping to appeal to the *Veronica Mars* generation.)

I love the idea of a weight-loss memoir . . . especially the bit with Paris and the hose. However, despite my best efforts, I keep losing (and then finding) the same damn five pounds. My most recent drop came from when I got food poisoning and I'm still counting it as a win. But I'd probably have to start really losing weight for real before I could chronicle it, don't you think?

'Til then, I'm probably stuck with my knockoff *Veronica Mars*.

Sigh,

Jen

Dear Dean Wormer,

In *Animal House*, you told Bluto that fat, drunk, and stupid was no way to go through life.

I beg to differ. Fat, drunk, and stupid is a perfectly fine way to go through life. . . . After all, it's worked out nicely for me.

Best,

Jen Lancaster

Like I Haven't Heard That Before

"Today on the bus a guy called me a fat bitch."

I'm standing in the kitchen folding a softened stick of butter, a cup of warmed sour cream, and a mound of fresh-shaved Parmesan into my world-famous mashed potatoes while I recount my day's activities to Fletch. There's a maple-glazed pork roast browning nicely in the oven and white-chocolate-chip macadamia cookies cooling on a rack farther down the counter. I've already sautéed the almonds and am waiting for the green beans to blanch so I can toss the whole lot with yet more butter[1] before serving the meal.

"That sucks," he sympathetically replies. "What happened?"

"Well, I waited on the corner for a cab for, like, twenty

---

[1] I'm about a tablespoon of heavy cream away from having the National Dairy Council sponsor our dinner.

minutes, and none came, so I jumped on the Western Avenue bus to take it to the Blue Line." I stir the potatoes before sampling them. "Hmm. Do these need more horseradish? Taste." I attempt to walk over to Fletch, but our dogs, Maisy and Loki, attracted by all the delicious smells wafting from the kitchen, have firmly stationed their combined 165 pounds of bulk directly in my path. "Move!" I bark. They back up about an inch and plant themselves again. They know very well that in fifteen minutes I'll be feeding them bites of pork roast off my fork and thus are going nowhere.

I continue, "A couple of stops after I got on, this hippie girl boards with a stroller, and the first thing I think is, 'Oh, honey, you *are* a baby; you can't *have* a baby.'[2] Anyway, instead of standing in the area meant for strollers up front, she moves toward me. I get up—ostensibly so she can take my seat—walk to the very back, and sit down." I taste the potatoes again. "You know what these need? Wine."

"Wine?"

"Yes. I mean, in a glass. For me to drink. Pour me some? I can't get around these idiots." I gesture at the dogs, and they both leap up to snap at the butter dripping from the wooden spoon. I'd say these are the most lazy, self-indulgent creatures on the planet, but that would discount my rotten cats, who keep hopping onto the counter and trying to grab the spoon with their paws. Listen up, creatures: If anyone's licking this butter, it's going to be *me*.

Fletch grabs some of Trader Joe's finest five-dollar Pinot

---

[2] Also, a patchwork vest? No.

Grigio for me and a bottle of water for himself. He pauses before selecting a glass from the cabinet over the coffeemaker. Every shelf is packed with flutes, tulips, goblets, martini glasses, and rocks tumblers. We've got the proper vessels for ports and sherries and Rhine wines and cognac. You can have a beer in amounts varying from eight to thirty-two ounces in pilsners or pints. Some glasses have obscenely long stems, some have no stems at all, and some have delicate flowers etched in thin crystal.

The thing is, they're completely unnecessary. We have something like three friends who will brave our dogs' enthusiastic expressions of affection. Sure, it's funny to *hear* stories about how our pit bull, Maisy the Love Monster, can leap four feet in an attempt to kiss visitors, only to split lips and blacken eyes, but it's less charming when it's *your* head that's bleeding. Our shepherd, Loki, stands more than five feet tall on his talon-tipped hind legs and has a penchant for salad tossing,[3] so his greetings are less than desirable, too. And, since only two of the three people still willing to enter our home actually drink, our stash of beverage containers is a tad overwhelming. I have no idea where they all came from and am equally dismayed that despite intentional carelessness, none ever seem to break. I can't bring myself to get rid of perfectly good stemware, so we live with them hogging up an entire set of cabinets.[4]

....

[3]Please consult UrbanDictionary.com if you don't know what this means; I'm not explaining it.

[4]What would I like for Christmas? How about something to put *in* our 726 glasses?

Daunted by the lot of them on display, Fletch finally chooses one of our fifteen multipurpose models and pours me a healthy belt of white wine. "Here you go."

"Thanks!" I take a quick sip to wet my throat. "So, I'm just about to get off at the Armitage stop and I see the hippie chick making her way to the front after shoving her kid's stroller in the area by the back exit. I keep my eye on said stroller because who the hell walks away from her baby on a crowded bus? I mean, we're in Chicago; yeah, it's relatively safe, but not let-a-stranger-watch-your-most-precious-cargo safe. Then this guy comes up and stands next to the stroller, and I get nervous because the mom's not even looking back at us. I mean, who is this guy? Is he going to abduct the kid? And why the fuck is he wearing a straw fedora, especially with his stupid beard? My first thought when I saw him was, *Hey! It's Panama Jackass!*"

After being removed from the counter 926 times, my cat Bones hops up for the 927th. I place him back on the ground and continue. "So I freak out because I'm concerned for the baby's safety, and suddenly I'm the bus's reluctantly appointed air marshal. Should I throw myself in front of the door if the guy tries to touch the kid? Yell for the driver? Steal his retarded hat? The thing is, if I get involved in an attempted kidnapping, I'm not going to make my one o'clock hair-color appointment with Dante, so what do I do?"

Fletch nods sagely. "That's quite the moral dilemma. Save a child or get your roots done. I hear Mother Teresa struggled with similar issues."

I wave him off. She wore that towel on her head all the

time. No one even cared about her hair. "Turns out everything was fine. The mother started having a conversation with him, and I realized they were together." I pause to take another sip of my wine. Mmm; cool, crisp, and five dollars' worth of delicious!

"Crisis averted?" He absently scratches Loki under the chin and is rewarded with a handful of dog drool.

"Yes, or so I thought. When we got to Armitage, I had to get off, and the dad and his kid were in my way, so I'm all, *'Excuse me; this is my stop.'* Dad turns to me, and I see he's really young, too. I didn't realize it at first because I was so focused on his extraneous facial accessories. Looking closer, I saw he was all disheveled and his eyes were sunken and hollow. Total newborn-sleep-deprivation syndrome. Then he says, *'Why don't you exit up front?'"*

Fletch gives his hands a quick predinner scrub and dries them on a dish towel. "Yeah, why didn't you?"

"Couldn't—the aisle was too crowded." I desperately hate having to squeeze through. Makes me feel like I'm stepping on people and sticking my butt in their faces as I try to ease out, and really? No one wants that. "So I'm looking at the dad, taking in how tired he seems. It was raining out, and I felt bad that these parents had to take their baby wherever they were going on a bus. They were visibly exhausted, and if they had their child out in this weather, it was probably because he was sick and they were going to the doctor. Plus it was cold and neither of the parents had on coats, so I was sympathetic." I've already drained my glass, so I shake it at Fletch in a *more, please* gesture, and he dutifully complies.

He's like my sous chef, only for liquor. "And yet this hair"—I point to my newly streaked locks—"is not going to blond itself, so I had to get off, right? As I tried to exit again, the dad scowled at me, not moving an inch, and that made me mad."

"Don't make me angry. You wouldn't like me when I'm angry," Fletch says in his best David Banner impression. "Is that when you turned green and exploded out of your clothes?"

I throw my hands up in the air. "Listen, did I *not* just save his baby from being kidnapped? I mean, can I get a little credit here for having an entire plan of attack mapped out? I was about to be a goddamned *hero*."

I see a smirk playing at the sides of Fletch's mouth. "Your *plan of attack* entailed what? Filing your nails? Yelling for the bus driver? Eating a candy bar?"

"*No*. First, I'd snatch the kid back with a bunch of lightning-fast Sydney Bristow roundhouse kicks to his head—which would really hurt with my pointy boots, by the way—and once the baby was safe, I'd chase him down and go all MacGyver on his ass, handcuffing him with only my purse straps and knockoff Chanel sunglasses."

Fletch looks dubious. "Considering you'd rather watch infomercials for an hour than cross the room to get the remote, I have a hard time reconciling your action-packed *Alias* fight scene with reality."

I wave a potato-covered wooden spoon at him. "Oh, please. With the adrenaline in my system, I could have totally done it. People can lift cars off their kids when they need to."

"Not lazy people," he counters.

Aarrggh. I'm not lazy. I'm simply judicious about excess movement.

"You're missing my point!" I exclaim. "The point is, I almost got *involved*, and I hate that, so how about a little fucking gratitude on his part?"

"You're mad at the guy for not reading your mind?" he asks.

"Do you want to argue with me or do you want to hear my story?"

"Have I got a choice?"

I choose to ignore his snarky commentary. "*Anyway*, I *did* give up my seat for the mom, even if she chose not to take it, so it seemed like the guy should have been polite when I tried to exit. Again, I said, '*Excuse me. This is my stop,*' to which he replied, '*Hey, man. There's a baby here. Why don't you think about someone other than yourself?*'"

After twelve years, Fletch is well aware of what will turn me into the Jencredible Hulk. He shakes his head and simply says, "That poor bastard," and then removes his glasses to wipe off the potato specks that hit him when I gestured a bit too hard with the wooden spoon.[5]

"Listen, I was sorry he and his little lady didn't have access to a car to take their kid to the doctor. And I felt bad I was all bundled up in a toasty warm trench coat and sweater, while they both shivered in thin shirts and stupid vests. But

[5] When Fletch smiles, the crinkles around his eyes make him look like Ed Norton. But with his hipster horn-rim glasses on, he's a ringer for Tom Arnold. (It's weird.)

the bottom line is, a baby doesn't give you license to do whatever you want. Newborn or not, you cannot block my exit. I took all these factors into account, and then I smiled at him, and in the most compassionate voice I could muster, I leaned in close and said, *'Bite me.'* Dumbfounded, he stepped back and let me pass." I bang my glass down on the counter for emphasis, and it weathers the impact heroically, damn it.

"Let me guess—this is when he called you a fat bitch?"

"Exactly! But that's not the end of the story."

"You called me out of a lunch meeting at work last week when Bob Barker announced his retirement,[6] so I assume the guy didn't punch you or I'd have seen you both on the news."

"Nope. But as soon as he called me a fat bitch, I snickered and replied, *'Yeah. Like I haven't heard* that *before.'* Then I stuck my tongue out at him and climbed down the stairs." I open the oven and remove the world's most gorgeous pork roast. The maple syrup will make it delectably sweet, while the Dijon mustard in the glaze will give it a savory bite. According to the meat thermometer, it's now exactly 170 degrees. I turn off the oven and tent the roasting pan with aluminum foil so the juices redistribute themselves. "Dinner in ten. And I'll need a refill." I pass my glass over the head of two slobbery dogs.

"What's the magic word?"

"Um . . . now?"

---

[6]His last day was June 15, 2007, and no one ever acknowledged my proposal to make his final show a national day of mourning.

"Nice try."

"Pretty please with pork roast on top?"

"Better. Somewhat." He fills the glass again and comes over to put his arm around me, causing the dogs to temporarily scramble before reassembling themselves right next to me. "Listen, Jen; I'm sorry if he hurt your feelings. You know you're fine just the way you are, even if you are deeply, profoundly bossy." Fletch then kisses me on the forehead before opening the cabinet under the coffeemaker to grab placemats and napkins.[7]

I unload plain white crockery plates from the dishwasher and use them to set the table. "Sweetie, that's the problem! He *didn't* hurt my feelings. The issue here is that I've been called 'fat bitch' so many times that I'm totally desensitized to it. I *should* have been bothered. I *should* have wanted to kick a lung out of that guy. Instead, I was simply amused, and that feels wrong somehow. I suspect it's a self-esteem thing."

Fletch snorts. "Right. You're a raging narcissist. Sometimes I hear you saying '*I look pretty*' in the mirror when you think I'm downstairs. Your self-image? Hardly a problem."

"You think you're telling me something I don't know? My self-esteem is so out of proportion, I'm no longer in touch with reality. I mean, I'm a size twenty-four. I'm the poster child for rampant you-have-such-a-pretty-face-isms. No matter how you slice it, I'm fat. Not husky, not Rubenesque, not

---

[7]Retrieving these items is his job because I kind of don't like to bend. I also refuse to carry anything heavier than my purse.

big boned, but fat. Porcine. Beefy. *C-h-u-n-k-y*. Shoot, I'm about two sizes away from not being able to shop in the big-girls section of the department store,[8] and yet I'm like an anorexic."

"If you're anorexic, you're doing it wrong."

I swat him with a dish towel. "No, no, I mean anorexics look in the mirror, and even if they're eighty pounds, their organs are failing, and they're on life support, they still see a fat girl. I'm a hundred pounds heavier than I was in high school, my veins are full of crème fraîche, and yet I look in the mirror, take in the hair and makeup, and think, *Damn baby, you fiiine.*"

Fletch nods, saying nothing.

"Seriously, check out my face. I have almost no wrinkles, even though I routinely tan myself into shoe leather. The fat totally fills them out. That's why I don't have those gross neck cords yet, either."

"If you're *fiiine*, then what's the problem?"

"I'm almost out of my thirties. I always thought I'd have my shit together by now; I'd be thin, I'd be out of debt, I'd be nice out of habit and not just when I wanted something, and maybe I'd own a home. Yet here I am hurtling toward the big four-oh in an overpriced rental with student loans and a paltry savings account, and when someone calls me a fat bitch, I

[8]FYI, the more upscale the store, the harder it is to locate the "women's" department. At Wal-Mart, they call it "Women's Plus" and hang a giant sign over the section right up by the front doors. At Saks, they call it "Salon Z" and hide it up three escalators and behind the human resources department.

simply accept it as fact. Right now, I can live with being a renter, I can live with being broke and fat, and I can live with being a bitch, but the minute you add 'middle-aged' to the equation, I'm afraid my world is going to collapse on itself like a dying star."

Fletch shakes the wine bottle at me, and I hold out my glass. He quickly refills and says, "As for buying a home and paying off debt, we're working on it. It would be easier if we moved to the suburbs—"

"The land of strip malls and minivans? Soccer moms and church socials?" I interrupt. "Right. If we moved to say, Wheaton, we'd need to buy a home with a basement or an attic."

"Why?"

"So I could hang myself from the rafters. I live in the city. Period. We're not having this discussion again."

Our city-versus-suburb debate has been raging for the past year. Financially, a move twenty miles west makes a great deal of sense, but the thought of it makes my heart cry. At this point, I'd much rather deal with the occasional drug transaction in front of my house than waste away in Wheaton, mingling exclusively with the Illinois version of the Stepford Wives.

Fletch continues, "Even without a move, we're worlds away from where we were when we were both unemployed, so don't give me the 'broke' business, because it's not true. Are we having pork roast tonight and not plain spaghetti with salt like that one time? Yes. Do you have to work temp jobs anymore? No. Did you not just deposit a healthy royalty check you earned from your first book? Yes."

I shrug. We had so little money for so long that sometimes I forget we aren't destitute anymore, even though we worked damn hard to get back to this point. He continues, "You want change? Lose the bitch. Be nicer to people. Stop telling them to 'bite you' and threatening to kick them until they're dead." Fletch gets up to turn off the overhead lamp and lights a couple of candles on the table.

I consider what he's said while plating up our dinner, but I get distracted by what I'm serving. The potatoes are so full of butter, they're actually yellow, and the beans glisten in the flickering candlelight. I slice the golden pork into mouth-watering slabs, trimming off two of the most egregious chunks of fat and tossing them to the dogs. Then I dice up four smaller bits for all the cats. They all wolf down their pork and immediately clamor for more.

"I'm afraid it's not that easy. I've had this mean-girl thing since birth. The fat's a fairly recent occurrence. Maybe it would be easier to fix that?" I grab my own dish and sit, ignoring my chair's creaking protest.

Fletch looks thoughtful for a moment. "Losing weight would be healthier, and even though you balk now, you'd be happier if you shed a few pounds."

"You think?" I take a bite of my meat, and tiny flavor fireworks explode in my mouth. . . . It's magically pork-tastic!

"I do. And I'd help you."

"Hmm. Would you maybe offer me a system of rewards, like ten pounds equals a free facial or something? I don't follow through well unless there's a treat involved."

"If bribery motivates you, sure." He reaches across the table to pat my hand.

"What about fifty pounds—would you, say, take me to Las Vegas?"

"That would be cause to celebrate, so, yeah, I'd take you to Vegas."

I chew thoughtfully for a minute before putting down my fork. "Okay. I guess I could give it a try. But only because I really want to see Steve Wynn's new hotel and not because I *have* to. Because I?"—I wave my hands down the length of my body, much like Barker's Beauties do when demonstrating a fabulous hi-fi—"am *fiiine.*"

"You'll try?" Fletch asks. "Well, good for you for recognizing change is possible." He raises his water bottle and clinks it against my glass, chipping the rim, which I take as a positive sign from God. Or possibly Crate and Barrel.

"Yes, sir, I'm going to do it. Although if I drop fifty pounds, maybe I should go somewhere more exciting than Vegas, like Italy or somewhere. I guess I can decide later. Regardless, I'm doing this." I take a bite of my transcendent mashed potatoes and glance over at the cookies waiting on the counter. "I am so totally going to do it." I take another bite of my pork roast. "Starting tomorrow."

Dear Ben & Jerry's,

Just so you know, a pint of Chunky Monkey *is* considered one serving. Please either adjust your nutritional labels accordingly or create a smaller package.

Best,
Jen Lancaster

CHAPTER TWO

Pack Your Knives and Go, Mom

My friend Stacey is over for our regular Wednesday night Bravo-viewing party. Currently we're watching *Top Chef*, but we've previously covered *Project Runway* and *Top Design*. Stacey and I had a rough moment early in our friendship when I told her I'd never seen *Project Runway*. She looked at me as though I'd said I didn't like chocolate and that shopping for shoes was a waste of time. Fortunately, before Stacey became an author she was a teacher, so she happily educated me in the Way of the (Tim) Gunn, hence the beginning of our Wednesday night tradition.[9]

Normally our Wednesday nights are at Stacey's house so we don't disturb Fletch, who's often busy working well into the evening. Apparently it's difficult for him to concentrate on projects when we're squealing over our girl crushes on

[9]Make it work? Indeed I did.

Padma and shrieking every time Marcel ruins a perfectly delicious dish by adding foam.[10] And although our arguments about the relative cuteness of Contestant Sam the Hot Diabetic versus Master Chef Tom Colicchio are logical and articulate, they don't help Fletch get out customer quotes more quickly.[11] However, Fletch worked all weekend and he doesn't have much to finish tonight. Plus, I wanted Stacey to see our pretty new living room set, so the viewing party is here this evening.

Stacey and I are nestled into opposite corners of the new couches in my matchbox-sized living room. I'm especially pleased because they're a nod to the balance we've already found in our lives. Back when we were dot-com thousandaires, I insisted I couldn't be happy unless I got the seventhousand-dollar Italian leather sofa that had been featured at MoMA. Fortunately, Fletch had the good sense to say no, not only because of the cost, but also because the couch was backless and the oddly tufted buttons made it feel like sitting on a bag of rocks.[12] During the following period of extended unemployment, our ratty old couch served as a reminder of exactly how far we'd fallen, and every day I dreamed of being secure enough again to finally get something new.

----

[10]Maybe this makes me a food philistine, but I can't stomach the idea of garnishing a lovely dish with what looks like something that shot out of a cat's mouth.

[11]BTW, the correct answer is Sam the Hot Diabetic because bald is not the new black.

[12]Jen's Life Lesson #324: Aesthetics can't be the only criterion considered when purchasing a couch the price of a used Honda.

Recently I got my first royalty check, so after months of price comparison and discussion, we found a set we loved at the Macy's outlet store. The pieces we finally settled on had been marked down so low, it would have been irresponsible *not* to buy them. After a thorough debate on their merits over a stack of blueberry pancakes,[13] we had to practically fist fight an investment banker and his charming young wife and toddler who'd discovered them when we went to the diner for breakfast. While Fletch explained to the family in no uncertain terms that the pieces were *ours*, I dashed to the cash register and paid for everything. The sale was complete before they were even done taking measurements. Charming Young Wife shot daggers my way when I returned lording my receipt and asking their kid to stop jumping on *my* new sofa. I imagine the term "fat bitch" was bandied about in their Volvo station wagon on the way home, but who cares? That's fat-bitch-with-a-new-discount-couch to you, lady.

I can't tell you how much I love this whole set. The couch, ottoman, and love seat are made from shiny brown Italian leather, but the style is classic with nicely padded arms[14] and chunky cherrywood legs. The pieces are thick enough to withstand dogs jumping on them and cat-claw puncture attacks, and I'd say they're ideal . . . except I didn't realize that when you buy furniture, you have to take length, width, *and* depth into account. This explains what Charming Young

---

[13]And bacon. And hash browns. And possibly a half order of biscuits and gravy.

[14]No more accidental head clunking for me!

Wife was doing with the measuring tape that day at Macy's.
Now to get from the living room to the kitchen, we have to
turn sideways.

Whatever.

It was totally worth it.

Maisy, smelling vaguely of corn chips, has wedged herself against me on the couch, and Loki, refreshed from another round of salad tossing, waits expectantly at Stacey's
feet for a similar invitation that is not forthcoming. He rests
his head on her lap and gazes longingly up at her.[15]

"How's the diet going?" Stacey asks.

Since we met recently, she has no idea of the lithe sorority
girl I once was, dancing to "Cruel Summer" at the Delta Sig
house in my size-seven boy-cut Forenzas. She didn't know
me in high school, either, back when my hip bones stuck out
so far they used to rub white patches in my Gloria Vander-
bilts.

You'd think I'd be in mourning for the shape I once had,
but my life isn't much different than it was when I was slim.
Sure, I have bad days when I wish I could swap my body for
Jessica Alba's, but who doesn't? Shoot; Jessica Alba probably
has a pair of fat jeans in her closet. I'll admit, once in a while
my weight embarrasses me, like when I was the only fat person at the health and fitness fair.[16] And sure, I may have died
a thousand tiny deaths earlier this fall when *Cosmopolitan*

---

[15] The length of that dog's eyelashes should be illegal.

[16] Please see chapter 7 of the best-selling *Bitter Is the New Black* for more details.

UK did a photo shoot to accompany an article I'd sold them *after* I'd just gained twenty more pounds. But due to the magic of airbrushing, the experience was far less traumatic than I expected.[17] Given a choice, I'd rather shop in the juniors' section than the women's, and if I could stop sweating while I eat, that'd be a bonus, but overall I'm still the same me I ever was.

"Not great," I admit. "At this point, I've *decided* to lose weight but haven't actually done anything about it."

"Have you dieted before?" she asks innocently, scratching Loki on his snout. His tail thumps in delight.

Stacey and I met on an authors' panel. Before the event, I'd read some of her books and completely fell in love with her writing. Many of her heroines are plus-sized characters who aren't starving themselves thin or filled with self-doubt and self-loathing. Her books consistently deliver the message that it's OK to be happy with who you are, so I was excited to meet her. After the panel, we bonded over a million commonalities and we discovered we're neighbors, so we've been fast friends ever since. Together, we are Stennifer.[18]

I have to stop snorting with laughter before I give Stacey a straight answer. "Yeah. This ain't exactly my first trip to the ol' diet rodeo. I've been on them hundreds of times, yet I've only had long-term success a few times."

---

[17]What didn't help? When my brother Todd spent five minutes on the phone pretending he was the art director, saying, "*Pssshht!* We're going to need more ink! *Pssshht!* We're going to need more ink!" What *did* help? Offering the art director a dollar per pound erased.

[18]And that dessert cart is *ours*.

Ever the problem solver, Stacey presses on. "OK, so you've proved you can get results. Could you do that again?"

"I don't know. The first diet that comes to mind was after my freshman year of college when I gained a bunch of weight."

Fletch comes out of the den and joins us in conversation. "You know what your problem is? Too much tequilas and popcorns," he says. He's referring to what one doctor told me when I went in for a back spasm at Purdue's student health center. The doctor delivered this statement with a poke in my almost-nonexistent belly, cracking himself up. I didn't find him at all funny, especially given the bulimia affecting half of all the girls I knew on campus.[19]

Fletch sits down next to Stacey on the dog-free couch. "I didn't gain weight because I was boozing. Freshman year, I drank ultragirly stuff like Fuzzy Navels and butterscotch schnapps, and you can only have so many of those before going into diabetic shock." Stacey and Fletch grimace at my candy-coated taste in beverages. "Oh, don't give me those faces. What, like you've never had Amaretto and Dr Pepper?" They both frown. "Pear brandy and pineapple?" Stacey turns up her nose, and Fletch visibly shudders. "Or made a peppermint slushy out of fresh snow and Rumpelminz while sledding down Slater Hill?" They vehemently shake their heads.

Pfft. Their loss.

....

[19]FYI, I responded to him by saying, "Is this how they teach you appropriate bedside manner at the University of Grenada?"

I continue, "The real culprit was my dorm's cafeteria. They served the kind of meals I'd never had at home. You know how people wax on and on about all the wonderful foods their moms make? Not me. My mom has always prided herself on her ability to alter recipes. Nothing makes her happier than cutting out even the most necessary portions of oil and sugar. She was obsessed with cooking healthy years before it ever became trendy. Like, when we were kids, our pancakes weren't all light and fluffy, drenched in butter and syrup. Ours contained lumpy brown flour and handfuls of palate-shredding wheat germ, topped with a thimbleful of Log Cabin maple-flavored syrup and a tiny smear of margarine."

"Sounds like multigrain granola pancakes—maybe your mom was just ahead of her time?" Stacey says.

"Ever had Kool-Aid made without sugar?" I ask.

"That'd just be red water," Fletch says.

"Yeah, ask me how I know. And have you ever tried a castor oil–raw egg–orange juice smoothie? Imagine drinking battery acid, only less delicious." Stacey looks disturbed. "Here's another example—cookies in my house were made not with milk chocolate chips and sugar but carob and unsweetened applesauce."

Fletch winces and Stacey says, "Ugh. What were those like?"

"Like eating a handful of damp sand." One time my mom's zeal even prompted her to make her signature apple pie with slices of zucchini.[20]

---

[20]Only once, though, because my dad threatened divorce.

"Was she a bad cook or just overly health conscious?" Stacey asks.

"The latter." Mom always made great stuff for holidays, and the buffets she set up for parties were spectacular. She'd serve wonderful treats like teriyaki wings and baked ziti and little Swedish meatballs, but none of these dishes ever worked themselves into our dinner rotation. Instead we had her homemade chicken soup about once a week, made with water instead of chicken stock, and she'd boil the bejesus out of the vegetables. She never separated the chicken carefully enough, so the soup would be all bland and mushy except for the tiny, stabby bones. "I got really turned off of food and became an incredibly fussy eater. I spent seventeen years opting for wheat toast in lieu of whatever dinner she'd cooked."

"Trust me," Fletch adds, "her mom could make an Ethiopian villager politely back away from the dinner table, claiming he'd had a big lunch."

I nod. "When I got to college, I had food I'd never really tasted before, like chicken-fried steak, au gratin potatoes, Pop-Tarts, and ranch dressing, and I *lost my mind*. Plus, there were shakers of real salt on the table and not the ridiculous NoSalt foolishness we kept at our house. And butter! Pat after pat of *real* butter, stacked in small golden packages on the salad bar! And I could put as much as I wanted on my toast!" I smile, thinking of how the plain, dry baked potatoes I could never choke down at the family dinner table turned deliciously decadent, piled high with sour cream and bacon bits and melted Velveeta. "Had I not roomed with a dietetics major who'd appointed herself my own personal Food Police, I'm sure the damage would have been much greater than fifteen pounds."

Stacey waves me off. "Wait . . . fifteen? This whole story led up to you only gaining *fifteen* pounds? Girl, please; I gained forty freshman year at Brandeis. We all did."

Fletch asks, "Was it a huge party school?"

"No, but every night around eleven when we were studying, people from local restaurants would go up and down the halls of our dorm selling anything you could think of—egg rolls, fried rice, pizza, burritos . . . It was insane. My dorm perpetually smelled like a food court."

Fletch and I are incredulous. He says, "No one did that at Purdue. None of us had any money."

"Not a lot of Jappy girls in Indiana," Stacey reasons.

"Question, then—how did you lose the forty pounds?" I ask.

"I'll let you know when it happens." Stacey and I laugh, but Fletch looks like he still can't wrap his mind around the fact that anyone could gain weight in college. He lived off campus his freshman year and existed on bologna omelets. Every time I pile his breakfast plate high with rashers, he reminds me how three pounds of turkey bacon lasted him a whole semester. Drinking might be the only reason he didn't starve to death. She asks, "What about you? How'd you shake it off?"

"When I got home, my parents decided I was 'fat,' so they put me on a diet and had me do a weekly weigh-in. I had to lose two pounds or I was in trouble."

"What kind of trouble?"

"Don't know. I always lost two pounds."[21]

My mom was so damn mad at me after my freshman year, especially once she saw me in a bathing suit for the first time. I went from 135 pounds to 150 and you'd have thought I'd flunked out given her reaction.[22] She always used to tell me her greatest fear was that I'd walk across the stage at my high school graduation overweight. *Really?* I remember thinking. *With forty girls in my school who'd either gotten pregnant or had babies,* this *is her issue?*[23] Had I not been so affected by reading novels about anorexia like *The Best Little Girl in the World* when I was younger, I bet I'd have developed an eating disorder in response to her obsession with my weight.

I clearly remember how annoyed I was every Friday morning, stomach rumbling, standing on the scale in our tiny first-floor bathroom. My mom would crouch down to examine the numbers while my dad made sure I didn't try to cheat by pressing my hand down on the towel bar. (He didn't catch on until the third week. Heh.)

I desperately hated the whole process, especially because I had no choice in the matter. I knew being heavier didn't change who I was, and I was furious at being forced

---

[21]Jen's Life Lesson #566: You *will* lose weight if you eat nothing but lettuce and laxatives the day before you're forced to step on the scale. But, um, that's *all* you'll be able to do that day.

[22]I saved that for my sophomore year. I rule!

[23]Obviously there wasn't a lot to do in Huntington, Indiana, in 1985.

to alter something about which I felt perfectly fine. And who cared if I weighed fifteen pounds more than when I competed in the Miss Huntington pageant? It's not like I won and had to worry about going to Miss Indiana with excess baggage.[24]

The worst part of that summer was the exercise. The second I got up and before I'd do anything else, I'd pop Jane Fonda's workout into the tape player, huffing my way through the sixty-minute advanced version before I'd allow myself to have my first of three meals of wheat toast.

To this day, I hate Jane Fonda.

And leg warmers.

I'm still OK with toast, though.

The only thing I liked was swimming laps in our pool, which ended up being the main reason I was able to get back to my pageant weight. But, really, I have to laugh when I think of what my family considered 'fat.' I'm just shy of five foot eight, and 150 pounds was well within normal limits, especially since I have a big frame and *b-o-o-b-s*. I'd gone from a seven to a nine, and I hadn't even broken into double-digit pant sizes at that point.[25] Plus it was the eighties. At least five pounds was hair and product.

Stacey asks, "Looking back, are you angry with them?"

"Now? God, no, not at all. The benefit of hindsight tells me weight wasn't the real issue. They were trying to come

---

[24]Besides, I could think of forty local girls right off the bat I was thinner than. Weight Watchers is wrong—nothing tastes better than self-righteousness feels!

[25]And even if I had, a size twelve is *not* fat—just ask Meg Cabot!

to terms with the fact that their moderately obedient child went away to college, and a drinking, swearing, moderately independent young adult returned in her place, you know? More importantly, I looked fantastic when I went back sophomore year. Totally let me date guys in better fraternities."

"Glad you had your priorities straight," Fletch chimes in.

I continue, "I wish I had that kind of external motivation right now, because it's certainly not coming from within. I'm conflicted—I know I *need* to do this. I mean, I don't want to have a heart attack, and a stroke would totally mess up my smile, and yet I can't get past the idea of not eating what I'd like."

"Me, too. Intellectually, I understand why it's important for my body to carry less fat, but I can't say I'm unhappy with who I am, regardless of my shape." Stacey has beautiful hair, perfect features, and a positive self-concept, and I swear men throw themselves at her wherever we go. She doesn't need to lose an ounce to be her gorgeous self.

"Exactly! We should start a Girls with High Self-Esteem and Possibly Cholesterol support group. Seriously, though, I know I should eat less and exercise more, so I started going to the West Loop Gym about a year ago. I'm there a lot, but I just don't see results."

"Have you done any personal training? I work out with mine three days a week, and I'm down about thirty pounds since last year. What's important is, I *feel* good."

"Oh, yeah," I reply. "I had a few sessions with a trainer last year. The problem was, I'd work my ass off, and then

I'd come home and reward myself with something delicious."

Stacey nods. "It's hard not to."

"When I go to the gym now, I'm still waiting for the endorphins to kick in. It doesn't matter if I kill myself every day, I've yet to experience anything like a high," I tell her.

Stacey shifts, and Loki takes this as an invitation to join her and Fletch on the couch. "I love working out with my trainer, Gabe, because he's a really good friend. But doing it on my own? Not so much. I dislike every single step I take on the goddamn treadmill. Like, when does it get fun?"

"Lately, I've been on this kick where I don't eat anything I can't pronounce," Fletch tells us. He's dropped ten pounds with this little trick since the Bus Incident.

Fucking show-off.

"Yeah, I tried that, and then I read the label on a package of Hostess cupcakes. It's amazing what I can pronounce," says Stacey.

"I'm more of a fruit-pie girl myself, but I totally agree," I reply. "Bottom line is, the weight went on so easily—seems like it should come off the same way."

"But so far you've done nothing," Fletch mentions.

"Thank you, Captain Obvious," I snap. "It will happen, just not tonight, OK?"

"Whoa, sorry. Just trying to participate in the conversation." Fletch moves Loki and his potentially leather-puncturing claws back onto the floor. Loki goes over a few feet to lie on his squashy down bed, where visions of salad tossing will soon dance in his head. "Maybe you should start the show?" he deflects.

I press PLAY on the TiVo remote and *Top Chef* begins. Five minutes of braising, sautéing, and roasting later, I look sheepishly at Fletch and Stacey and ask, "Um, is anyone else hungry?"

TO: carol_at_home, wendy_at_home, jen_at_work
CC: angie_at_home
FROM: jen@jenlancaster.com
SUBJECT: scenes from a parking garage

Setting: In the car, circling the lot two levels underneath Nordstrom.

Me: My God, it's crowded in here. We're never going to find a space.

Angie: *(gestures toward cars parked perpendicular to those already in spaces)* Well, why don't you park like that?

Me: Those are the valets'.

Angie: *(squints at a Lexus SUV with a Notre Dame alumni sticker on it)* Wow, the valets really have nice cars.

Me: *(turning to look at Angie, incredulous)* I meant they're valet *parked.*

Angie: Oh. I guess that makes more sense.

Scene ends as I almost drive us into a pole because I'm busy laughing myself into a pants-wetting asthma attack.

See you soon?

Jen

P.S. Ang, I wouldn't mock you if you hadn't infected me with the plague.

P.P.S. Ten points to you for not mentioning how much weight I've gained since I saw you last. Thank you for taking my delicate little feelings into account.

Talking (Terrible) Turkey

"I stand up, and my ass knocks over someone's wine-glass, like, four tables away. No lie. And now I'm too mortified to ever go to that restaurant again," I tell Angie. I'm lying on the guest bed in the office with my legs angled up and feet against the wall, my default phone position since high school. Normally I'm loath to talk on the phone, but recently we switched cable providers and now our service is a flat rate. My hate for the telephone is neatly eclipsed by my love of free long distance.

"I'm sure it wasn't that bad," Angie replies. "Besides, I saw you a month ago, and your butt was fine. I'd have noticed if it was seventeen feet wide." Of course, Angie is a mom and routinely lies all day—for example, *That fluffy bunny on the side of the road is covered in delicious raspberry jam! And he's napping; shhh, don't wake him!*—so I'm not so quick to believe her.

"Don't be so sure. I was wearing black pants and a girdle. They're very deceptive."

In the background, I hear Angie's youngest son saying, "Mommy's on the phone and Daddy's at work—so who will make me a sandwich, I wonder?"

"Do you have to go?" I ask. "The last thing I want is my rampant obesity causing your children to starve. And by the way, when the hell did I begin to criticize myself? A month ago I was fat and happy. But ever since I made the decision to drop a few pounds—way less easy than it sounds, by the way—I've become obsessed with my size, and in so doing I've inadvertently allowed my inner critic to have a voice. And you know what? She's a *bitch*. Like now when I see my underpants in the laundry, I no longer think *Soft! Cotton! Sensible!* Instead I hear her say *Damn, girl, these panties be huge*."

"Your inner critic has terrible grammar."

"I know, it's the only way I can take away some of her power over me. Anyway, should I call you back?"

"Nope, not to worry; lunch is handled. Hang on a sec." After a quick discussion of the merits of peanut butter versus turkey, and crusts on or off, I can hear Angie working on the sandwich as we talk. Over the summer we chatted one night while Angie stripped a bed, changed wet sheets, comforted and repajamaed a toddler, and chased down a car of speeding teenagers while shaking a brick at them, never once interrupting the conversation or setting down her margarita. The only reason this woman isn't president of General Motors is because she's chosen not to be.

"The other mothers on the PTA are terrified of you, aren't they?"

"Naturally." She laughs. "Back to the restaurant—what'd you do about the glass?"

"I was so embarrassed, I wanted to crawl in a hole and die, but the guy was cool. The waitress got him more wine, and he wouldn't let me pay for it, so it was best-case scenario. But I'm bothered that certain body parts are trailing behind me creating mayhem and wasting perfectly lovely Bordeaux. And lately? I've noticed I'm developing a bit of a shelf back there. My inner critic calls it an ass plateau. Seriously, it's a fleshy blob that sits right above my crack, like a fanny pack or perhaps my tailbone's version of a helmet. When I see you I'll let you rest your drink on it."

"What's stopping you from dieting?"

"Sloth? Lack of proper motivation? The new Democratic Congress? Honestly, I don't know why I'm not doing more, because I'm certainly thinking about it 24/7. Then my mind goes back to a life spent not eating cookies and I wonder why I'd even bother, since life wouldn't be worth living. The good news is I bought another tanning package, and that's almost the same as dieting. You know, tanning is the new black."

I hear an audible gasp from the woman who thought she created an SPF 130 sunscreen by layering SPF 50 over SPF 80. "Yes, and so's melanoma. What did your doctor suggest?"

"Don't know what she suggests yet—I'm not going to see her until late this afternoon. My plan is to have her put me on antianxiety medication because I can't sleep at night."

"You've still got the insomnia?"

"Yeah, I still feel pretty stressed, but it's more like free-floating anxiety over financial stuff than episodic. Although the stress is somewhat lower now that I got caught up on my student loans." Yeah, *you* try to not have a panic attack when the student loan guy tells you he's going to send the Department of Justice to your house to break your ankles and take your couches and dogs.

Okay, fine, he didn't exactly do that.

He simply suggested I follow the payment schedule as I'd promised to do in a binding legal document.[26]

"Did you use your royalty check?" I hear a muffled banging on the other end of the line. Angie's either building her own chicken coop or testing her formula for cold fusion.

"I did. Oh, and get this—when I told my mom about finally taking care of this debt, she said, *'You're just like that Osama fellow,'* which . . . what? I said I had no idea what she was talking about and she replied, *'You know, your Illinois senator—Senator Osama. When he got his book deal, the first thing he did was pay off his student loans.'* I told her if she couldn't differentiate between the terrorist *Osama* bin Laden and the Democratic senator Barack *Obama*, she may want to taper back on her 24/7 FOX News viewing."

"Speaking of your mom, how was Thanksgiving? Did they come up?" Most years, my parents drive to Chicago from their home in Indiana and take us out for a lavish dinner

---

[26]Besides, I imagine that if the DOJ seized my dogs, we'd have a *Ransom of Red Chief* situation on our hands.

at Lawry's. We love going there because the restaurant is in Marshall Field's old private residence and it feels like we're having dinner at an obscenely wealthy elderly relative's house. The place is all done up in Christmas decorations and there's festive music, and everyone's dressed in their holiday finery— it's more like a party than a restaurant, and there's enough pie for everyone! We gorge ourselves on prime rib, creamed corn, and my favorite dessert ever, a chocolate bag filled with fresh berries and mousse.

We started this tradition about ten years ago, after Fletch and I got out of college. We both had entry-level jobs and were required to be at work the day after Thanksgiving, too. My parents would have spent the day with my brother's family, but we lost them about twelve years ago. Don't worry— they're fine. That was the year my mom decided to extend her fat, salt, and sugar moratorium to Thanksgiving. I'm not sure if it was the accidental turkey jerky or the yeast-roll baseballs that dealt the killing blow, but my brother and his wife ran back to her family's butter-drenched, chocolate-covered cele-bration in southern Indiana and never looked back. (If they had, they'd have seen a pile of unsalted, unbuttered, un-touched carrots.)

Instead of spending Thanksgiving alone or in the car for eight hours, we improvised, and a tradition was born. How-ever, my relationship with my mother can be volatile, and we generally end up missing every third holiday because we're not speaking to each other, as was the case this year.

"Nope, but my sister-in-law's family didn't celebrate until Saturday, and now that my parents and brother live within walking distance of each other, they spent the day together. Since we were here, Fletch decided he'd cook."

"Uh-oh. Was the fire department involved?"[27]

"Not this time. We followed a menu from this guy on Food Network, and it was great."

Angie's a budding Martha Stewart, and everything she prepares is delicious, homemade, and perfectly nutritionally balanced. But there's always a chance she's hiding a flask and a Nixon-esque Enemies List in her pinafore apron, which is exactly why we're such good friends. "I love Food Network! Unfortunately, the kids turn up their noses whenever I serve anything even remotely gourmet, so I don't try too often. Get this—last week James was on a play date and the other kid's mom fed them SpaghettiOs. James never had them before and he just went crazy! He kept telling the mom, *'You'll have to give my mother the recipe for these!'*"

"Stories like that make me reconsider my whole children-are-the-devil stance."

"Yeah, I imagine I'll think twice before selling them into white slavery." I can practically hear Angie smiling through the phone. "Anyway, from what I saw this year, if we hadn't gone to my grandmother's house, I'd have done Tyler Florence's meal."

"Hey, that's exactly what we chose! Except I couldn't get his name right, so for a whole week, I kept telling everyone we were having a Tyler *Durden* Thanksgiving."[28]

....

[27]This would be funnier were it not such a reasonable question.

[28]The first rule of Thanksgiving Fight Club is, don't talk about Thanksgiving Fight Club.

"I don't get it." With four kids under thirteen, Angie doesn't see many R-rated movies. For her, it's pretty much anthropomorphic penguins and Ellen DeGeneres starring as a cartoon fish.

"Not important. All you need to know is, when Fletch and I work together, we do a good job. Our dinner was fantastic, although we used two pounds of butter cooking the turkey alone."

"If you're going to do Atkins, that's not so bad."

Before I can respond, my caller ID clicks and I glance at the number; it's my doctor's office. "Hey, Ang, I've got a call on the other line. Can I ping you later?"

"No problem. Have a good day!" Then Angie hangs up for an afternoon of laundry folding . . . or possibly of brokering a lasting peace agreement in the Middle East. You never can tell with her.

Last month when Angie was visiting, we had some of our mutual friends over and the conversation turned to stress management and therapy. By the way, how great is it that mental health is no longer a taboo subject? Ten years ago we'd have never had this conversation.[29] Turned out practically everyone in the room takes some sort of medicine for either depression or anxiety—Paxil, Prozac, Effexor, Zoloft, Valium, Ativan, Xanax . . . the only

---

[29]My mother says people are OK with talking about mental health now because of all the hard work she put in as a therapist.

side effect seemingly being that suddenly everyone's a pharmacologist.[30]

As we spoke, I began to realize that our systems are struggling more and more to cope with daily stressors, which led me to think about evolution. Since the days of the caveman, our bodies have changed to adapt to their environments. Seems like we should automatically produce more serotonin or endorphins or whatever feel-good juice it is we need to function, but this seems no longer to be the case, hence our need for medical intervention. Then it occurred to me that the problem may be that advances in technology have happened so quickly that we've totally lapped the natural progression of human evolution, which just seems . . . wrong.

Finding no plausible solution, I decided *screw it* and had another margarita, quietly noting that I should discuss cake-free methods of stress control with my internist.[31]

That Monday my doctor put me on a course of Zoloft. At the same time, I came down with a horrible cold[32] and was out of commission for about two weeks. But even after my symptoms cleared up, I couldn't shake the fatigue. I barely left the house because even the idea of climbing the stairs to

---

[30]Please note: MS Word totally knew how to spell most of these drugs. Telling, no?

[31]Some people are destined to be deep thinkers. I am not one of those people.

[32]Angie brought with her the collective germs of sixty-eight preschoolers, having subbed in her son's class the day prior to her arrival, which is essentially as dangerous as licking a petri dish full of live cultures.

shower was exhausting. I found that I couldn't sleep at night, but that's only because I couldn't get out of bed until noon.

The thing is, I wasn't stressed or anxious—far from it. Mentally, I felt terrific. It was such a relief to get rid of the constant blathering that goes on in my head, and Fletch remarked about how much calmer[33] I was. Yet I was sleeping sixteen to eighteen hours a day and I couldn't figure out why. I even missed a doctor's appointment because the idea of walking to the corner to get on the bus at the godawful hour of eleven thirty a.m. was too much to bear. Obviously a trip to West Loop Gym was out of the question.

I got up one day at the crack of ten thirty a.m.[34] and promptly fell back asleep on the couch. A few hours later I woke up to the sound of a garbage truck idling in front of my house. The damn thing was parked there for almost an hour, and I could barely hear my TiVoed episode of *Extreme Home Makeover*, or, as Fletch calls it, *The Ty Pennington Paints a Wall and Makes You Cry Show*. I kept looking out the window, thinking *I am vaguely annoyed*.

Then it struck me—when am I ever *vaguely annoyed*? I'm generally a mad-as-hell, want-to-beat-you-with-a-nail-studded-plank, track-you-*and*-your-kids-down kind of annoyed. And where was my bizarre assumption that the truck had been sent by some waste-management goons to harass me? Or that a group of Chechen rebels had stolen it, had

---

[33]Read: less neurotic.

[34]And only then because Fletch poked me with a suit hanger and asked if I was dead.

packed it with homemade explosives, and were going to destroy a piece of the adjacent expressway as soon as they finished their coffee? I mean, at no point did I even *think* about calling Homeland Security, currently the third preset on my speed dial after Domino's Pizza and the place that delivers Philly cheesesteaks.

I realized that although I was totally copasetic, some essential element of *me* was missing. I didn't have the nervous energy making me apeshit crazy, but I also didn't have the nervous energy making me dash off ten pages at a time about my current obsession.[35]

Where the hell *were* my obsessions anyway? I mean, not once since I started taking the pills did I put on camo makeup, lie on my stomach, and stake out the weirdos next door with binoculars. I took big sips of my canned soda, never once worrying I'd choke on a fingertip or a syringe; nor did I cautiously peer inside the toilet before sitting down to make sure there was no alligator inside. What was up with *that*?

It finally dawned on me that the meds were the culprit, and I stopped taking them cold turkey.[36] I figured whatever the withdrawal symptoms might be, they couldn't be worse than losing the essence of what makes me *me*, however flawed that may be.

But now I'm having trouble sleeping again, so I'm off to beg for new drugs.

---

[35] I refer you to my greatest work—*Hasselhoff: The Chest Hair Manifesto.*

[36] Please consult your physician (and not me) for appropriate medical advice.

I *love* my doctor! She's the first one I've ever had who I don't actively dread going to see, which is likely because of her bedside manner. I mean, outside of a social situation, how many doctors have you met who insist you call them by their first names? Plus, her personal style is to die for. If I saw her on the street, I would think she was incredibly cool and confident, the way she carries off her spiky blond Annie Lennox haircut. Last time I was here she was clad in a vintage Pucci dress and baby pink motorcycle boots. Wonder what she'll be in today?

In the waiting area of her office are paintings by local artists and a bunch of signed photos—looks like she's treated Cameron Diaz and Sean Penn and a ton of famous athletes. I dig going to Chicago's version of the doctor to the stars.

Of course, it's not accidental that I'm here. Years ago I worked in health care and learned how to check out a physician's practice history. Dr. Awesome's credentials could not be more flawless, so I've never questioned or second-guessed her judgment.

Exactly on time, she calls my name, so I follow her to the examination room. We enter an immaculate space, and she gestures for me to sit in the chair next to the computer rather than on the exam table. I dig how she conducts herself—it's like we're going to have a conversation and not some scary, impersonal exam.

We settle into our respective seats, and Dr. Awesome asks me the reason for my visit. I explain how I've been having trouble falling asleep because of stress and I'd like to do something about it.

"Is the stress you feel new, or has it been ongoing?" she asks.

Back when I was a salesperson, I worried about making my numbers and completing projects. The stress I felt when I was unemployed was obvious, and when I started temping, my anxiety was linked to a combination of boredom and misplaced aggression. (I dare you to try to keep smiling when a high school graduate details a three-point process of stapling documents together and then quizzes you on it.)

Now that I'm writing professionally, the anxiety is more free-floating because I have no control over the business portion of bookselling. What if someone else writes a story like mine first? Or better? What if everyone hates my work? Or worse, completely ignores it?

"Yes and no," I reply. "Here's the thing—back when I was doing sales, if my numbers were low, I could channel my stress by working harder. I could make more phone calls, give more quotes, take more meetings, create more proposals, but in my new career as a writer, there's no set of rules to follow to guarantee success. It's a big, fat crapshoot, hence the insomnia."

"I understand. Tell me, Jen, what's your activity level like?"

Just shy of cadaverous?

"Um, it's OK. I was doing really well last year going to the gym. I even had a trainer for a little while, but for Christmas she gave me a size medium sweatshirt—like that would *ever* fit me—and a bill for six hundred dollars for sessions we hadn't even had, and I stopped seeing her. Then I got busy with my second book, and . . . well, here we are." Vanity had previously driven me to hit the gym when I thought I was going to be featured in some magazines as part of a publicity push. Turns out everyone just used photos of the book cover. Regardless, I still look pretty good right now. I mean, I've got a glowing tan and a faboo haircut, no less than four shades of blond perfectly showcasing said tan, and the whole package is tied together nicely with proper accessories and well-tailored pants. What's not to like?

Dr. Awesome scans her computer screen and furrows her brow, tapping a finger to her lips. "Your weight troubles me. According to your chart, you've put on more than thirty pounds since last year, and that's without weighing you today. Do you feel like the gain came on because of the stress, or is the stress causing you to gain? Or would you say it's your lack of activity?"

I would say it's the ten pies I've eaten in the past two months.

"Um, the stress is causing my gain?" I totally sound like I'm guessing. Which I am.

"For a course of action, we need to up your activity level immediately. I believe your weight and your stress are linked, and . . ."

Ugh. I don't want to hear this. Avoiding her earnest eyes, I look down at my feet.

And then I look at her feet.

And then I shout, "Oh, my God. You're wearing leopard-print Manolo ballet flats! I didn't know those existed outside of my dreams!"

And here's where we get to Jen's Life Lesson #1012: Never interrupt your doctor to discuss her taste in designer footwear.

A flash of recognition crosses my fun, stylish doctor's face. Suddenly she doesn't want to dance around my feelings about my anxiety or hear how I camouflage my weight with pretty hair, cute shoes, and shapely ankle–revealing capri pants. Her entire demeanor changes. Her spine stiffens, and she leans forward in her chair, delivering what amounts to a death sentence.

She talks way too candidly about the danger presented by my high blood pressure and elevated cholesterol level. She delivers a long, blood-curdlingly descriptive monologue about diabetes and gallstones, moving on to the horrors of coronary heart disease and stroke, with a side of breast cancer and cirrhosis of the liver and, for good measure after taking in my savage tan, squamous cell carcinoma.

In painstaking detail, Dr. Awesome describes the number of agonizing, wasting ways I will die if I don't change my eating and fitness habits, like, immediately.

Dude.

Dude.

Ouch.

Tough love *sucks*.

But tomorrow I begin to change my life.

For real.

Dear Resident at 2331 North x—— Street,

Our office has received numerous calls about the state of the front of your home. Although we encourage the recognition of national holidays through tasteful adornment, it is now December, so we respectfully request that you dismantle your Easter décor, like, immediately.

Best,

Jen Cognito, Association President[37]

P.S. Throwing down a cylinder of Morton table salt is not the new "shoveling." Kindly attend to the snow on your sidewalk, or fines shall be assessed.

---

[37]Get it? Get it? Jen Cognito? Like "incognito"? Get it? No? OK, just me, then.

Two Fat People Admit Defeat

"Since when is macaroni and cheese diet food?" Fletch asks as he closes the front door behind a retreating army of service professionals.

"Um, *hello*? Near-death experience? I'm supposed to comfort myself with lettuce? I think not," I reply. I tuck back into the melt-y, breadcrumb-crusted plate of happiness in front of me after pulling a quilt fashioned from old college sweatshirts around my shoulders, trying to fend off the arctic wind currently blowing through my living room.

Not long ago we started running the heat when fall finally turned to winter. I noticed an odd smell coming from the basement, and Fletch explained that all gas furnaces do that. I disagreed vehemently, and we squabbled about it until today, when I couldn't stand it anymore and called the HVAC guys.

Apparently our chimney has caved in, and all sorts of loose bricks and mortar are blocking the gas our furnace is *supposed* to vent. The toxic fumes can't escape, and what I've smelled is the paint melting inside our furnace, and had I actually listened to Fletch, we'd have been exploded or poisoned at some point in the very near future![38]

I continue, "I figured if I was going to die this weekend, I was *not* heading to the afterlife with nothing in my stomach but broccoli, so I broke out one of the servings of macaroni and cheese I froze for just such an emergency." I keep a number of emergency rations in the freezer. Fletch looks down at my plate and back at me. "Okay, fine. Two servings. Whatever. We almost *died*, you know."

"We're not in danger anymore," he counters.

"Maybe we're not *right this minute*, but my system is in the delayed kind of shock only Italian ham and three kinds of melted cheese can fix." I'm anxious to change the subject. "What did the furnace guys say?"

"One of two things—either we get a whole new furnace that doesn't need to be vented through the chimney, or we hire a chimney sweep to clean out all the debris. They suggested we try that first."

"How much will that cost?" I take another bite of the creamy concoction, and it's smoky and delicious. The key to really perfect mac 'n' cheese is pancetta. Dice and sauté it first; then set it aside to mix with the elbows and cheese sauce before it goes in the oven. Use the pancetta drippings as a base for the roux and whichever mild white cheese you prefer, but whatever you choose, do your taste buds a favor

---

[38]He so owes me a Coke right now.

and toss in some fontina because there's almost nothing that melts more smoothly and—

Fletch interrupts my reverie. "Are you listening to me, or are you thinking about your macaroni?"

Busted. "Um, I'm listening. Of course. You were saying it would cost how much?"

"About six hundred dollars."

"Ouch." Although I presently have such house lust, I actually dream of escrow and have already picked out paint colors and backsplashes, at times like this I don't mind being a renter. I fear I lack the responsibility homeownership requires. I mean, last week I gave myself food poisoning eating pie left over from Thanksgiving—twice—and still buy cereal based on the prizes inside. Plus, there's no way we can buy a home in the city as nice as where we live now. Our place is a hundred-year-old row house that's been completely renovated[39] and filled with top-of-the-line appliances and fixtures. We've got a full basement, a garage, three bathrooms, and a gourmet kitchen with no less than forty-seven pristine white cabinets, fortunate considering our barware situation. Better yet, we have a small, grassy front lawn and a twee little backyard that I've turned into a tropical paradise with $2,000 worth of landscaping and my own backbreaking labor. If we didn't live next door to idiots who patch their broken windows with plastic bags from the grocery store, this place would be perfect.[40]

. . . .

[39]Except for the chimney, apparently.

[40]To be fair, the letters I've sent them from the fictitious homeowners' association have had an impact, and now they use bags without print on them. Progress, I say!

More important, we have the first landlord I've ever liked, so I refrain from cackling *Gee, that sounds expensive!* in the background while Fletch describes the possible solutions to her on the phone. I return my attention to lunch and my daily dose of FOX News. I hear him brief our landlord and then call the chimney sweeps before returning to the living room.

"What time will they be here?" I ask.

"Not 'til Monday morning."

"But today is Friday." The HVAC guys red-tagged the furnace and water heater and cut the gas to both, so until the chimney is swept, getting warm or washed in our house is not an option.

"Still wearing your days-of-the-week underpants, I see," he dryly replies.

"No." *Yes.* "What's our game plan, then?" I drop my fork and have to scramble for it before the dogs get there first. Ha! Victory! I wipe it on a napkin and continue eating.

"Our landlord said she'd pay for us to take the dogs and go to a hotel."

"What about the cats?"

"Two dogs and four cats in a hotel room sounds far worse than no heat or hot water. The cats can stay here. It won't go below about sixty degrees with the way this place is insulated, so they'll have to deal with being a little chilly. That's why they have fur."

"They'll mutiny!" I love our cats, but I got them in college, so they're all between twelve and fourteen years old, and now it's like living with a group of loud, pushy, cranky senior citizens who take extraordinary pleasure in vomiting in your shoes. The dogs won't even walk past them in the hallway, they're so scary. "Sounds like we're not in any danger with the furnace and hot-water heater turned off, right?"

"Correct."

I consider our options for a moment. "Let's just stay here."

"You wouldn't rather go to a hotel?"

"Nah. We'll be all right."

Fletch narrows his eyes at me. I am *never* amenable, especially when it comes to being physically uncomfortable. He strictly adheres to my HHT credo, meaning I can't be held responsible for my actions should I ever get Hot, Hungry, or Tired. (Special dispensation is made for instances that are humid, cold, and boring, too, e.g., any outdoor sporting event.) "What's your angle?"

"No angle. We survived with our utilities being shut off when we were unemployed and broke; this is no big deal. Also, I don't want the hassle of packing up and heading to a hotel."

Okay, that's kind of a lie. Truth is, we just dumped our satellite service and switched to cable with on-demand. There's a whole season of *Real World/Road Rules Challenge: The Duel* cached in the player's memory.[41] Although neither Miz nor Coral is participating in this challenge, big Beth from *The Real World*'s second season in Los

---

[41] I used to TiVo it until I was thoroughly mocked for being the oldest person on earth to watch fine, fine MTV reality programming.

Angeles is. Beth's almost as evil as Tonya and her Kidney Stones of Doom from *The Real World Chicago* cast, which means *someone's* getting bitch slapped, and I can't miss it. Of course, if I had my druthers, I'd cast Puck from San Francisco because he's always stirring shit up, Cyrus and Montana from Boston for their snarky commentary, Mormon Julie from New Orleans for the hate factor, and the oh-so-oily Veronica because she makes out with everyone and every—

Ahem.

He shrugs. "As long as you're fine with it, we can stay. I guess we'll shower at the gym."

"Wouldn't be the first time," I reply. We joined West Loop a couple of years ago specifically so we could bathe after losing gas service. We took advantage of their free trial offer but ended up liking the place so much that we decided to join. After paying our gas bill, we funded our membership by listing a couple of things on Craigslist, including an exercise bike. The bike sold the very first day, largely due to the ad I posted:

TWO FAT PEOPLE ADMIT DEFEAT

Two fat people are looking to dump their Excel 395 Recumbent Magnetic Exercise Bike for $100 OBO.

Although we don't know from a lot of firsthand experience, this terrific bike comes with:

- Adjustable seat (extralarge to accommodate even the biggest caboose)

- Adjustable tension (which apparently would have been an excellent cardiovascular workout, had we ever gotten past the second level)

- Computerized speed, distance, odometer, timer, and calorie display

- Less than 250 miles on the odometer

- Cup holder (and, really, isn't everything better with a cup holder?)

Don't need an exercise bike? No problem!

The Excel 395 also makes a great clothes-drying rack.

Please buy our bike and get it out of our house so it's no longer a daily reminder of how we failed in our quest for fitness. Also? We're tired of dusting it. Thanks!

P.S. It will fit in an SUV, but we can also deliver it for an additional fee, although do you really want two sweaty fat people having simultaneous heart attacks in your stairwell?

P.P.S. Naturally, we'll need cash because we'll probably use the money for pie.

I continue, "Now there's no way I'll skip my workout if I have to go there to wash my hair anyway. Problem solved. Except . . ." I trail off.

"Now what?

"I won't be home on Monday."

"I will, so I can let the chimney sweeps in."

"I kind of wanted to see them."

"Why?"

"No reason."

Fletch looks puzzled for a minute, and then chokes back a laugh. "You think Dick Van Dyke and a band of sooty Cockneys are going to sing and dance in the basement, don't you?"

"No." *Maybe.*

As Fletch wanders off to the kitchen for more coffee, he calls, "Oh, I forgot to mention it—the HVAC guys said the trapped gas was making us sick. They said once it's vented, we'll have a lot fewer headaches and far less lethargy, and we'll feel much better because of the improved air quality." He heads into his office at the back of the house, and I can hear him turn on the space heater before closing the door.

I chew on this information for a moment. This is great news! (Except for the us-almost-dying-from-toxic-gas part.) The leak means all the lying around I've done lately is technically not my fault. My problem hasn't been lethargy; it's been chemistry! Nuts to you, you vicious inner critic! Now you can go back to helping me mock others! No wonder I didn't pop out of bed, don spandex, and head to the gym for a prebreakfast workout like I'd pledged to do every night this week when I went to sleep. How was I supposed to take the dogs on their power walk when my system was being compromised by noxious fumes? And my body was slowly being poisoned, no wonder it craved Snickers bars and not salads!

But, I wonder, how do I explain all the years of lazy *prior* to our gas leak?

TO: stacey_at_work
FROM: jen@jenlancaster.com
SUBJECT: Next Week?

Sorry to have missed you last night—let's plan a time to get together when you're back in town. Except for thinking up reasons I'm allowed to skip the gym, my schedule is almost totally empty. (Today's reason is because I have a cold. Yesterday's was the dogs seemed sad. Tomorrow I can probably milk the cold angle again, with the one-two punch of also being mad at my mother.)

See you soon?

Jen

TO: jen@jenlancaster.com
FROM: stacey_at_work
SUBJECT: Re: Next Week?

Some excuses I use to avoid the gym that you are welcome to borrow:

1. Mercury is in retrograde. As is my ass.

2. My pedicure color clashes with my only clean workout outfit.

3. My inner child thinks walking on a treadmill is stupid and boring and only doo-doo heads do it.

4. My iPod needs to charge.

5. There is a marathon of *I Love the 80s* on VH1, and I miss A-Ha so much.

6. I have a tapeworm on backorder.

7. It's raining.

8. It's snowing.

9. It's sunny.

10. It's mild with a 42 percent chance of precipitation later in the day.

11. There's a full moon and I am suspicious that there are at least four guys at my gym who are werewolves. Okay, maybe just in need of a good back waxing, but better not to risk it.

12. That bitch with the perfect bod who always tells me in the locker room how hard it is for her to keep on weight no matter how much she eats is probably going to be there again,

and I might just kill her this time. Going to prison for homicide is so much worse than staying fat.

13. I dreamed about working out; that counts, right?

14. I'm having a good hair day.

15. I'm having a bad hair day.

16. I'm having a pulling-my-hair-out day.

17. Today is surely the day that George Clooney is gonna call to ask me out.

18. In which case when I get laid tomorrow, I don't want my quads to cramp up in the middle.

I get back Sunday morning. If you don't have plans in the evening, we could hook up for dinner or postdinner drinks. Otherwise, next week Monday and Thursday night both look good right now.

Have a great weekend!

biglove,

s.

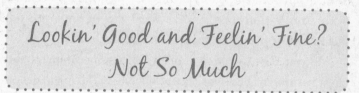

Lookin' Good and Feelin' Fine? Not So Much

*M*otivation.

    I squeeze my eyes shut and try to concentrate.

Motivation.

I clench my jaw and grit my teeth.

Mo-ti-va-tion.

I break down the word, saying it slowly in my head and concentrating on each syllable.

Motivation?

Yeah, I've still got nothing.

I stuck to a low-fat, low-calorie diet for a brief period, but then we had the gas leak (and resultant macaroni explosion), and now I can't seem to find the will to get myself back on task with exercise *or* nutrition. My motivation is as elusive as Britney's underpants.

If I'm going to get myself in gear, I need to figure out what drives me. (Fletch promised me rewards, but I've already lost interest in them.) I'm aware that I do well when I have a deadline, but anything with a due date is linked to compensation. Checks with my name on them certainly propel me toward achievement, and I'm sure I'd lose weight if I were being paid. Unfortunately, there aren't a lot of employers out there needing people to "be less fat." A pity, really.

Motivated by the thought of all the custom cabinetry and guest bathrooms $250-large could help buy, I tried to get on *The Biggest Loser* last year, but I acted like myself in the audition and the screeners cut me. I didn't even get past the initial casting call because obviously they didn't want strong, confident women who liberally employ the F word. (They'd have so many bleeps during my workouts, it would sound like an episode of *Springer.*)

Speaking of the Losers, it seems like the contestants stay on track because they hated how they looked and felt when they were heavy. Unfortunately for my waistline, I'm fine with both these things. In the casting process, I said in no uncertain terms that I'd never be the pusillanimous fatty who broke down and cried on the show. I imagine I'd be all, *Hey, when you pussies are done with your meltdowns, come and get me at the pool. And bring me a daiquiri!* With all the emotional upheaval in the program, I often wondered if participants wouldn't be better on a therapist's couch rather than the treadmill. Fletch and I would watch over plates full of pork chops and scalloped potatoes, giggling at everyone's Scary Problems.

Seriously, how could America *not* fall in love with me?[42]

---

[42] I mean, unless "contemptible" is not the new black.

Knowing the ass I'd have kicked on *The Biggest Loser* does nothing to help me find my motivation today. I really *should* be driven to change because of my health. Honestly, my doctor said some terrifying stuff, and I prefer not to die anytime soon, whether it's the result of a faulty furnace or my own gluttony. So you'd think my fear would propel me into the car and on to the gym, but it doesn't. There's an O. Henry level of irony here that I can finally afford the occasional pedicure again, yet being borderline diabetic, I might eventually lose my feet.[43] I'm scared enough to consider these factors . . . but not quite enough to be spurred into really doing something. I'm wrapped up in angst, not action. Sure, everything Dr. Awesome said was real and frightening when I was in her office . . . but now that it's a few weeks in the past, her dictates feel slightly less relevant.

Too bad I'm fighting with my mom at the moment, because parental involvement has always provided me with motivation to lose weight. After my freshman summer, I was in great shape for a long time. However, my weight started to inch up again during my third junior year.[44] This time the bloat *was* beer related, since I'd turned twenty-one. Because I was finally a legal adult, *no one* was making me stand on a scale against my will. And yet Mom's will was just as strong. So she—ever the crafty one—employed a different approach.

One day she and I were looking at my sorority composite photos. I began to bitch that my collarbones were almost only ones you couldn't see in the off-the-shoulder black

---

[43] And what of my shoes?!

[44] Yeah, yeah; yuck it up.

drape and pearls my sisters and I wore for the shot. Naturally, I thought I was cuter than everyone else,[45] but with my insanely competitive nature, I didn't like them being thinner than me. Sensing an opening, my mom leapt on the opportunity like Maisy on a Milk-Bone. She offered to "help me" before our photos were retaken in the fall. Oh, yes, she promised, my collar bones *would* be defined. Help consisted of her paying for membership at a fly-by-night diet center.

Without a doubt, the Nutri-Bolic center provided the worst diet food ever. My meals were mostly packets of dried powders claiming to be "soup" and "oatmeal," although none resembled any soups or oatmeals I'd ever tasted. Had I been in a coma, perhaps I'd have appreciated the thick, starchy liquid texture of my meals. Too bad I was conscious, because I found myself telling random strangers, "I just want to chew something, damn it!"

Interestingly, this "food" gave me a brand-new appreciation for all the staples of my mom's repertoire. I craved every atrocity to ever originate from our badly wallpapered, low-ceilinged, harvest-gold-appliance-having kitchen. Hot dogs shriveled in the microwave to cocktail-frank size, paired with stale buns? Yum! The three-bean salad that looked exactly like the organic matter we pulled from our pool's filter? Deelicious! Unseasoned rubber chicken served on a bed of still-crunchy brown rice? Bring. It. On! Even those grotesque onion-and-Worcestershire creations my dad, Dr. Ronald

---

[45]Except for Tracey and Holly, stupid, naturally gorgeous bitches with chiseled cheekbones and flawless skin.

McMengele, grilled just long enough to make the blood run down our arms when we picked them up were suddenly appealing.[46]

Consuming a thousand calories a day with very little protein, I felt lightheaded and weak every second for three whole months. I wasn't just hungry. I was famished. Starving. Ravenous. Not only did I want to consume my parents' cooking in vast quantities; I was in such a state that I'd look at the love of my life, a 140-pound Great Pyrenees mountain dog named George, and I'd fantasize about his tender, meaty flanks, charbroiled over a hickory-wood fire and served with a side of home fries.

I didn't lose weight that summer because I was eating sensibly—I lost it because I was starving. I dropped more than thirty pounds, but at the cost of a portion of my sanity.

The clothing store where I worked was right across from a drugstore in the Glenbrook Square mall. At the end of the day, I'd sail past the displays of Generra and Guess T-shirts in our front window to buy a Little Debbie brownie. When I got to my car, I'd open the package and spend five minutes smelling it and marveling at the smooth icing and dense, rich, nut-studded cake. No matter how hot it was, I'd keep the windows of my sassy little Toyota Celica rolled up so none of the scent could escape. Overcome with desire, I'd finally stuff the whole thing in my mouth, chew it to a fine paste . . . and then spit it back into the wrapper. Had I not

[46]Jen's Life Lesson #1240: Calling your father's gourmet, handcrafted burgers a "Ray-Kroc-of-Shit" will get you grounded, even if you're twenty-one years old.

been so concerned with keeping my teeth white and esophagus intact, bulimia would have been a viable choice. Regardless, the simple act of having solid food in my mouth—even if I didn't digest it—kept me from going all Shannen Doherty on everyone.

One dark day, my coworker Meredith left a cup of ice cream in the break-room freezer, which I discovered when I reached for my container of plain yogurt. I meant to sneak only a tiny spoonful of rocky road to wash away the sour taste of the unsweetened Dannon, but the second it hit my tongue, I *lost it*. With three deft bites, I swallowed the entire thing *and* licked the cup dry. The way I panicked and stuffed the empty container back in the freezer, you'd have thought I was holding a smoking gun.

Even though twenty different girls worked in that store, and despite my tacit denial, Meredith clearly knew I'd eaten her ice cream because I hardly talked about anything except food. As Meredith and I folded the acid-washed jeans and organized racks of scrunchies, I'd chatter on about the boutique where they sold the giant cookies and the calzones at Sbarro and all of my favorite pies, listed alphabetically. Meredith would smile and nod well into the third hour of my "All Things Arby's" [47] soliloquy, in what I assume was an attempt to keep me from losing my mind and biting our customers.

Poor Meredith. We worked together only when I was following that insane diet, so she never knew I wasn't completely batshit crazy.

....

[47] What, like you've never composed a sonnet about potato cakes?

Since I can't find any compelling reason to cart my big ass to the gym, I decide it would be fun to see whether I can locate Meredith online and confess my crime. Maybe I can even find an address where I can send her the seventy-five cents I still owe her. But before I can pull up Google.com, I'm hit with stabbing pains up and down my arms and in my chest.

Oh, dear.

The good news is, I'm fine. I took an aspirin and antacid and felt better. The issue was less "heart attack" and more "too many slices of cheesesteak pizza from Philly's Best."

The bad news is, Dr. Awesome wanted to see me again anyway. And now I'm here in her office, and her hideous nurse is *making* me get weighed after I've dodged the scale during my past few visits.

After five minutes of what I consider to be a highly unprofessional argument, we compromise and the nurse finally agrees that if I just step up on the damn thing, she won't say the numbers out loud.

While my weight registers, I position one hand over the digital display and one over my eyes. Somehow the nurse finds this to be a personal offense. Oh, come on; I'm not the first person to do this. Stacey says she turns around when her trainer weighs her, and she's never once mentioned his agitated foot tapping or disgruntled sighs.

The thing is, I've got a pretty good idea of my number already because I have a bizarre talent: within a minute, a pound, a degree, and a dollar, I'm somehow intuitive enough to predict the time, my weight, the temperature, and how much my groceries cost.[48] Based on the way my pants have bitten into my flesh since I finished the second book, I'm afraid to let the scale confirm the scary digits floating around in my head. I mean, I know, but I don't really want to *know*.

With quiet resignation, the nurse writes my weight in my chart and tells me I can step off the scale. "All right, it's over," she says with a voice far sharper than the situation merits. What*ever*. If weighing in is such a treat, why don't we put you and *your* childbearing hips up here, lady?

The nurse leads me back to the exam room, and as soon as I sit down, I whip out my bottle of hand sanitizer. When I worked for the HMO, I was in and out of doctors' offices all day long. Not coincidentally, I was always sick from touching germy doorknobs. I've since become completely OCD, and this is the fourth time the Purell has been out of my purse since I've been here.

Nurse Big Hips instructs me to sit on the paper-covered table, and she takes my blood pressure, only the cuff feels a whole lot tighter than usual. Shortly thereafter, a thermometer is jammed in my mouth and I correctly guess that my temperature is 98.4.[49]

Last time I was here, there was a question about my blood pressure. I'd attributed the inflated numbers to my having run for the bus, and I would have thought nothing more of it,

---

[48]No, I don't know why I've never yet been on *The Price Is Right*.

[49]Surely there is a carnival somewhere *dying* for a person with my kind of skill.

but for the past month, I've noticed an odd tingling/numbness in my arms. Yesterday after my initial bout of pain, they still felt weird after I had aspirin and antacid, so the doctor insisted I come in.

After Nurse Booty leaves the exam room, I seek out the hand sanitizer again to rub the area where the BP cuff was because what if the patient before me had tuberculosis or chlamydia? I dig around in my glorious new handbag for the bottle.

Okay. You caught me.

I admit it.

I bought a new purse with my royalties, too.

Sure, said royalties came from the book I wrote about spending all my money on designer bags and then going broke, but the irony isn't lost on me, and I promise I learned my lesson.[50] Plus, it's the first new purse I've gotten in about five years, which anyone would agree is totally reasonable, especially since it *isn't* Prada.

I love this bag so much, I promise to carry it every day until it completely disintegrates. It's a large brown and tan satchel with glossy leather handles and a leather bottom, and it's got tassels and some random equestrian-looking hardware on it. I bought it specifically because it's large enough to comfortably carry a variety of items—restaurant doggie bags, books, Fletch's BlackBerry, etc.

I've never had such a big bag, so I'm totally taking

----

[50]To fully disclose, I also got my hair colored with this money. I apologize for nothing.

advantage of it. This puppy is *full*. I can even carry a bottle of wine in it, though I'd caution anyone else before doing so. A week ago Fletch and I attended his company's holiday party, which was kind of weird because everyone he works with is so short. When we sailed in, I swear we were a head taller than anyone else there.[51] Anyway, I had a good Cabernet tucked away to take to another fete later that night, and the weight of it turned my lovely handbag into a military-grade battering ram . . . which I learned only after accidentally nailing the dour company president in the crotch.

Jen's Life Lesson #8897: Making a "hitting someone's Yule log at the Christmas party" joke totally *is* funny. It's not my fault none of the wee folk in his company have a sense of humor.

After cleaning my hands again, I pull out my book and begin to read, having learned the hard way that the doctor's computer cannot be used to access my Gmail. In my defense, they shouldn't have left me bored and shivering shirtless on a cold metal table for half an hour that one time.

When Dr. Awesome enters, I tell her all about my arm pains. After a few questions and possibly some whining on my part, she rules out cardiac infarctions and theorizes that the numbness and tingling are much more likely due to carpal tunnel syndrome or pinched nerves in my elbows.

Oh. Well . . . good.

---

[51]Plus, no one was particularly nice, so I had to bite my tongue to not ask how things were going on Middle-earth and if anyone had been back to the Shire lately.

The doctor begins to narrow down potential causes. "Have you had any changes in your activities in the last month, like maybe taking up tennis?"

"I would never chase balls," I say solemnly, in my nod to all things Cher Horowitz.[52] "I have been reading a lot of *In-Style* in the bathtub, though. It's their holiday issue, so it's pretty thick. Do you think that's the problem? I could switch to a lighter magazine."

With a quick frown, she continues. "How much time do you spend on the computer?"

"Hmm . . . ," I say, mulling over the question. The honest answer *is, I cruise the Internet almost every waking moment because the world is anxiously awaiting my expert opinion on all things Tori Spelling and it would be selfish of me not to share it. Oh, that is, except when I'm busy watching TiVo'd episodes of* The Real World: Denver. *And by the way? All the snow dumped on Colorado recently? That was totally God's way of punishing them for this season's utterly contemptible cast.*

"I'd say maybe an hour or so."

The interrogation continues, and the doctor pokes, prods, and manipulates my limbs and soon determines the problem. Apparently I bend my arms too much, and to make them stop tingling, I have to remember to straighten them out more often. Dr. Awesome suggests I get wrist guards and also wrap my elbows in Ace bandages, inserting a pen or a ruler as a brace so I'm not tempted to crook them unnecessarily.

---

[52] Other personal heroes include Elle Woods, Patsy and Edina, and Lucille Bluth, of course.

Yes.

This is officially the dumbest reason I have ever sought medical treatment, thus displacing the time the squirrel bit me. Fortunately, I *finally* convinced her to prescribe me some Ambien to help me sleep, so I feel as though I've accomplished something.

The trade-off is that Dr. Awesome wants to revisit the whole blood pressure business, and she orders a battery of tests. First up? Blood work!

Jen's Life Lessons #5644–5647: (5644) Those who think I'm a baby about being weighed have obviously never tried to extract any of my fluids; (5645) if Nurse Badonkadonk thought she disliked me before, she had another thing coming; (5646) I'm fat everywhere *except* my veins; and (5647) snappy retorts in the manner of *"Heh; this is why I'm not a heroin addict!"* only serve to prompt more needle-based digging in both my arms. Eventually the nurse has to tap a vein *in my hand*, ignoring my suggestion that perhaps my blood would rather just stay inside me, where it belongs.

Now I'm off to another room for an echocardiogram. Dr. Awesome promises my heart is fine and says this test is just a precaution. I've had one of these before, so I'm not as much of a nancy pants about it. Nothing about it is painful, except the thought of someone seeing me *n-a-k-e-d*. As I strip from the waist up, I examine the computer system in here. There's a small webcam on top of the monitor, and according to the screen saver, it's used for facial recognition log-in. So cutting-edge! Unfortunately the camera broadcasts whatever it sees onto the screen, and I accidentally turn in front of it while struggling to get out of my bra. I'm treated to an extreme close-up of my own bare rack, and the first thought in my head is *Worst. Porno. Ever.*

I put on the flimsy cover-up and engage in more hand cleaning. This time I use the office's scrub sink, finishing with a couple of generous squirts of their sanitizer. When the nurse returns, she covers me with a bunch of stickers and attaches electrodes all over my arms and chest, including *way* underneath my left *b-o-o-b* and down my legs. I laugh about being glad I shaved and she ignores me. Ugh. One paper gown later and I'm suddenly Henny Youngman. I'm embarrassed for me. No wonder she's not a fan.

The test is over quickly, and before the nurse leaves, she tells me that there are ten sticky electrodes on me and I can peel them off myself. I search and search but can find only nine. The last one's probably stuck behind an errant *b-r-e-a-s-t*. Yeah, really looking forward to that twisted little Easter egg hunt when I get home.

Now I have to go next door to the radiology center for chest X-rays. Again I'm required to strip to the waist. Aarrggh. Aren't they using, like, *lasers* or something? What's the difference between seeing through my polo shirt and sensible bra and seeing through a gown of the same thickness? As long as they note that the little alligator-shaped blob over my heart is a logo and not a tumor, what's the big deal?

My argument falls on deaf ears. The technician excuses herself while I disrobe *again*, and when I'm done, I lie on the big table in front of a large donut-y tube with my book until she returns.

"Ma'am? This is a *chest X-ray*. You have to stand over there," she says. "And naked from the waist up means you have to remove your pearls."

Pfft. Not in my world, lady.

I comply and hold as still as I can while she snaps images from behind the big shield. As I hug the chilly metal plate, it strikes me that this is yet another wake-up call. I hate anything vaguely medical, and everything I'm doing today has been garden-variety and relatively noninvasive. What if I really were having a heart attack yesterday and not just an adverse reaction to compulsively looking at cat pictures online?

What if my bad, lazy habits cause heart disease or a stroke? How will I handle going through the related (and braless) medical procedures? Shoot, I'm afraid of getting BriteSmile and Botox—there's no way I'll have the fortitude to deal with something real like a stroke or cancer. Although I like to think of myself as tough, my actions today speak volumes. There's a world of difference between shouting at people in traffic and facing a wasting disease with dignity and maturity. I mean, I lost my shit over standing on a scale. What if something were really wrong?

When we're done and I'm dressed and sanitized again, I keep replaying the day's unpleasantness while I head to my car. I've lacked the motivation to do something about my weight because I've been convinced I both look and feel good.

I'm starting to wonder if I'm not operating on a false premise here. Honestly, maybe I *don't* feel all that great. I get winded carrying laundry up from the basement. And I sort of don't like bending because it makes my pulse throb. Walking from the parking lot to the store shouldn't be a challenge, right?

Thoughts racing, I unlock the car and climb in. I suspect if I were living a life where I truly felt good, the possibility of a heart attack wouldn't have crossed my mind yesterday.

But it did.

Shit, I can't have a heart attack. Heart attacks happen to *old* people. And how can I be *old*—I'm still breaking out on my chin, for Christ's sake. Yeah, I'm going to be forty, but forty is the new thirty! Forty should be about buying a house and a snappy new car, not about interviewing private nurses and buying hospital beds.

This is all wrong. How did I even get here?

I place my hand on the gearshift and notice a small black smudge near my knuckle. I rub it, but it doesn't go away. I'm so distracted by the swirling vortex of thoughts, I *lick* the offending spot to remove it.

Uh-oh. *That's* going to cost me. Ten bucks says I'm about to come down with a serious case of Hand-Lick Fever. Outstanding. Can't wait to hear what Dr. Awesome has to say about *this* bit of stupidity, as I'm sure I'll be back with flulike symptoms in the next week. I artfully dodged her on my way out of the office, so I spared myself the tail end of the Why You Should Be Less Fat Lecture, Part Infinity . . . at least this time.

As I pull into the garage, I lift my gigantic handbag out of the car and feel the same tingling numbness in my arm. I swap the bag over to the other side and the same thing happens. I calculate and realize I've been carrying this heavy-ass bag *exactly* as long as I've had the arm pain.

Today just keeps getting better and better!

After I recover from my bout of the flu, I decide I prefer being healthy and feeling good, if only because I'm not spending my disposable income on medical supplies. This time it was just Kleenex and Vicks VapoRub, but who knows the expenses heart problems entail?

Changes must be made.

But the only way I'm going to be able to enable change is if I get a real measure of where I'm starting. In my head I know how much I weigh, but I should probably hop on the scale to confirm it.

Clad in only my underwear, I loom in front of my scale for fifteen minutes. Each time I place a toe on it, my whole foot jerks back as though the scale's on fire.

Try as I might, I can't bring myself to stand on it.

Shit.

I *have* to weigh myself to get a baseline measurement so I can track my progress . . . or do I?

The bathroom is directly off the room I use for my home office, and when I glance at my desk, I notice my digital camera. I quickly put on a pair of Lycra workout pants and sports bra and yank my hair out of its ponytail. I apply a sparkly coat of lip gloss, contour my cheeks with a dark blush, and don my favorite string of pearls because I'm going to document my weight loss *photographically*! This is genius, especially with the advent of digital cameras, because it means no pockmarked teenager can make fun of me from the confines of his or her photo-developing booth. And how great will it be to arrange all the pictures together once I'm done, like a flip-book? I'll call it *The Incredible Shrinking Jen*!

To begin, I have to figure out where I should stand and how to work the camera's timer, but before I do I take a long, hard look at myself in the mirror.

I look . . . nice.

My teeth are superwhite,[53] my hair is bouncy, and if I saw me on the street, I'd totally think I was cute. If I were single, guys would want to date me because I wouldn't be the kind of pain in the ass who orders the lobster, takes a bite, and declares herself full. Clean-plate club, baby!

Sure, there are a couple little lines around my eyes, but they're small and positioned in such a way that when I smile, they enhance my grin rather than detract from it. Moving down, I can't see the collarbones I worried so much about in my composite photo anymore, but at this point I imagine everyone's tired of looking at starving starlets' clavicles on the cover of *Us Weekly*, so this is no great loss.[54]

---

[53] I swear by Crest's Vivid White Night Effects toothpaste.

[54] Hey, Hollywood? You know who thinks skeletons are sexy? Necrophiliacs, that's who.

My shoulders are broad, and I look like someone who doesn't need the bag boy's assistance getting her groceries to the car, thank you very much, even if my arms aren't as round as I'd like. My chest is well proportioned to my frame, and I imagine with a few less pounds and the right corset, I could dress up as the St. Pauli Girl next Halloween. (That is, if I didn't detest costumes.) And sure, gravity's been a bitch, but that's why I invest in good bras.

Then there's my stomach, where much of my weight is carried. I should hate it, but it's smooth and brown and solid, kind of like . . . a perfectly baked loaf of bread. And who hates bread? Certainly not me! Yeah, my midriff is *fat*, but it's not blobby, dimpled, rippling fat. It's . . . *pretty* fat, if that's possible.

I continue my inspection, and I get to my hips and butt. I'm not a fan of my new ass-teau, but it's behind me, so it's not like I have to look at it all day, and besides, that's why God invented girdles. Plus, it's proportionate to the rest of my body, which I much prefer to being pear-shaped. Everyone likes apples more than pears.

I take in my legs next. They are, in a word, powerful. My father was thisclose to being a professional football player, and I've inherited his fantastic legs. They've never been slender or dainty; rather, they're incredibly well muscled. Sure, once you get north of my knees they're squashy, but my calves look strong enough to win any ass-kicking contest.

Smiling at my reflection, I give my hair another good shake before placing the camera on my makeup table. I set it and pose in front of the chocolate brown doors to my bedroom closet. Using my best posture, I suck in my gut and tilt my head slightly down and to the side in order to capture the best light. I hold the pose for another ten seconds until I see the flash go off.

I check the camera's display, but it's so small and blurry, I can't see anything. However, if my initial assessment is on target, I bet I look pretty good. Shoot; maybe I should consider plus-sized modeling. After all, I've got the clichéd such-a-pretty-face—maybe I could even make a few bucks? Or possibly get free clothes? Or *handbags*!

Sometimes they have famous plus models visit the girls on *America's Next Top Model*. How cool would that be? I love both Mr. Jay and Miss J., and Tyra Banks would so want to be my best friend, even if I will have to break it to her that she is *not* the new Oprah. But friends are obligated to tell each other the truth, right? We could drink margaritas together and eat ribs and then drop by Miss Janice Dickinson's house, where the fun would really begin!

Anxious to begin my television career, I rush back into my office to download the photo. I can barely sit still while my computer takes its sweet time. Come on; come on!

After what feels like hours, the image appears on my monitor. It's showtime!

And . . . now all I want to know is this: how the *fuck* did Jabba the Hutt get into my bedroom, and why is he wearing my pearls?

So now I don't feel good *or* look good.

Now what?

The last time I lost any significant weight was the spring of 2000. Inspired by all the gorgeous tulips blooming in the center of Michigan Avenue, I decided I wanted a big-city wedding the next year, and Fletch and I began to make plans.[55] At the time, everyone was doing Atkins, evidenced by all the baggies of cheese and turkey in my office's kitchen and the screaming when a bread basket was proffered during corporate lunches. I tried it, too, and the weight simply fell off. I loved never feeling hungry but found myself dying for stuff like grape juice and would have committed murder for five minutes alone inside a Krispy Kreme store. But I kept up the carb-free regimen until I bought a book on wedding planning, realized that with my demanding job I didn't have the bandwidth to coordinate caterers and florists and photographers and the like, and tabled both the wedding and the diet. Three Croissan'wiches later, the weight came back. And it's been here ever since.

In terms of dieting, Atkins was the least offensive, and it was fun to gobble down a juicy steak while gloating about how much thinner I already felt. I bet if I kick-start my weight-loss quest by going low carb, I'll have some initial

[55]This was back when I felt I deserved a three-carat princess-cut ring from Tiffany, so I also researched places where Fletch could sell a kidney in order to afford it.

victories on the scale that I can use to segue into a healthier long-term way of eating!

Resolved: Nothing motivates like success, so Atkins it is.

And now I'm off to buy some cheese.

TO: angie_at_home
FROM: jen@jenlancaster.com
SUBJECT: Quh Muh Gahhhhhhhh

HAnngie,

Pink! Pink liqueuerr! Called X-rated! Yum from drinkpinkvodka.com!
Sold at Cosatco!! Tastes like bitingin into a fresh mango and grapefruit
and passiopnmfruit and swirly swirly with frenchg vodka—YUM! Oner
of these and an Ambien and all of a sudden leggings MAKES TOTAL
PERFECT FUCMOINGH SENSE! Like, GEENIUS! Pants you wearrs
under you skirts? Yes! Brillianbt'1!!1!!

Now I want to amek phone calls untless Fletch stops me :[

Laaqaaaaaatttttteeeerrr,

Jennnnnnn

TO: angie_at_home
FROM: jen@jenlancaster.com
SUBJECT: Um, hi, about last night . . .

Ang,

So, this is probably why the warning label on my new bottle of sleeping pills says DO NOT CONSUME WITH ALCOHOLIC BEVERAGES, NOT EVEN ONE AND NOT EVEN IF IT'S PINK AND FRUITY AND GIRLY, YOU DUMB ASS.

On the plus side, I'm totally not hungover after last night's whoops-I-forgot-I-was-on-Atkins celebration.

However, Fletch is mad at me because I lost my mind in the fifteen minutes he was down in the basement folding laundry when the cocktail and Ambien kicked in at the same time. He came back up because of all the banging. He caught me throwing away the mini–food processor he'd bought to grind spices. Apparently I'd filled it full of ice and was angry "it doesn't make drinks."

I'm back on the Atkins horse today. For lunch I had one and a half Burger King Texas Whoppers minus the bun.

Shameful.

Talk soon,

Jen

Shame con Queso

Shouldn't Atkins be easier?

I mean, I'm all for the concept, which is that obesity isn't caused by calorie intake but by excess sugar in the bloodstream. Dr. Atkins theorized that carbohydrates are the problem, and once they're eliminated, the body goes into the state of ketosis.[56] Once in ketosis, the body stops burning glucose and instead fuels itself on fat reserves. This, in layman's terms, means I can inhale all the beef tenderloin I want as long as I don't order the baked potato, too.

Again, *in theory* this plan rocks, especially since I've previously been on the kinds of diets where I didn't take in enough protein and felt like I was going to die until I totally lost it and ran to La Bamba (home of the "Burrito as big as your head") for super steak, extra guacamole, and hold the

---

[56]Wouldn't this be a great place to have an informative footnote about what ketosis is?

hot sauce *right now; faster, please, goddamn it!* I dig the idea of Atkins because there's something deliciously naughty about being able to dish up as many pork chops as my dish (and tummy) will hold.[57] And who doesn't like to station themselves next to the cheese platter at a party?

The problem with Atkins is in the execution. During the induction phase, almost all foods are banned except for meats and some dairy. The dairy part's tough because I can have heavy cream in my coffee, but I'm not allowed to drink a glass of milk. Fruits are strictly verboten, as are all but a handful of my favorite vegetables. I'm allowed to make the thickest sandwich in the world, chock-full of my favorite deli meats and slathered in mayo, but then I'm stuck trying to fashion a bun out of a slice of lettuce because bread is a no-no, unless I get the low-carb bread, which is as flavorful as a shoebox and retails for close to six dollars per loaf. Sure, I can cook up *mucho, mucho queso fundido* (a mouth-watering Chihuahua-cheese-and-chorizo-sausage dip), but it's not even fun to eat because there are so few vehicles available for dip transport. Pork rinds are allowed, but I'd rather eat the pigskin off a football. The last time I made *queso fundido* I found myself eating cheese dip off of slices of cheese. Very wrong, and not in the good long-dirty-weekend-with-Vince-Vaughn[58] wrong way. Also? I had a hell of a time making a balsamic reduction with Splenda instead of sugar.

....

[57]According to the 1972 version of this diet, which is the book I am using. A later version modifies these rules and restricts the liberal application of stuff like butter, which sounds a lot less fun.

[58]Prior to his post-*Swingers* bloat, of course.

Presently, Fletch and I are grocery shopping, normally one of my favorite activities. But tonight it's like a horror movie: every time I turn around, there's more forbidden food—bread! Pastry! Orange juice! White rice! Fried chicken! Yogurt! Potato chips! Ice cream! Angel hair pasta! Chocolate cake! Aaahhhhh! Fletch finally insists I keep my eyes on only the contents of our cart because he's tired of hearing me gasp every five seconds.

We're almost done when I screw up by strolling down the liquor aisle. Drinking is completely out of the question during the induction phase of Atkins. I can add a cocktail or two in the second phase, but I fall off the low-carb wagon so often that I've technically never made it to the second phase. The longest I've ever gone is about thirteen days. Thus, gazing upon bottle after bottle of all my favorites—Stoli raspberry-flavored vodka, Kahlúa, Molson, and all the other beers, wines, and spirits I love—causes me to have the kind of meltdown that will ensure mockery well through our golden years, e.g., *Hey, Jen, remember when looking at a bottle of Jose Cuervo made you cry at the Jewel?* Yes, laugh it up, asshat. We'll see what's so funny when I put you in the crooked nursing home we saw on *60 Minutes*.[59]

Later, when we're home and the groceries have been put away, I dine on a pile of grilled hamburger and a sadly tomatoless salad swimming in bleu cheese dressing. For dessert I have cream cheese mixed with lemon zest and Splenda,

[59]Yet another *Simpsons* quote, this time from episode 65, season 4, "Itchy & Scratchy: The Movie." Not the Best Episode Ever, but from the Conan O'Brien years, so still pretty damned good.

served over a bowl of sugar-free Jell-O. Blah. I'm not hungry by any means, but I'm certainly not satisfied, and I'm pretty sure I'd kill or die for a slice of pie right now.

I'd also love a glass of wine, but that's not an option. Then I remember I finally picked up my prescription of Ambien. Although a part of me is all, "Woo! Recreational drugs!" I do need them because my insomnia's been especially bad lately. Ever since the Christmas party, things have been weird at Fletch's company. They expanded the business too much this year and spent a lot of money on dumb stuff, e.g., taking all the employees to a luxury tropical resort for a week, even *after* they knew they'd be ending the year in the red. There's a dot-com-bomb feeling about the place, and I wonder how much longer Fletch is going to have a job. We're financially prepared if it happens, but I'm not so keen on going through *Layoff: The Sequel,* if for no reason other than the inevitable stress eating unemployment inspires. Lest you forget, I created the Twinkwich[60] last time we were out of work. Fletch has been searching for other jobs, so hopefully he'll be out of there before anything happens and I'm compelled to eat nineteen cheesecakes in response.

Fletch has already gone to bed, but my Ambien hasn't kicked in yet, so I decide to spend a little time on the Internet before turning in. I catch up on the blogs I follow and check my mail. I notice I've gotten an e-mail from Amazon telling me about some new Barbie products I might be

---

[60]A Hostess Twinkie and Ding Dong paired in a sandwich of nerve-calming decadence. (Basically it's homemade Prozac.)

interested in because last Christmas I bought a bunch of Barbie stuff for my niece. Although she likes Barbie, she has a number of interests, including soccer, basketball, gymnastics, ballet, reading, etc. My sister-in-law prefers to encourage those interests, so buying Barbie stuff is a task I've assigned myself.

Back when I was my niece's age, I loved Barbie with a singular passion. Almost any other toy I received was tossed aside with disdain. I owned tons of Barbies, and I'd carry all of them around in this battered leather suitcase that had been my grandfather's. It was lined in Barbie-pink silk, and whenever I'd play, I made it into Barbie's condo, using the sock and underwear compartment as her sleeping loft.

My favorite Barbie wasn't a doll at all; it was a life-sized bust of Barbie with hair I could brush and style. Plus, I could put makeup on her and swap out her jewelry, and I considered this important practice for being an adult. Critics say playing with Barbies gives little girls unrealistic expectations of what they're supposed to look like when they grow up, to which I respond, "*Pfft.*" If it hadn't been for Barbie, I'd never have learned to apply liquid eyeliner!

I wonder if they even make those Barbie heads anymore. I do a quick search on Amazon, and I begin to page through different models—the Barbie Fashion Fever Grow 'N Style, the Barbie Glamour Pup, the Barbie Primp and Polish, the Barbie Bling Bling, etc. Suddenly, I'm hit with what feels like tractor trailer full of pillows, and the next thing I know, it's morning and I'm waking up in the guest room, a foot away from my computer, which is still open to Amazon.com and whirring away.

Weird.

"Hi, I'm in my underpants and I'm all greasy."

There's a certain stillness at the other end of the line before Angie asks, "Is this a bad time?"

"No, no; I'm just out of the shower, getting ready for the gym. I'm putting on lotion. But I've got my headset on, so I can talk," I reply. Inspired by all Angie can do with her hands-free phone, we recently purchased one of our own. "You might hear some grunting, but that's just me struggling into my Lycra pants."

"Grunting? You positive this is a good time?"

"Absolutely! Plus, I'm dying to hear the squirrel update." Angie's husband, Jim, is a professor at a large midwestern university and he's brilliant, which is why stories of him being terrorized and outsmarted by a flying squirrel are so hilarious.

She's already snickering when she replies, "Things are not going well. It's been almost two weeks, and still no one's seen it. The maintenance department set every variety of baited trap—rattraps, mousetraps, and even those have-a-heart living traps. You can't move in his office without bumping into one. The more traps they set, the angrier the squirrel gets. Two days ago it destroyed all the plants in Jim's office, and I just got an e-mail from him because . . . because . . ." Angie sputters with laughter before continuing,

"Because he can't *call*. The squirrel has chewed through his phone lines. The more they do to try to catch him, the more punitive he gets."

"I love this squirrel! I picture him with a tiny Rambo headband and a couple gun belts slung over his shoulders. What do Jim's students think when they come to his office and see all the traps?" I ask while smoothing leave-in conditioner in my hair.

"Oh, they know all about it. Jim starts each class with a Flying Squirrel Report. And his classroom has giant plasma screens and he's already shown them the photos of those flying squirrels he found on Google. Judging from the pictures, they don't fly so much as parachute."

"Maybe if I'd had a fun finance professor I wouldn't have cut class so much," I muse.[61] I load loose powder onto my brush and tap off the excess before giving my face a quick dusting.

"Someone at your door?" she asks.

"Nope, that's just me putting on powder."

"Wait, what? I thought you were going to the gym."

"I am."

There's a brief yet ever-so-slightly judgmental pause at the other end of the line, and Angie finally says, "You wear *makeup* to the *gym*?"

"Well, *yeah*. I may be the fattest person there, but I'll be damned if I'm going to show up completely unadorned."

"Crazy-person alert!"

---

[61]Nah, probably not.

"Not at all," I counter. "The way I see it, I can be heavy, I can be close to forty, and I can have a naked face, but no more than two at the same time. Right now the only one of those factors I can control is the makeup, so here I am." I blend all four colors of my blush and apply it to the apples of my cheeks, sweeping backward. "I don't put on full makeup. I mean, yes, I do foundation, the Bobbi Brown two-step under-eye concealer, powder, blush, eye shadow, and liner. Um, and mascara—you know, the kind with a base coat that goes on gray and then the top coat that makes everything thick and dark. Oh, and I fill in my brows and apply lip gloss. Or I use lipstick, depending on how tan I am and which looks better with my workout shirt. But that's it."

"Isn't that just about everything, Tammy Faye?"

"*No.* I leave off the iridescent shimmer powder and I don't use the brightener in the corners of my eyes. I'm *way* less radiant than usual."

"Okay, then. As long as you're not *radiant*. Speaking of, how's the gym going?"

I shrug. "I guess it's all right. If I weren't on stupid Atkins, I'd be doing better. Apparently carbohydrates give you energy in addition to a fat ass, and I can barely eke out two miles. On the upside, I've been going consistently, mostly because I only tan if I hit the treadmill first."

"Aw, Jen, no! I thought you were trying to get healthy. And skin cancer? Is so not healthy." Angie is also patently disgusted with my newfound love of those plastic Croc clown shoes, particularly in the ridiculous colors. I have them in pink, green, purple, and white with flowers painted on them.

Angie refuses to leave the house with me if I'm wearing them when she visits.

"Tanning is OK if I'm exercising. Yes, I'm increasing my risk of melanoma, but in so doing, I'm decreasing the risk of heart disease. I'm not knocking time off my own personal doomsday clock, but I'm also not adding to it. It's a draw, and that's fine. Besides, my biggest obstacle is craving carbs. I can't stand wanting bread so much. Makes me feel too much like Reggie."

"Reggie? Remind me—was he your Newfoundland or Great Pyrenees?"

"Neither. Reggie was our Japanese exchange student, re-member?" We volunteered to host him because my mom thought it would be so culturally enriching. Turns out he left Japan to escape his culture, and he was practically more American than we were. He lived with us for three years, and we never learned a damn thing. "Reggie was on the wrestling team. Before big matches he'd starve himself into a lower weight class, and whenever you'd ask how he was, he'd say, 'I'm trying not to eat.' Everything went by the wayside— schoolwork, TV, friends, normal conversation—and all he could focus on was his own hunger."

"And that's how you feel right now?" I hear vaguely fa-miliar scraping noises in the background that sound almost like Angie's buttering toast. But that would be impossible because Angie's pledged to diet along with me even though she doesn't need to.

Scrape, scrape.

God, I'm so preoccupied with bread right now, everything sounds like toast. Angie is probably just installing a travertine backsplash with marble she hand-tumbled herself. It's not breakfast; it's masonry! Plus, she wouldn't be eating, because she started a fat-flush diet and she's only drinking liquid for the next five days. She's testing it out, and if it works, I'm going to try it, too, although I wonder if I put a loaf of sourdough and Irish butter in the blender, would that count as a beverage?

"Exactly! Funny, but when I'm not dieting I can go hours and hours without thinking about food. Some days when I'm busy it might be four in the afternoon before I remember to eat something. But now that I'm doing Atkins, all I can think about are bagels and donuts and Lucky Charms cereal, and I'm making myself crazy. So what do I do? How do I deal with this? How are you managing the whole not-eating thing?" There's no response on the other end of the line.

"Ang? Angie? Are you there?" I ask. My phone service, although supercheap, is not always reliable. Occasionally I'll get disconnected and keep talking for long stretches before I realize the other party is gone.

She finally replies, "I'm here. But I'm, um, not fasting anymore."

"Really? You were so gung ho. What happened?"

I hear her take a deep breath. "A Russian family just moved in next door. They were busy unpacking, so I had my kids shovel their sidewalk. To thank us, they brought over this incredible homemade date-nut bread, and it would have been rude of me to not serve it and share some coffee with them, so I broke the fast."

"Well, I figured drinking nothing but cayenne-pepper water would get old pretty fast. How much did you lose before you ate the bread?"

Another long pause. "None."

"All that effort for nothing? That sucks. How long were you on it?"

"Um . . . about three hours."

"Ang, that's not a fast; that's skipping breakfast."

Before she can reply, I hear a sweet little voice in the background say, "Your barn door is open!" before collapsing into a fit of giggles.

"I take it James is home from preschool?" I ask.

"Yep. Someone taught him that last week, and he's been saying it nonstop. It's like the funniest thing he's ever heard. That's the great thing about little kids—you can tell them the oldest, most hackneyed knock-knock joke, and they think you're Seinfeld. Anyway, you've got to go, and I have to make the little guy soup and a sandwich. Have a good workout!"

"Talk later!" I say, removing my headset.

But I'm not going to have a good workout.

Because all I can think about right now are tomato soup, grilled cheese sandwiches, and buttered date-nut bread. I hate Atkins so damn much.

I'm getting pretty tired of my routine at the gym. Every time I go, it's the same thing. First, I walk on the treadmill for a while. I try to spice it up by reading a trashy book, as those tend to hold my interest best. Sure, I'd love to improve my mind and body at the same time, but it's hard for me to concentrate on Dostoyevsky *and* not falling on my ass, you know? My goal is to work hard enough that I get a little triangle of sweat in the V of my T-shirt, which generally takes about half an hour. If I'm feeling adventurous, I might crank up the incline to three or four, but not for terribly long because I don't like to feel it in my shins.

After the treadmill, I hit the elliptical machine, which requires even more hand-eye coordination, thus no books. My gym has four big plasma-screen televisions, but I can't read the subtitles while I'm bobbing up and down like a big, fat, well-groomed piston. I do the elliptical for as long as I can stand; unfortunately, it's only about five minutes at a time, not only because I have no energy but also because I'm bored. The problem is, I normally think I'm the most fascinating person ever to don a pair of Air Nikes, but the second I hit the elliptical, every interesting thought I ever had exits stage left to hang out at the juice bar until I'm done. I wonder if I get an iPod, will my workouts improve? I try to finish up the session on the bike, but only if one's available. Although my gym has a ton of bikes, only two are recumbent. Since the pointy little seats on the other bikes remind me of that awful scene from *Caligula*, I refuse to ride them.[62] Exit only, thanks.

In an effort to wake up my fitness regime, I try something

---

[62]Yeah, I know selling my recumbent bike was a bad idea. Thanks for not mentioning it sooner.

different. Since I'd rather be *s-o-d-o-m-i-z-e-d* by a bike seat than go to an actual exercise class with real, live people who have the ability to point and laugh, I check out the cached videos that come as part of my cable service. Honestly, I've never even accessed this screen before, but as I do, I am pleasantly surprised. My gosh, there are so many choices here! Tae Bo and toning and thin thighs in minutes! Pilates and power core and walking with weights! I can even work out with the Girls Next Door (from Hef's harem), but I'm kind of wary of the exercise they might have me do. My concern is *not* how my Kegel muscles look in a swimsuit, you know?

I click through the listings and finally settle on yoga. Everyone likes yoga, right? I see all the stars in my gossip magazines trotting to class lugging their mats . . . which I'll admit bugs me. Couldn't the yoga center provide nice, squashy, sanitized mats as part of the price of admission? Or couldn't folks like Gwyneth Paltrow and Madonna task one of their minions to carry them? Regardless, the idea of having longer, stronger, more flexible muscles appeals, and there's the whole Zen aspect of it, too. I'm starting to feel Fletch's job stress, and if I can't relax myself, how am I supposed to help him stay calm?

I select the video and press PLAY. I'm ready with my own nonskid yoga mat, yoga straps, and yoga blocks, all laid out perpendicular to the (yoga) television. I'm wearing my yoga pants, and since I don't have a yoga top, I just threw on one of my big Champion workout tees. I light a couple of sweet-smelling candles in order to make the room more ambient, and draw the curtains. Then I undraw the curtains because it's too dark, plus it's the middle of the afternoon on a Thursday and we've already received the mail. Unless anyone comes to the door—which isn't happening—no one from the street can see me.

OK, let's begin. The video's new age-y instructor starts with deep breathing. She's all ropey and leathery. For someone who's supposed to be a paragon of fitness, her body certainly looks like a bendy strip of beef jerky. Whoops, wait; I forgot to breathe while I was snickering. Yes. Let's breathe! Breathing is nice. In. Out. In. Out. I'm "scooping out my abs" and "pressing into my sitting bones," which I assume means "suck" and "tuck." In. Out. Look at the rise and fall of my chest. In. Out. In. Out. The instructor wants me to really *feel* my breath. (What does that mean, exactly?) In. Out. Innnnnnn. Ouuuuuuuut. Very nice. She says I'm getting rid of my toxins. Lovely! Perhaps I can breathe out all the wine I accidentally drank last night when I forgot I was on Atkins.

And I was so close to getting to level two, damn it.

Innnnnn. Ouuuuuuuut. Terrific. That bottle of wine is practically evaporating every time I exhale. There's some whale music playing in the background, and combined with the sugar-cookie-scented candle, it makes the whole room feel entirely pleasant. Look at me, breathing with the best of them!

Time to stop sitting on the floor? Alrighty. I use the couch to help hoist myself up. (There may or may not be some grunting involved here.) So, now I'm supposed to do some sort of flop-over-type move. With my legs in a V, I lunge forward with the instruction to "open up my chest," which . . . gross. How's the idea of my splayed chest cavity supposed to be relaxing? Ick. I lunge and splay, lunge and splay, being careful to stay centered, which I'm interpreting as "don't tip over."

We move on to a pose called Warrior. I like that. *Warrior.* Yes, I am a warrior and my enemy is Fat! I shall splay *your* chest cavity, Fat! Look at me, lifting my pelvic floor![63] Lift, lunge, lift, lunge, to the sky, to the sky. Yogi Beef Jerky says I'm supposed to feel the nature swirling within as I tuck my tailbone. Huh. All I feel right now is the Riesling swirling within. I'm going to have a hard time vanquishing Fat if I accidentally spew semisweet German wine.

We're on to Downward-Facing Dog. Dumb name. I guarantee you my dogs have never stood on the tips of all their paws, arching their ample rumps in the air. You want a dog pose? Then either wipe your mouth on my pretty pink bedspread or drag your butt across a freshly steam-cleaned carpet. Actually, this pose looks way more like the way my cats stretch, right before they run to the basement to poop in a box and then dash back up to walk all over my counters. (The stretch cool-down includes napping on my cashmere sweaters, with sharpening claws on the new couch optional.)

Perhaps there *is* something to calling this move Downward-Facing Dog, because not only have Maisy and Loki woken up, but they're fighting over who gets to lick me on the

---

[63] Who knew my pelvis had a floor? Although I think this has something to do with the Kegels.

face while I press into the floor with my hands and feet. I push them away, and they come right back at me with cold, wet noses. Shove and extend. Shove and extend. Extend . . . extend . . . and *Aaah! Stop fucking goosing me!*

I have to pause the video while I corral the dogs in the other room. They howl in protest, and I tell them they are harshing my mellow and Yogi Beef Jerky's going to be pissed. I rewind and get myself into Downward-Facing Dog. Damn, this is *hard*. It uses all my nonexistent push-up muscles, and I'm totally shaking as I try to hold the pose, made a jillion times more difficult because my big cottony T-shirt keeps bunching up around my head and suffocating me. Push and extend and spit out cotton, the fabric of our lives. Frustrated, I finally rip the whole damn shirt off and throw it across the room, leaving me in nothing but yoga pants and a particularly ugly bra covered in faded pink cabbage roses.

I'm just about finished with Downward-Facing Dog when I hear a noise that makes my blood freeze. No, it's not the crack of a gunshot or the tinkle of an ice cream truck; it's the sound of feet clattering up my front steps. Before I can pull myself up, I come face-to-ass with the UPS delivery man, and I peer at him shirtless, backward, and upside down from between my legs, over the spare tire that is forcing my cabbage-rose-clad rack up around my neck, and through my uncurtained window.

And this? Right here? Is why I hate exercise.

The UPS driver turns ten thousand shades of red and drops the huge box, sprinting away from the door and required signature. He's already down my street and back on the expressway in the seconds it takes me to stand up and throw on my shirt.

Mortified but curious, I open the door and bring in the box. It's about the size of a coffee table, and it's addressed to me from Amazon.com. Huh. I don't remember ordering anything recently. The reserves from my royalty check are dwindling, and I've been really, really careful about spending money. I enter the kitchen, pushing aside the doggie gate, releasing the beasts, who promptly show their gratitude with more goosing.

I root through the junk drawer until I find a box cutter. I slit the box open along the seam and . . .

Aaaaaaaaaaaaahhhhhhh!

Head!

Box!

In!

There's a motherfucking human head inside this box!

Which means a serial killer read about my fear of lifting a toilet seat and finding a severed head and *he's sent me one*!

I am too freaked out right now to figure out how he'd (a) get my address and (b) convince Amazon to ship this to me. Sweet Jesus, a head, *a head*, oh, my God, I'm going to diiiiiiiiiiiiiieeeee!

The room gets dark and spinny and I feel my knees go out underneath me. I grab on to the box as I go down, and right before I hit the floor, I spot a soothingly familiar shade of pink.

Wait.

Severed heads aren't pink.

With sparkly earrings.

And golden blond tresses.

And shimmery rose pink lip gloss.

Upon closer inspection, I realize it's not a human head at all. It's a Barbie Fashion Fever Grow 'N Style hair-styling head.

What the . . . ?

How did . . . ?

I pace around the kitchen, gingerly holding the head at arm's length as I work out the details. I scan the receipt and see that it was me who ordered this, but I have no memory of that. I check the date on the order and cross-reference it with the white-board calendar we keep on our fridge.

Wait a sec; I ordered this the day I started on Ambien. Dr. Awesome did warn me about rare instances of people sleep-eating and sleep-driving while on Ambien, but she said nothing about sleep-Barbie-ing. At the moment I'm almost grateful at being busted by the UPS guy while doing downward-facing flab-hang, because this? Is *way* more embarrassing.

I stuff the box in the little den off the kitchen, saving all the packing receipts so I can send the damn thing back. I mean, really; I'm almost forty—what the hell am I possibly going to do with a *Barbie head*?

After taking another Ambien last night, I wake up in the guest room again this morning, and notice that *someone* during the night has not only retrieved and unpacked the

Barbie head, but also styled her with a big back-combed updo, thick black eyeliner, off-white lipstick, and a Pucci-style head wrap.

Well, how about that?

My shame looks exactly like Nancy Sinatra.

TO: angie_at_home
FROM: jen@jenlancaster.com
SUBJECT: To carb or not to carb, that is the question

Hey,

Help me out—I'm trying to figure out whether or not I should shitcan Atkins and try something new. Here's what I've come up with by way of pros and cons.

PRO QUITTING ATKINS:

100% less crying when Fletch eats a plate of cookies and a glass of milk

Having my veins filled with blood again and not just bacon grease

Peeing in the toilet rather than on my hand while holding a ketosis stick

Using the same soiled hand to cover up my stinky ketosis breath

Booze, sweet, sweet booze

Not having the urge to primal scream when encountering once-beloved cheese counter

All things french fried, cottage fried, waffled fried, mashed, scalloped, au gratined, hash browned, totted, boiled, chipped, Lyonnaised, puffed, broiled, parsleyed, and baked

CON QUITTING ATKINS:

[crickets]

[crickets]

Yeah, that's what I thought.

But if I end Atkins, then what do I try?

Jen

P.S. Three more Barbies arrived in the mail today. WTF is wrong with me?

I Wish I Could Quit You, Olive Garden

I'm heading to New York tomorrow for some meetings, and I'm almost beside myself with anxiety. The thing is, I'm not worried about my appointments even though they're important. Rather, I've spent the last week agonizing over the flight. I'm particularly nervous this time since I haven't flown anywhere for about four years. Intellectually I understand I'm much safer "up there" than on the road and can quote the stats inside and out. The issue is that I've yet to convince my central nervous system that I'm not going to die in that aluminum tube; hence, terror sweat.

I used to handle flying just fine, but that was before a plane I was on ran out of gas and we had to make an emergency landing at Midway because we couldn't make it to O'Hare.[64] Touching down to refuel at a different airport

---

[64]For those unfamiliar with Chicago's airports, one could *walk* between them if necessary. Also, how do you run out of gas? Shouldn't that be the first thing the pilot checks once the doors are closed?

didn't scare me—what did was seeing the line of ambulances and fire trucks lined up waiting to extinguish/resuscitate us. I was also on a flight where we made an unscheduled stop because the passenger right behind me had a heart attack, and I've experienced turbulence so rough the flight attendants cried, so at this point I'm a bit surprised when any flight goes as planned.[65]

Naturally, I've driven Fletch crazy with my constant obsessing.

"Hey, honey?"

Fletch glances up from the eggs he's poaching on the stove. Ugh, eggs. I can barely stand them anymore. I've eaten so goddamned many eggs, it's only a matter of time until I grow feathers and a beak. "What's up?" he asks.

"I'm worried about the flight."

He struggles to remain patient. "Really," he states. "Why this time? Is it because you're not sure you can take out a terrorist by swinging your heavy purse at him, or are you back on the I'm-worried-we're-going-to-crash-in-the-Andes-and-the-other-passengers-will-want-to-eat-me thing from yesterday?"

Admittedly, I may have been more than a tad fixated on this for the past few days.

"Well, yes, of course I'm still worried about those things. But what occurred to me this morning *really* terrifies me. What if I've gained so much weight since I last flew that my

---

[65]BTW, did you ever notice when you say you're a bad flier, everyone thinks this is the perfect time to tell you about all of their flying traumas? Well, guess what? *These stories don't help.*

seat belt doesn't buckle and the stewardess has to give me one of those extenders? Or, oh, God, worse yet, what if the employee at the check-in desk takes one look at me and says, *I'm sorry, ma'am; you're going to have to buy a second seat to get on this flight.* Then I really will die. From shame."

Fletch switches off the burner, covers the sauté pan, and sits down across the table from me. He takes my hand and gazes lovingly into my eyes. "I'm just curious," he says. "At what point did you lose your fucking mind?"

"What do you mean?"

"Up until recently, you were the most confident person I knew. You're the one who says everyone else is too thin and you're just right. Now that you're actually losing weight, you're completely fixated on body image, and you never were before. Doesn't make any sense."

I consider this for a few moments before responding. "I don't know. Maybe it's because before I started dieting, I never thought about my weight or what I ate."

"If you keep obsessing, you're ultimately going to fail because no matter how much weight you lose, you will never think you're thin enough. That's a recipe for unhappiness right there. Anorexia, too."

I snort. "From your lips to God's ears."

All right, all right; I'm aware that eating disorders are diseases and people die from them and they're no laughing matter. They're scary, and so many young women legitimately suffer. In my own circle of friends, I've seen lives ruined in the relentless pursuit of perfection, and it's so sad. But, still . . . could I please have one for a week or so? Just to get a nice start? Back in the day when I briefly considered bulimia, I could never bring myself to stick my fingers down my throat. I tried to do it mentally by picturing greasy liver and onions served in a dirty ashtray, but my imagination's not that good. I was all about the binge, but I could never master the purge.

Fletch sighs and returns to cooking. Taking a slotted spoon from the ceramic crock next to the stove, he gingerly picks up each egg, pausing to let the water drain. "I'm serious, Jen. You've got to be a little more Zen about everything. Give yourself credit for the progress you've made and you're going to feel much better. Ditto on flying. Get a grip—everything is going to be fine."

He plates up our food—I'm having Atkins-approved poached eggs with a side of Canadian bacon, and he's eating the same thing, except he's also having a side of multigrain French toast. I watch as he puts a neat little pat of the extra-rich European butter on each slice, and then covers the stack with pure maple syrup. He heated the syrup first, so the butter melts instantly and the heady combination begins to ooze down the side of the toast. I feel myself salivate as he slices into his first bite, and my eyes follow the trajectory of his fork from plate to mouth and back again. I would kick kittens for one small taste right about now.[66]

Fletch notices me staring at his breakfast with naked lust. "I'm sorry—do you and my French toast need a moment alone?"

---

[66]But on the bright side, at least I'm temporarily distracted from visions of planes falling out of the sky.

God, I am the worst dieter ever. Here I am on a plan that allows, nay, *insists* on plenty of protein and enough volume to never feel hungry, yet all I want is the six-month-old frost-laden French toast Fletch found at the back of the freezer. Even though I'd be allowed to eat ten rib eyes or an entire wheel of Tillamook cheddar, I would give up my favorite triple-strand pearl necklace to drink the syrup puddle on his plate.

"No, no; I'm fine."

"Excellent." He continues to tuck in to the stack.

"Hey, it looks like there's a light powdering of cinnamon and sugar on the crust."

He turns his plate to examine its contents. "Yeah, I guess there is. Now, what else do you have to do before you leave? You have your ticket, and your hotel is confirmed?"

"Yep. Everything's set, and I'm even done packing. All I have to do in the morning is stash my makeup in my carry-on." I pause to choke down a bite of my Canadian bacon. "Is that as good as it looks?" I gesture toward his plate.

Fletch raises a beleaguered eyebrow at me. "No. It's kind of stale, if you want to know the truth." He takes another bite, and a bit of butter-syrup drips off the side. I feel something on the side of my mouth, and I think I may actually be drooling. Shameful. "Are you looking forward to tomorrow? This is your first trip back to New York in how long?"

"Six years." I break the yellow part of my poached egg and make yoke swirls with my knife. "So, your French toast . . . is it, um, lightly crunchy on the outside but all soft and warm inside?"

He shrugs. "Yeah. Anyway, what's the plan? You land at LaGuardia, take a cab into the city, and then what?"

"I check into the hotel, and then I go to my publisher's office to meet up with my editor and publicist. And then we're all going to go out for drinks with my agent." I'm going on a temporary Atkins vacation while I'm there, but I'm totally going to watch my fat and calories.

"You know where yet?"

"No." I gaze longingly as Fletch dips a piece of Canadian bacon into Lake Deliciousness, its sweetness providing what I'm sure is a wonderful contrast to the ham's saltiness. "How's the European butter in combination with the syrup? Would you say it's a flavor party in your mouth and everyone's invited? Is it richer and nuttier than regular butter?"

He lays down his fork in disgust. "The only thing nutty in this kitchen right now is you. Here." He slides his plate over to my side of the table. "Have a bite if you want it, but if you don't, then stop grilling me. Either way, we're going to have a conversation that doesn't include carbohydrates, agreed?"

"I'm sorry; I'm sorry. I won't say another word, I promise." I slide his plate back over to him . . . after I decide against licking it.

"What else is on your mind?" he asks gently.

"Other than imagining myself hurtling to the ground in a flaming metal shell and landing on a desert island with Kate, Jack, Sawyer, and Locke, and . . . Hey! Come back! I promise to stop."

Reluctantly, Fletch returns from the living room, but now

he's got his laptop with him. He's working from home today because he wanted to spend a little more time with me before I left. I bet he's regretting that decision right now.

"I am never discussing plane crashes with you again. Or bread," he says.

"I can't—"

"Not pumpernickel, not rye, not seven grain, not hot-cross buns. Understood?"

"Bread is all I think about."

"*You must stop Atkins.* Every time you're on it, you make everyone around you crazy and you gain back more than you lost."

"This is the last time, I swear. I need its quick success before I go tomorrow. When I get back on Saturday, I'm going to start cooking meals from the Weight Watchers cookbook."

"Sounds reasonable. I went through it, and I like a lot of what they suggest. Are you going to join, too?"

"Ugh. No way. The last goddamned thing I want to do is sit around and listen to people talk about their *feeelings* about birthday cake."

"Yet you've discussed nothing but your fear of death and donuts around here for the past three days."

"Oh, please; this is totally different. Remember when I went to Weight Watchers when we lived in Lincoln Park?" I ask.

Fletch taps something out on the keyboard of his Black-Berry.

Mmm . . . berries.

"Not really, no."

"About ten years ago? Remember? I wanted to shake off the twenty pounds I'd gained since graduation?"

"Not ringing any bells."

"I went because my friend Terri in New Orleans was doing Weight Watchers at the time and she really liked it. Remember? She dropped quite a bit of weight and was still able to go out for drinks occasionally, so I thought, *Hey, sign me up.* I went and it was kind of ridiculous. Seemed like everyone in the meeting blamed their weight on someone else, and the entire discussion centered on how evil it was when someone had a birthday at work and brought in dessert. I only went the one time."

He snaps his fingers. "Yes! I vaguely remember you flailing around the apartment afterward, screeching, 'Cake, cake; oh, God, not cake!'"

"The meeting was a Janeane Garofalo bit come to life."

"And you're 'above' all of that?"

"No, I want to see what I can accomplish on my own. Weight Watchers seems like a last resort for people who can't control themselves. And that's not me."

"Five minutes ago I thought I'd have to wrestle a sticky plate away from you."

"I can control myself—when I choose to. I've simply chosen not to."

"If you say so. But it seems like the sooner you seek help, the easier the whole process is going to be." Fletch's cell phone rings, and he glances down at the display. "Sorry, I've gotta take this." He walks into the den and shuts the door.

Whatever. I'm doing fine, and I see no need to employ any sort of help. I gained the weight on my own, and I can lose it on my own. Besides, my immediate concern is, what happens if my plane crashes and I live and I don't have a blow dryer and everyone on the island thinks my stupid natural curl makes me look like Hurley?

I eat and drink my way from Morningside Heights to Tribeca. There are no carbohydrates left in Manhattan when I finally leave the island. And when I try to fasten my seat belt on the plane on the way back, I struggle for five minutes before I can click it into place.

Whatever weight I lost over the past few months has found me again.

Sigh.

Jen's Life Lesson #301: Never watch food commercials when dieting.

Every time I see an Olive Garden ad, my Pavlovian response is to drive to their nearest location as quickly as possible. This is shameful on so many levels—first, there are eleventy billion better, more authentic[67] Italian restaurants out there; second, many of them are within city limits, and third, the fact that we're in this car headed to the one in Schaumburg means I'm totally off Atkins. A-fucking-gain.

I'm never, ever going to make it out of the induction phase.

I wish I could quit you, Olive Garden.

What's worse is, I'm contemplating everything I'm about

---

[67] I studied Italian for years and know for a fact that "*hospitaliano*" isn't a real word.

to stuff in my mouth, so I'm really not tuning in to whatever it is Fletch is saying.

". . . which is so wrong, because a true pilsner has a pale body and a crisp, *dry* finish, not sweet," says Fletch. "So Joel says, '*A sweet finish? And you call yourself a microbrewer?*'"

"Wait, what? Joel[68] is back? I thought he was in Iraq until this fall."

"He *is*. I was talking about an e-mail I got from him. Were you even listening?"

No, I was thinking about breadsticks.

"Yes, of course! Joel. Beer. War. Yes." Joel was on leave over New Year's, and he and his wife came to our house for what was supposed to be a classy dinner party but eventually turned into a bourbon-fueled, mildly homoerotic wrestling match. My pretensions were painfully short-lived as I was forced to host in a pair of sweats, having grown too fat for all my pants. By the time Fletch challenged Joel to a duel at four a.m., wrasslin' seemed like the most appropriate way to welcome in the New Year. But before stuff got too boozy, I totally grilled Joel about his confidential assignment in Baghdad. You'd think five kinds of cheese would loosen his tongue, but not so much.[69]

"Speaking of Joel, I saw this story on the news about an

---

[68]Fletch's army buddy Joel, previously known as Hurricane Joel for his propensity to speak in capital letters, is possibly the worst beer snob to ever walk the earth. Every time I drink a Miller High Life in front of him, a piece of his soul dies.

[69]I would never, ever help terrorists, but I can say that if they believe the finest wedge of Whole Foods Gruyère is their key to unlocking American military secrets, they're going to be sorely disappointed.

organization that sends care packages to combat troops. And they don't just send them to Iraq and Afghanistan—they also ship them to places like Djibouti and—"

"Wait, *where*?"

"Djibouti, and I had no idea we had troops stationed there. Anyway, they ship candy and books and—"

"Where on earth is Djibouti?"

"The Horn of Africa, not that far from Yemen. So I was thinking—"

"Oh, my God, Fletch. Fletch!"

"What?"

"Ask me where Djibouti is!"

"Pardon?" With an eye on the rearview mirror, he passes the slower drivers. Which, according to him, is every single person on the road.

"I said, ask me where Djibouti is!"

"I'm aware of where it is. I just *told* you; were you not listening again, or can you not find Africa on that big blue ball on a stick we keep in the den?"

"Please ask; I promise it will be worth it."

"No." Zoom, zoom; eat our dust, other motorists.

"Just play along for once in your life."

He grips the wheel more tightly and squares his shoulders. "No."

"Please! I won't commandeer a bite of your dessert if you do, I swear."

Through clenched teeth, Fletch asks, "OK, Jen; where's Djibouti?"

"In my pants!"

I spend the next ten minutes braying like a jackass, rendering further conversation impossible until we get to the restaurant.

Having yet to learn a thing about moderation, I stuff myself with breadsticks dipped in Alfredo sauce, calamari squeezed with lemon and doused in chunky marinara, chicken Roma with a thick dusting of freshly grated Parmesan, cheesecake, and about fifteen Italian orange cream sodas. I take in enough calories to sustain an African village for a week. Oy.

Shortly after we get back in the car, I begin to whimper.

"Now why are you complaining?" Fletch asks. "With all this traffic, I'm not speeding. Look." He gestures toward the speedometer. "I'm not even going forty."

"Your driving is fine," I moan.

"Then, what's the matter?"

"I ate too much," I wail, unbuttoning my pants and pulling down my zipper. "And now my Djibouti hurts."

After the setback at the Olive Garden, I decide to give Atkins one last chance after reviewing the Weight Watchers cookbook. I'm guessing Dr. Awesome wouldn't approve of this way of eating, but I'm desperate for some real progress. If I had a tiny bit of tangible success, I know I'd be motivated to eat better and exercise more. As it is now, I'm so sapped of energy that I haven't even been to the gym in a few weeks.

Fletch has had a rough week in the office, so I decide to humor him by ordering dinner from his favorite rib joint.

Ribs, especially those covered in sugary barbecue sauce, are an Atkins no-no, so I pick a green salad covered with grilled chicken. Yawn.

When the food arrives, I'm upstairs cleaning the bathroom, so Fletch assembles our plates. The house rule is, we eat at the kitchen table unless we have delivery, and then we get to have dinner *and* watch television. Woo! When I sit down next to Fletch, the smell of barbecue wafts up to greet me, and there's no less than two pounds of food piled on his plate. "Mmm, something smells incredible. What did you get again?"

"I'm having the rib sampler—there's baby backs, spareribs, and rib tips." He gestures to each cut of meat with a giant half-eaten bone as he names it, and it kind of looks like he's playing the drums in the Flintstones' band. He also has a huge chunk of cornbread and a giant pile of French-fried sweet potatoes on a side plate because he has so many ribs, the sides wouldn't all fit. "Want to try some?"

"Um, I probably shouldn't . . . but it smells so good." Here's the thing—I'm a huge fan of barbecued ribs, but I'm also incredibly fussy about them. Seems like everywhere I order them they're too spicy, too tough, or too fatty. Maybe there's too much cartilage or they're so stringy, I get tired while chewing them. It's rare that I ever happen upon the correct juxtaposition of meaty, tender, and slightly sweet, but not for lack of trying. I'm always so excited to get them, yet I'm perpetually disappointed.

I prepare myself for another letdown as I sink my teeth into a spare rib. The meat falls off the bone the second it hits my mouth. The sweet sauce has the perfect amount of heat—not too spicy, but with enough of a red-chili-powder kick to wake my every taste bud. It's delicately smoked and juicily perfect; I can tell exactly how low and slow it has been cooked. This easily ranks in the top ten. "This is transcendent," I tell Fletch, placing the rest of the rib back on his plate.

"Go ahead and finish it. There's plenty more." he says.

But I can't. If I have one more bite, then I will go in the kitchen and toss back the pound of meat that's still sitting in the take-out container. I desperately want to roll around in that damned barbecue sauce, but if I do, then I'm going to go out of ketosis and I'll have to start the induction phase *again*.

I open up my salad and begin to eat it instead. Suddenly the crisp bed of romaine is far less appealing than I imagined it would be. I stab a bite with my fork and reply, "No, that's OK. Thanks, though."

I continue to stab, chew, and shoot angry glances at Fletch's glistening pile of sweet, sweet meat.

Stab. Chew. Glower.

Stab. Chew. Glower.

"Um, Jen? You OK?" Fletch asks.

"I'm fine." Stab. Chew. Glower.

"Are you sure?"

"*Yes.*" Stab. Chew. Glower.

"Jen, if you want ribs, have ribs. There's a ton of them," he reasons. He sounds exactly like I did in college when my best friend, Andy, was trying to quit smoking. I knew it was much healthier for him to be a nonsmoker, but he was such a bitch that I finally convinced him we'd both be happier if he just smoked already.[70]

"That's the thing," I reply. "I've had every single thing I've wanted for dinner for the past three years. Maybe if I'd had a salad once in a while, I'd have earned my own slab of ribs right now." Stab. Chew. Glower.

"Want me to eat in the other room? Is this torturing you?"

"No. I'm fine. I'll just enjoy my *salad*. Mmm, lettuce-y!" Stab. Chew. Glower. I watch as he takes a bite of his cornbread and a giant drop of golden butter plops onto the ottoman. "That bread is literally dripping with butter," I accuse.

He's quiet for a minute, and I see him surreptitiously trying to wipe the excess butter off the sides of his mouth. "Your, um, salad looks very nice. What kind of dressing did they give you?"

"Boring bleu cheese."

Stab. Chew. Glower.

Stab. Chew. Glower.

Fletch hands me the television remote. "Here; you can drive," he says.

"Wow, thanks!" I reply. "Is this you throwing me a proverbial bone because of my stupid salad?"

"No. I can't work it because my hands are covered in gooey, delicious barbecue sauce." To emphasize his point, he sucks the sauce off each finger and smacks his lips.

---

[70]Something tells me that Fletch and I would be terrible at an intervention—like we'd show up with wine or something.

I shriek, "Evil! You're evil! What an evil thing to say!"

He shrugs. "I figured if you're going to be passive-aggressive and scowl at my food the whole time, I'll one-up you by being aggressive-aggressive."

Yikes. You see? This is what not having carbs does to people.

"Oh, Fletch, I'm sorry," I backpedal. "My salad is fine. The chicken is grilled nicely, and there are whole chunks of bleu cheese. The cheese is nice and sharp, and the bacon bits are chewy and not crunchy. The dressing is thick so it doesn't sluice through the leaves. Actually, it's kind of a great salad. The thing is, even if this is the best salad in the world, it's not a barbecued rib and it never will be and it makes me sad."

He smiles. "It's okay."

"No, really, it's not. You might not want to be so quick to forgive me, because somehow I'm still mad at you even though you didn't do anything."

He frowns at me and takes a purposefully enormous bite. We finish our meal in a thick silence (except for all the intentional and prolonged finger licking), and afterward I go upstairs to replace the towels in the bathroom.

While I fold the fluffy white cotton fabric and place the squares neatly on the bars, I realize that not only am I still hungry, but also I've made Fletch mad. The only reason I picked at him was because I wanted some damn carbohydrates. Dinnertime is usually one of our favorite opportunities to connect and really talk without distraction, but ever since I started this diet, our meals have been rife with tension because I've been unhappy with whatever's been on my plate.

Christ, he's already under enough stress at work—the last thing he needs is to catch a bunch of shit from me just because I'm not having Tater Tots.

Is *this* what I have to look forward to as I try to live a healthier life? Complaining about my meals and thus ruining it for everyone around me while they try to eat their ribs?

Sure, I can be a stress eater and have been known to snack out of boredom, but the thing is, I truly love and appreciate good food. Dining is one of my greatest pleasures. But right now I feel like I've been denied every flavor that makes life worth living, and I'm cranky and unsatisfied, and I'm taking it out on the one person who could use a little extra compassion right now. I really have to wonder why I'm even bothering to try to lose weight.

So far it's just not worth it.

from the desk of the logan square–
bucktown neighborhood association
. . . .

Dear Mayor Daley,

Can you please include better fast-food joints in your plans for urban redevelopment in the Logan Square–Bucktown area? As is, there are no decent hamburger places for miles and miles. There's no Rally's, no Checkers, no Jack in the Box, no Hardee's, no Carl's Jr., no Red Robin, no In-N-Out Burger, and no Culver's ButterBurgers. For God's sake, we don't even have an Arby's.

What the hell? Did we lose a war or something?

Also, I called 911 last week because one of my stupid neighbors was working on his forty-year-old hoodless purple Plymouth and kept driving it around the block at seventy miles per hour. When I called the police, they were very rude. They kept asking me what the license plate number was, and I kept telling them I couldn't see it because they were driving by too fast. I gave them the car owner's address, but apparently that wasn't good enough. They asked, "How are we supposed to identify the vehicle without a plate number?" And I replied, "It's the only forty-year-old purple

Plymouth with no hood making seventy-mile-an-hour laps around the block." They never came, and now I'm pissed. Please fix.

BTW, a really good hamburger would probably go a long way toward unruffling my feathers. Think about it.

Best,
Jen Cognito, Association President

Gentlemen, Start Your Cheesecakes

"Wrong. No. No way. Uh-uh. Over my, and by extension, your, dead body."

"I'm presenting this as an option."

Fletch has just gotten home from work and has joined me in the guest room, where I'm working on my first piece of fiction. He sits down on the bed across from where I'm positioned at my computer.

"Well, stop thinking about it, because it's out of the question. You probably just had a bad day and your judgment is off," I reply. I cross my arms to emphasize my point.

"We have the cash reserves," Fletch counters.

"Yes, and they're in case the unthinkable happens, and not because people at work are *mean* and you want to *quit*."

"You're oversimplifying the situation, and you know it."

He's right. He was hired to be a high-level business strategist, inking long-lead-time deals with CEOs. However, the company is in such a panic for instant sales and cash, they're having all their sales executives do entry-level stuff like make cold calls to IT directors, exactly the kind of work Fletch did ten years ago when starting his career. They also eliminated bonuses.

"I know; those asshats lured you away from your very secure, albeit boring, telecom job with promises of fat bonuses and complete autonomy, and now you're reporting to a high school grad about how many 'dials' you made today."

"Exactly. That's why I want to give notice."

"Don't you see?" I ask. "They're trying to drive you out, not because of your poor performance, but because they made bad business decisions. If there was ever a shadow of a doubt they weren't going to be economically viable for the long run, they should have never rallied so hard to get you to join the organization." I take a quick breath and try to return my voice to a less shout-y level. "The thing is, if you quit, they don't have to give you a severance package and they don't have to pay unemployment."

"I'll get another job in a heartbeat."

"Ha! Where have I heard *that* before?"[71]

Fletch counters, "Things are very different now. We have resources . . . my 401(k), an IRA, stocks, et cetera. And I'm getting ten recruiter calls a week." He adds, smiling, "Plus we have our 'savings account.'" (Which is actually a big beer pitcher full of quarters.)

I pull up our online bank account and examine the

---

[71]Oh, yes; in my book *Bitter Is the New Black*. Pick up your copy today!

balances. "There's no reason to burn these resources un-necessarily, and I guarantee none of this"—I point at the screen—"will last as long as you think. We pledged we'd never cash in our 'savings' at the Coinstar again."

Fletch says nothing, scanning the figures over my shoulder. I continue, "Make them fire you or lay you off, because you can't walk out of there on principle alone without what's due to you. Otherwise, you'll have left your phone company job in vain, and if I have to worry about income, I'm going to inevitably eat so much, we'll need the jaws of life to break me out of this house. Am I making sense here?"

Fletch nods slowly. "Yeah, you're right. Walking out is a bad idea, but after the day I had, it seemed like a reasonable alternative."

"Whatever's bothering you now is going to get worse because they want you to check out voluntarily."

Fletch looks thoughtful. "Honestly, it's probably just a matter of a couple of weeks anyway. I'm guessing they'll do a big purge before they get stuck paying out commissions at the end of the month. I've already packed up almost every-thing, so I'm ready to be cut loose as soon as they give the word."

I give him a quick pat on the head. "You always do the right thing." I close the window for my banking information and return to what I'd been doing.

Fletch lies back down on the bed and closes his eyes for a couple of minutes, deep in thought. "Hey, wait a minute." He sits back up. "If money's such a concern, shouldn't this be a team effort?"

"Of course." I nod. "That's why I'm working on my novel."

"The *Veronica Mars* meets *The Net* thing? How's it coming? Did you send the synopsis to your agent?"

"Yeah, and Kate said she dug the premise. And I could so easily convert it to a screenplay."

"Nice. How much progress have you made?"

I squirm a bit. "Enough." Fletch totally supports my writing career, although he normally doesn't read my stuff. I bounce almost all my ideas off of him, but he says he's already lived everything I describe, so there's no need for the blow by blow. He's right, except he may not realize I, um, *adopt* some[72] of his funniest lines and attribute them to myself.

"Can I hear what you have?" he asks.

Uh-oh.

I shift uncomfortably in my seat. "It's, um, really rough. And since when do you want to know about the details? You always say you're a big-picture guy."

"Maybe I'll bring a different perspective."

"Sure, OK, but it's so, so rough. You should wait until it's more polished."

"Jen, I'm familiar with your writing process. It's a rough draft, which means your draft? Will be rough. I'm curious to see how you work in the network security aspect of the story."

"I'm . . . not really there yet."

---

[72]Read: all.

"Then how did you explain about the protagonist being a hacker? Everything hinges on that plot point, right?"

I am so freaking *pwn3d* right now.

"Err . . . still fleshing that bit out."

He begins to look suspicious. "And the mystery surrounding her family?"

I pluck my T-shirt out of my armpits because I've started to sweat. Hard. "Oh, yeah . . . that bit of exposition isn't appropriate to address yet."

"Then read me the part where she gets busted by the NSA."

Straws. Me. Grasping.

I bolt out of my desk chair. "Dogs! Maisy! Loki! Who wants to go outside? Huh? Who needs to make a potty? Oops, no; I can't read it now; the dogs haven't been out in hours. OK, guys; let's go!" Both of them gaze languidly at me from their side-by-side position on the guest bed, barely thumping their tails.

Fucking traitors.

Fletch narrows his eyes. "Have you even finished a chapter yet?"

"Ha! Of course!" I squawk. "Of course I have! Not completed a chapter? That's crazy talk! You know what we should do? We should go buy you a new belt. You love belts, and you've been bitching that your oxblood-colored one is getting ratty. Let's go to Coach! Right now! Belts! Yes! You had a terrible day and deserve something extraspecial." I dash over to my closet to put on shoes. "Ready!" I grab his arm and try to pull him off the bed.

"Jen." His voice becomes very serious. "How much have you done?"

"Plenty!" I giggle nervously. "Good and plenty! Like the candy!"

His patience has worn thin, and he looks me directly in the eye. "Is this book going to be ready to send to editors in the next month? Otherwise, if tapping into our reserves is going to give you palpitations, and you don't have any writing to sell, the most logical solution is that you start temping again, at least for a short while."

I gasp so hard, I suck all the air out of the room. Noooooo!

"Now, are you gonna show me what you've got?"

Very, very slowly I pull up the Word document, temporarily titled *Jen Rocks Fiction*. With a heavy heart, I click it open. "Keep in mind, the opening line can make or break a book, so it's got to kick serious ass."

"Uh-huh."

"Really, would *A Tale of Two Cities* be the same without 'It was the best of times, it was the worst of times'?"

He leans back against the dogs and they respond by licking his cheeks with much enthusiasm. Suck-ups. If you little bastards think we're going on walkies later, think again. "Yes."

"But you don't disagree it's important. If I were to say, 'Call me Ishmael,' you'd know in a heartbeat I meant *Moby-Dick*, right?"

"Is this a quiz? 'Cause if you say, 'Tyler gets me a job as a waiter, after that Tyler's pushing a gun in my mouth and saying, the first step to eternal life is you have to die,' the answer is

Fight Club. Quit stalling. We've established the importance of an opening line. Move on to the part where you read me what you've got."

I clear my throat. "This is the scene where the heroine is getting ready for a big job interview at the college placement office. So here goes: 'I look like Donald Rumsfeld in this outfit.'" I stop to gauge his approval.

He chuckles. "I like it; it's very *you.* Continue."

I was hoping he wouldn't say that.

"Um . . . that's . . . that's kind of all I have right now. But it's superintriguing, right? People will want to know what's next."

"You've been writing for three months, and all you have is one line? In three months? One line?" He's not mad so much as incredulous.

"It's a really good line," I insist. "And fiction is a lot different than nonfiction. With nonfiction I just have to describe the scenes as they happen around me, and the pages sort of write themselves. With fiction I have to make everything up."

He glances down at his fingers. "So far you've made up eight words."

"Yet the story has taken shape nicely in my head."

"Then it's a shame the oral storytelling tradition is dead or you'd be all set. What have you been doing up here? I thought you were working all this time. You spend hours, no, *days* on this computer. Tell me you haven't pissed away three months playing Big Kahuna Reef."[73]

---

[73]But I mastered all fifty levels!

"Don't be silly. I've done all sorts of stuff. I've been very busy dieting. And, um, researching what I need to know about her character," I bristle.

Fletch leans over me to pull up my cache of Web sites, and I watch him scan the list, his eyebrows going higher and higher with each line he reads. By the time he gets to the end, they've practically disappeared into his hairline. "Really? Because it seems like you've mostly been cruising YouTube. How can you sit there and lecture me on what I should be doing to support this household when you're doing nothing but watching *a goddamn panda sneeze*?"

I'm silent for a minute because he's completely right, so I have to level with him. "The truth is, I really tried to do something with this novel, but I've been so hungry that every time I began to type I ended up with a fourteen-page 'Ode to the Oreo.' I'd talk about how my character opened the bag and how the smell of chocolate cookie practically smacked her in the face. And then I'd describe grabbing a pitcher of milk—ooh, *whole* milk—and how it would pour out all cool and smooth and rich, and then she'd twist open two Double Stufs, toss away the clean sides, and stack the other two together to make her signature 'Quad Stuff.' Then she'd dunk this heady concoction, this Mother of All Oreos, into the cold milk, and she'd pop the delectable bite into her mouth and—"

"You're doing it again."

"No, I'm explaining where my time went. I'd write all this ridiculous stuff about cookies, and then I wanted to actually *see* someone eat Oreos—"

"Sort of like watching food porn?"

"Exactly! So I Googled Oreo commercials, and a bunch of them were on YouTube, and I'd never really been to YouTube before, and you would not believe the shit they've got there! Dogs on skateboards! Cats falling off televisions! And, of course, sneezing pandas. I, um, kind of got distracted, but the good news is, it got me to stop thinking about cookies, which is why I was able to write such a great opening line. If you think about it, finding the sneezing panda was a good thing."

He kisses me briefly on the forehead. "The reality is, if we want to keep our safety net, we don't have time for you to be a temperamental artist, scanning the 'interwebs' to be inspired by pandas with sinusitis. I know the deal was, you'd stay home, write, and run the household, but our situation has changed."

I know when I've been defeated. "I'm not going to argue because I can't. You're right, and . . . the possibility exists I've been taking advantage of the situation."

"Maybe there's a compromise here?" He looks thoughtful for a moment. "I'd say you haven't been properly motivated. You do much better with a deadline. How many times have your manuscripts been late?"

"Never."[74]

"Could be a hard-and-fast end date is what you need. How about we agree that if you don't have something to show Kate by the time my company lays me off, you return to temping until I start working again?"

---

[74]Am kind of a nerd that way.

My natural charm is not going to get me out of this. "I have no grounds to say no deal, do I?"

"Not a one."

"But it took me months to come up with the opening line. How am I supposed to finish a whole novel in the next few weeks?"

"Perhaps"—he smirks—"*Jen Rocks Fiction* isn't the book you work on next. What about nonfiction? Don't you have any more neighborhood stories to tell?"

"Not unless someone new moves in." Because it's winter, things have been kind of quiet around the 'hood. Maybe a little *too* quiet.

"Well, what else do you have? Didn't your friend suggest you do a book about dieting?"

"Yeah . . . great idea, but that seems like a whole lot of work. If I wrote it, I'd actually *have* to lose the weight, and it would be a struggle not to lapse into the Oreo Zone again. Don't get me wrong. I want to be thinner and healthier—I'm just not sure I should stake my whole writing career on my ability to avoid Ding Dongs. After all, Atkins has been a holy disaster, and so far all I've done is messed up my metabolism and discovered I have a penchant for cookie-snuff films."

"Let me ask you this—would you rather arrange travel and fetch coffee for some random executive or write a book about losing weight?"

"Can't it be neither?"

"No."

"Then it's a tough call."

"Well, at least mull the book thing over." He stands up

and brushes the dog fur off his wool pants. "Listen, I'm going to go change so I can hit the gym and work out some of this tension. Are you coming? Here's a perfect opportunity for you to test your mettle."

"Um, maybe next time?"

"All right. I'm going." As he heads down the hall, he calls, "And stop watching that damn panda video."

A-choo!

Too late.

Pretty Fat Memoir Proposal

by Jen Lancaster

It's time to stop sweating while I eat.
It's time to stop driving one block to Starbucks.
It's time to stop having cookies for dinner.
It's time to stop *promising* to go to the gym
    instead of *actually* going.
It's time to stop treating my body like a fraternity
    party.
In *Pretty Fat*, I will do all of the above.
(If it doesn't kill me first.)

I'm so tired of books where a self-loathing heroine is teased to the point where she starves herself skinny in hopes of a fabulous new life. And I hate the message that women can't possibly be happy until we're all size fours. I don't find these stories uplifting; rather, I want to hug these women and take them out for fizzy champagne drinks and cheesecake and explain to them that until they figure out their insides, their outsides don't matter.

Unfortunately, being overweight isn't simply a societal issue that can be solved by positive self-esteem. Rather, it's a health matter, and here on the eve of my fortieth year, I've learned I have to make changes so I don't, you know, *die*. Because what good is finally being able to afford a pedicure if I lose a foot to adult-onset diabetes?

LANCASTER—*PRETTY FAT* PROPOSAL

It Seemed Like a Good Idea at the Time

OK, *maybe* I could write a book about trying to lose weight if for no other reason than the idea of putting on panty hose and answering someone else's phone fills my stomach with dread. Writing a book is a good idea, really, because I'd be forced to stick with a healthier way of life.

Here's the thing—no one is better than me at starting a project. But without an impending deadline, I'm awful at finishing anything. My basement is a testament to my short attention span. Shelves are stacked high with every hobby and habit I've ever abandoned. Decorative tiles and colorful grout from my mosaic phase share shelf space with skeins of yarn and various poke-y sticks from my knitting days. Next to them are Rollerblades still spotted with blood from my wobbly kneecaps and a dozen new-puppy manuals with their covers chewed off from my brief (and spectacularly unsuccessful) foray into dog training. Currently collecting dust are a sewing machine and a squash racquet—I told you I didn't chase balls—and course work from the week I decided I'd become a Realtor. There are stacks of Spanish-language CDs that I quickly abandoned once I decided it would be easier if everyone else simply learned to speak English. (And don't even get me started about the ten thousand diet cookbooks and exercise tapes I own.)

As evidenced by my experience with Atkins, I quit whenever things get hard or boring. The only way I know to achieve success is to back myself into a corner. For example, I waited tables in college and depended on tips to pay my bills. I also *hated* being a waitress, so every chance I got, I volunteered to go home early, except when I'd get to the end of the month and rent was due. On those nights, I'd drop a kited check off at my landlord's office. During my shift, I knew I wasn't allowed to take off for the evening until I'd earned enough to cover the amount of the check I'd written. This obligation pushed me to upsell liquor and to work the dessert tray like my shelter depended on it. Because it did.

Honestly, the only reason I've completed two books is that they both sold based on a proposal, rather than a full manuscript. My *obligation* is what drove me to put words on pages, not just blind inspiration. Left to my own devices, it's pretty clear I'd have never gotten past the opening lines of "Camille said you stole a bag from a homeless guy" and "Carrie Bradshaw is a fucking liar." If I were to propose a book about losing weight and it sold, I'd *have* to do it because I care too much about my career not to. My work ethic would motivate me to get healthy in a way that doctor's orders and vanity never have.

Also, writing a book beats the hell out of fetching coffee. So there's that.

☕

I *could* do this, especially since I've been way more successful in the gym lately, having added carbs back into my diet. I've really been pushing myself, so I'd wager I could physically handle the kind of work I'd have to put in for a book. Shoot; I've even worked out three times this week![75] With sweating and everything! I still desperately loathe the elliptical machine, but the effort has been easier ever since I bought an iPod.

Stacey suggested I load my iPod with audio books. She works out with them and says they help her mind disengage from all the "suck and hate" her body feels while doing cardio. I followed suit, and it was a good idea at first, but I found myself bawling during a particularly poignant moment in Joshilyn Jackson's *Between, Georgia* while doing tricep curls.

Fearing another emotional outburst, I tapped into the iTunes library. Dear God, this service is more addictive than Swiss chocolate and Internet porn served together in a Tetris-covered waffle cone.[76] I've since created the perfect

[75]So maybe three times in a week doesn't sound like that much. But it's three times more than I worked out in all of 2004.

[76]Plus, I appreciate working out with the confidence that Tone-Lōc and Marky Mark will never make me cry in the weight room.

mix of music to keep me going at the gym; it lasts about an hour, building at the beginning and slowing at the end. Were this list to be made public, the entire world would listen to it while getting fit and I would single-handedly destroy the diet industry, and then a lot of people would lose their jobs, and I don't want that to happen, so please don't share the following unless you *want* to be responsible for wrecking the economy, OK?

Jen's Superfantastic Treadmill Mix

Unwritten/Natasha Bedingfield

Since U Been Gone/Kelly Clarkson

Move This/Technotronic

Straight Outta Compton/N.W.A.

Somebody Told Me/The Killers

(What's So Funny 'Bout) Peace, Love,
and Understanding/Elvis Costello

Anything, Anything/Dramarama

Bust a Move/Young MC

Feel Good Inc/Gorillaz

Ladylike/Storm Large and the Balls

Funky Cold Medina/Tone-Lōc

Pump Up the Jam/Technotronic

Faith/George Michael

Hey Ya!/OutKast

Pump It/Black Eyed Peas

Do Me!/Bel Biv DeVoe

Push It/Salt-N-Pepa

Shine On/The House of Love

Fletch says I have the musical sensibilities of a strip club DJ, but he's just jealous. Come on, Kelly Clarkson *and* N.W.A.? Elvis Costello *and* Bel Biv DeVoe? Genius!

I have to admit, I'm starting to feel good, even if I don't look any different yet. Maybe there's something to be said for these endorphins after all? 'Til now I thought they were one of those largely fictional, Madison Avenue–type words used to sell products.[77] As a matter of fact, on the way home from the gym today I was in such a pleasant mood, I didn't even shout at the guy on the bike who cut me off, despite the fact that he caused me to slam on my brakes and spill my skim latte.

Hey, bike messenger dude? People have *died* for getting between me and my coffee.

I would have been well within my rights to bash him with my car door, but it didn't even occur to me. Watching him pedal along in the dead of winter didn't make me question his sanity. Breaking a sweat allowed me to understand that maybe he *likes* how he feels while riding a bike and he cycles not because he's a crazy person, but because it helps him stay

[77]I also think "ions" and "electrolytes" are scams.

healthy. Then it occurred to me that you never see fat people on bikes.

I mean, except in Queen videos.

Ooh, I should download some Queen!

Since I'm exercising consistently, that proves it's all the more possible to conquer the food thing. I just need to find the right way of eating. There's got to be a plan out there that doesn't leave me shaky, ravenously hungry, or so packed with cheese that I can never use the bathroom again. There's got to be a middle ground.

I've been asking around, and I've heard excellent things about the South Beach Diet, so I begin my Internet research. The very first thing I read is that I'm not supposed to consume any caffeine during the induction phase.

Pfft. Next.

Perhaps a quick glance at YouTube will provide proper inspiration. . . .

I'm resting my eyes for a moment because I kind of watched too much Internet video earlier. Did you know they stream whole television shows on the Web now? When did this little miracle happen? And why didn't anyone ever tell me how good *Survivor: Cook Islands* was?[78] I thought it was all people having to eat bugs, but it's full of yelling and plotting and all the other stuff that make me love reality TV so damn much. Bless CBS; they have the entire series cached for my viewing pleasure.

[78]I heart Yul.

I got to the point where Jonathan was voted out, and I had to lie down. I'm almost asleep in the guest room when the phone rings. I check the caller ID, see that it's Fletch, and answer.

"Hello?"

"Hey, it's me. It's official. I'm done. I just wanted to let you know I'm on my way so you don't have a heart attack when I come home midday."

I shake my head, trying to clear it. "Wait, what? You're done? *Done* done? Did you quit, or get fired, or laid off, or . . ."

"I'll give you the scoop when I get home. Real quick, though, because the valet's here with my car, I got severance; they're going to pay our insurance next month; basically everything ended best-case scenario."

"Congratulations? Or I'm sorry? I'm not sure which is appropriate."

"I'm pretty happy, so let's go with congratulations. See you in a few."

"Um, OK; see you then."

I get up from my nap. I look from my heeled professional shoes hanging in their little slots on the back of the guest room door over to my computer. The party is over and I'm getting back to work; whether it's writing or temping is still to be determined.

I turn on my computer and pull up a blank Word document, and I begin to type.

It's time to stop sweating while I eat.

"Any word on your proposal?" Stacey asks. Tonight we're at her place watching Bravo. *Top Design* is on, and it's just not catching our attention like *Top Chef* or *Project Runway*.[79]

"Nope, no decisions yet. I suspect my editor likes it, although she obviously won't confirm or deny this until after the deal is signed, if we even get to that point. And I haven't a clue as to what everyone else thinks," I reply.

Stacey gives me a sympathetic look. With four books under her belt, she's done this before and knows exactly how nerve-wracking waiting for an answer is. Stacey points the remote at her TV and mutes *Top Design*. "Any idea when they'll give you an answer?"

"God, I hope it's soon. The stress eating is killing me," I say. I pull a bag of Raisinets out of my purse. "Will my losing fifty pounds count if I gain twenty now?" I offer Stacey some, but she declines. I tear open the familiar yellow package and absently begin popping them in my mouth, one after another. I'm all about comfort foods right now. Candy is good, but I'd kill for something covered in gravy. Unfortunately, mashed potatoes lack a certain portability. If I could come up with a way to serve them on a stick, I'd make millions. "The worst part is, if the book doesn't sell, not only will I be fatter, but I'll be fatter at a temp job."

"How's Fletch's search going?"

"He's already got feelers out at places he used to work, and everyone's been receptive. He's had a couple of good in-

---

[79]Todd Oldham, you are *not* the new Tim Gunn.

terviews, and overall he's really upbeat. It's not going to be like last time, when he was out of work for a year."

"That's a relief, yes?"

"Totally. It's kind of a good thing, actually. If the book sells while he's home during the day, then I can use the car to go to the gym, since exercise will be a major part of the story. But if he were working and out on appointments, I'd be stranded 'til he got home."

"You can't take public transportation to the gym?"

"Not really. My gym is in the West Loop—it's only a few miles, but to get there I'd have to either switch buses three times or go from bus to train to walking half a mile. There's no way I'm putting that much effort toward getting on a treadmill, especially since the walk is bonus exercise. Fortunately, Fletch got a decent severance package, and he's so delighted to finally be done, he granted me a reprieve until the end of the month, which means I've got another week before I have to call my old temp agency."

"Tick-tock."

I wolf down another handful of Raisinets. "Fuckin' A."

"What are you going to do between now and then?"

"I don't know. Pace? Watch more reality TV on the Internet? Enjoy my last free moments not filling out other people's expense reports? What I *should* do is return the million e-mails I got in the past month while I was working on the proposal. Of course, the very first one I opened today said this: *'Dear Jen, I'm seventeen and I live in Australia. I love* Bitter Is the New Black! *But I have a question after looking at the old photos on your Web site—you have such a pretty face, but you seem to have let your body go. Have you ever thought about losing weight?'* So . . . yeah. If that's the kind of mail I've got waiting for me, I'm not that anxious to tackle it."

Stacey strokes her chin in an exaggerated thinking gesture. "Hmm. Are we planning to fly Down Under and stab her in person, or do we hire someone to do it?"

"Normally I'd send her such a scathing response, she'd be afraid to ever pick up a book again, but I get the feeling she was being genuine."

Stacey snorts. "You should *genuinely* tell her to call you in twenty-three years and then grill her on how very, very easy it was to maintain the figure she had at seventeen."

I stuff another handful of Raisinets in my mouth.[80] "What gets me is the 'pretty face' bit. 'Cause I won't mind being reminded I'm fat as long as you water it down first. Why not say, *Hey, I'm going to insult you, but first I will congratulate your fortunate genetics and appropriate application of Bobbi Brown cosmetics to prevent you from hitting me.* Shit; I kind of prefer being called a 'fat bitch.' At least it doesn't pull any punches."

"You're right—'pretty face' is only used to counteract addressing someone's weight. Nobody ever says, *You have such a pretty face; it's a shame you're a whore.*"

"*Ha!*" I bark. "How about, *You have such a pretty face; if only you weren't as dumb as a bag of hair.*"

---

[80]Not really helping my case much, am I?

"Ooh, *You have such a pretty face; too bad your children were spawned by Satan.*"

"*You have a gorgeous face, but have you ever considered flossing?*"

"*You have the prettiest face and the ugliest house.*"

"*You're a classic beauty in every way, except for your hideous personality, of course.*"

"*You're so lovely, so I wonder why your husband can't keep his dick in his pants.*"

"Nice one!" We exchange a quick high five. "The best part is how people say it like maybe you didn't notice you had great cheekbones *and* a huge ass. Or flawless skin and a handful of back fat. I wonder if people think weight is like a piece of spinach caught in our teeth and we wouldn't have known about if they hadn't been kind enough to inform us."

"Nothing would surprise me." Stacey gets serious for a minute. "Listen, I take total responsibility for my weight. I love food. I love movement a whole lot less. I'm well aware of who I am and what I look like, and I'm happy with the whole package. I have a great life, and I'm thankful for it. I work out with a trainer, but mostly because of how it makes me feel. Yet I admit it can be like a knife to the chest when strangers define me based on digits on scale."

"Amen," I exclaim, accidentally spitting out a Raisinet. I pick up the chocolate with a Kleenex and stuff it in my purse. Ten bucks says a month from now I'll have forgotten about it and will finally have said feared heart attack when I assume a rat shat in there. "I have to say, though, if someone gave me a pill tomorrow that would make me an instant size six, I would stomp through a meadow full of puppies to get it."

"Then you couldn't write a book about losing weight the hard way."

"True. And I am perfectly fine with that."

She gives me a sidelong glance. "Yeah?"

I grin sheepishly. "No, not really." We sit for a moment in companionable silence. Stacey appreciates exactly how much I want the challenge of working on a new book. Being able to sit down and put thoughts on paper, knowing these thoughts will be out there for others to read, is the most joyous feeling in the world.

If my proposal sells, this time it won't just be about writing. Writing this book means I'll be obligated to change my entire life, and I'm conflicted. I want to change my life . . . except I sort of like it. I mean, I couldn't be more delighted every Monday night after Fletch goes to bed when I come downstairs, pull up *The Bachelor* on TiVo, drink Riesling, and eat cheddar/port wine Kaukauna cheese without freaking out over fat grams. I'm perpetually in a good mood because I do everything I want. I love having the freedom to skip the gym to watch a Don Knotts movie on the Disney channel without a twinge of guilt. I've figured out how to not be beholden to what other people believe I should be doing, and when the world tells me I ought to be a size eight, I can thumb my nose at them in complete empowerment.

And yet a good part of me wonders if I'm not completely full of shit.

If this book gets green-lighted, I won't have any more excuses not to make the kind of grown-up modifications to my lifestyle that I should have made years ago.

And that's terrifying.

And exhilarating.

But mostly terrifying.

TO: angie_at_home
FROM: jen@jenlancaster.com
SUBJECT: Help!

The Food and Drug Administration announced they're going to ban
over-the-counter sales of ephedrine-based diet pills, which . . . DAMN.

Now what the hell am I going to do for a Plan B?

TO: angie_at_home
FROM: jen@jenlancaster.com
SUBJECT: Never mind

I just heard that Pfizer is coming out with a doggie diet pill to help combat obesity in overweight pets. Maisy would TOTALLY be eligible for it.

Plan B is back, baby!

Careful What You Wish For

We're on our way back from the grocery store, where we spent the whole time arguing about how much cheaper food is in the suburbs. Fletch argued the pros of moving to the suburbs, and I argued how the cost of food wouldn't matter because I'd bake my head in the oven like a Butterball turkey if forced to move there. Give me Libertyville or give me death? I choose death.

As we pull down the alley, Fletch nudges me. "Check it out." He doesn't open our garage door two lots down. Instead, we idle behind our new neighbor's house.

"What am I supposed to be looking at? The car? It's been up on blocks since the day they moved in." I shrug. Fine, maybe people don't put their cars up on blocks in swankier suburbs like Naperville, instead opting for the garage. Which is exactly what I would do. With the motor running.

"Look closer. I've been meaning to show you this for a

couple of days, but we kept driving down the alley the other way."

"Their dog can't be out, because there's no barking." Our new neighbors have a small white dog that looks like a Muppet. We don't know his name, so we call him Little Dog. He'd be cute except he's outside all the time, so he barks All. The. Time. Normally this would simply be an annoyance—hardly surprising for this 'hood—but this month has been bitterly cold, and his constant exposure is dangerous. Since Fletch and I are home during the day, we've been calling the Anti-Cruelty Society every time he's out for more than twenty minutes. Last week we watched the Anti-Cruelty van pull up to their house and we quietly cheered while the animal control people talked to the residents. Lately, they've been good about leaving the dog outside for reasonable amounts of time.

"Guess again."

"Rats? Are there more rats? At this point I've seen so many that unless they've got top hats and have formed a kick line, I can't even muster up the interest."

"Check out the box in the garbage."

I squint out my darkened window. "Torro Electric Snowthrower. They bought a snowblower; what of it?"

"Jen, don't read it—just look at it."

"Am I looking for the price?"

"Nope. Look again."

"Make and model?"

"You're going micro—think macro."

"Um . . . there's a hole in it?"

"Yes! You're getting warm."

"I see some painter's tape on it."

"Uh-huh. Warmer. Keep going. What do you notice about the hole? What purpose is the tape serving?"

Am I this annoying when I make him try to guess things?[81] "The hole is . . . argh, I don't know. Just tell me what I'm supposed to see, damn it."

"The hole is cut in a perfect arch. The top of the box is notched, and the seams are covered with painter's tape. Don't you see what this is?"

"A snowblower box."

"No! It's a doghouse!"

"What?"

"Those idiots built a house for their dog out of *cardboard*. After Anti-Cruelty talked to them, *this* was their solution. To stick the dog in a damp paper box. Held together with painter's tape. During the coldest weather we've had in years." Fletch shakes his head in wonder.

"According to that guy's bumper sticker, he's a union carpenter. Why wouldn't he use wood? How is a paper box supposed to protect his dog from the elements? No one uses paper to keep warm—it's a terrible insulator! That's why buildings have fiberglass pumped into their walls, and not just old term papers."

"Exactly."

"And the roof on that thing is caved in—it must not have been able to withstand the weight of the snow."

[81]Wait; don't answer that.

Fletch gives me a sly grin. "Perhaps he should have used load-bearing tape."

"Their half-assed attempts at taking care of Little Dog are even worse than when they weren't trying at all."

"Yep."

"Did you see they shaved Little Dog? First thing I thought was, *I guess someone got themselves into beauty school.* Then I got mad. It's ten degrees below zero out here, so why is now the time to divest this creature of his only protection against the elements?"

"Obviously because they were building him a deluxe doggie palace—out of cardboard—so he didn't need a fur coat."

"I've seen them playing with Little Dog. They're not vicious; they're *dumb.* We have to call Anti-Cruelty again. This type of stupidity has to be noted."

"Already did it," Fletch says.

"Cool." Fletch backs up to our garage. "I feel bad for the dog, but the doghouse is validating."

"How so?"

"Everyone has a friend who consistently has the worst job ever. She has a terrible boss and terrible coworkers, and her assignments are terrible. So she quits and gets another job, and everyone there is awful, and the stuff she has to do is either too hard or too easy or too something. It's like everywhere she goes, it's always worst-case scenario, you know?"

Puzzled, Fletch replies, "Not really, no."

I rub his shoulder affectionately. "That's because sometimes that friend is you."

"Hey—" he begins to protest.

I wave my finger at him. "Tut-tut, this isn't a you-centric example. My point is, sometimes you look at this friend and think, the one common factor in all your terrible employment scenarios is *you*."

Fletch says nothing, so I continue. "With me, I'm always complaining about the people we live around. When we were in Lincoln Park, I hated the drunk college students. In Bucktown, the yuppies made me nuts. In River West the fat girls and their bitchy boy companions made me want to take a hostage. And these were all entirely different circumstances, and the only common thread was me. Because of the law of averages, it's almost impossible to believe that every single person who's lived around me has been a moron, and that makes me doubt myself, especially when I still go around thinking every guy over six feet tall in the grocery store is you.[82] But then I see this stupid paper doghouse and I realize, at least in this one instance, *I am not the idiot here*. And suddenly my world makes sense again."

We finally pull in and begin to gather up bags. The message light is blinking on our phone. I listen to the message while Fletch doubles back to get all the heavy groceries, as I like to carry only the stuff that's either paper or in a box.

Pink cheeked and ruddy, Fletch returns a few minutes later, laden with soup, spaghetti sauce, and soda.

....

[82]I have a disorder I call False Fletcher Syndrome. Somehow I think every tall guy at the store is my husband and I end up throwing cereal into a lot of strangers' carts. I suspect it's my brain's reaction to all those trans fats under one roof.

My brows are knit and my mouth is pulled into a frown. "Bad news," I tell him.

With a serious expression he asks, "What's up?"

I point at the phone. "You got a message."

"And?"

"Looks like you're about to be the one common factor again."

"I don't follow."

"I'm going to be grocery shopping alone."

"You're speaking gibberish again."

I lose my frown. "Call your recruiter and start polishing your wingtips. You're going back to work."

And not a moment too soon.

Between the uncertainty of my proposal and worry about employment, I've been abusing controlled substances (that is, if you consider turtle cheesecake to be a controlled substance).

"Did your celebration include a 'special hug'?" Angie teases.

"You? Are *so* not funny," I reply. My friends think it's hilarious if they can make me squirm. Last time Carol was here, she and the rest of the girls talked about sex in a manner I found far too graphic.[83] I threw such a fit, Carol finally acquiesced and asked if it would be easier if she simply referred to anything explicit as "that special hug

---

[83] Meaning the conversation existed at all. You'd think someone who dropped as many F bombs as I do would be comfortable with intercourse discourse. You would be wrong.

married people do when they love each other very much."

"We had celebration *cake*, thank you very much," I retort. "With cream cheese frosting and little carrots piped on it. I got it at Whole Foods, and it must have weighed eight pounds."

"When does he start?"

"Not for a couple of weeks. He's still got to go through a drug screen and criminal check, but unless parking tickets or traces of boxed wine are felonies, he's in excellent shape."

"Did you tell your mom, or are you still incommunicado?"

At the moment, my mother is mad at me for being mad at her for being a jerk, which may or may not have been caused by *my* being a jerk. I know; I know. Don't ask. "Not talking." I sigh.

"This isn't the same fight from the spring?"

"No, this is a different fight."

"I can't keep them all straight." Almost every one of our girlfriends is engaged in some level of combat with her mother. How is it we all got along fine with our moms for years, yet the minute we hit our mid-thirties, wham, it's *Adolescence 2: This Time It's Hormonal*. Is it us? Is it them? I don't get it.

"I figure she's like the dogs when they get all stirred up for no reason. They lose their minds and run around the house like wild beasts, foaming and biting, bashing into each other and flying over ottomans, but eventually they wear themselves out and they're fine. I'm just going to wait until she's exhausted and panting on the big pillow by the hall closet. Then we'll talk and all will be as it was. But right now? Honestly, it's a relief to not have to discuss anyone's unemployment with her. I had a hard enough time dealing with my own anxiety back then, let alone trying to keep Mom from panicking."

"Your situation is different this time; why would she panic?"

"Because she totally doubts that Fletch and I have the capacity as adults to learn lessons. Do you realize that even though I wrote an entire book about all the crazy stuff I did to get a job, she's still tells my brother that I secretly was sitting around eating candy, happily racking up debt and waiting to be evicted?"

"You did eat a ton of candy."

"Not the point. The problem is, I have no credibility within my family. Zero. For example, I was down at their new place and I noticed a really strange smell, like the air was musty and damp. It gave the whole house kind of an old-lady whiff. So I said something about it with an eye toward problem solving, like, *'Hey, did you get this place tested for mold?'* My mother was furious that I was being negative and did nothing to address the strange odor. Then, a couple of months later, my niece was there with a little friend, and the little friend says, *'Your grammy's house smells like an old lady's house.'* Right after, I get an e-mail from my mom saying, *'Oh, the house smells a little off—there must be a problem. We're going to get it checked out immediately.'* So the opinion of a five-year-old stranger carries more weight than mine."

"That's some serious annoyance. With my mother, I could tell her any fact, like the sky is blue, and she wouldn't believe me. I could show her documentation, charts, graphs, whatever, and no dice. I could quote experts from NASA about atmospheric conditions. I could go all Bill Nye the Science Guy and detail the concept of Rayleigh scattering and bouncy air molecules and shit, but she'd never buy it. Yet if my brother were to say the sky is green and offer no proof, she'd suddenly be president of the Green Sky Club."

"On the plus side, at least you only have boys and there's no chance in thirty years your daughter will be tooling around in her hover car, bitching on her space phone about things you do."

"I'll probably have daughters-in-law at that point. But they'll expect me to torment them."

"And you won't disappoint."

"You got that right." Angie cackles. "What else is going on with you? Any book news yet?"

My call-waiting clicks, and I check the display. Of course my agent is on the other line. I'm just going to add "psychic" to Angie's ever-growing list of abilities. "Dude, Kate's on the other line. We may be about to find out. Gotta fly."

"Good luck."

Yesterday my agent told me there were no updates.

My offer didn't come until today.

Woo!

I try to call Fletch and tell him the good news, but he's

at the gym. I consider dialing the reception desk directly and having them grab him from the free-weight room, but I'm probably a bit too screamy to talk to anyone at the moment.

I know I've done this a couple of times before, but each time a book sells, it feels like a miracle. The experience is so surreal. This kind of stuff doesn't happen to me; it happens to people in movies. I want to call my publisher and ask, *Are you sure*? You're really interested in what I have to say? And you're willing to write me a check to do so? And then you'll take these thoughts—asinine as they may be—and put them in a format that will live on in the Library of Congress forever?[84]

Unbelievable.

I'm dancing around the kitchen with the dogs and a fat slice of carrot cake when a thought stops me in my tracks.

I sold a book.

Correction, I sold a book, the contents of which depend on my decision to change my body, my health, and my life.

The hard way.

Without surgery or drugs.

In terms of the deal, I'm not bound to lose a certain amount of weight; rather, my publisher is interested in the process, and if I happen to get positive results, all the better. Failure can be just as funny as success, sometimes even more so.

---

[84]To be fair, they're probably not housing my stuff next to Mark Twain's. But, still . . .

But let me be crystal clear here so there's no misunderstanding:

I am not about to have my inability to stop eating Ding Dongs documented for eternity in the Library of Congress.

This is the push I've been waiting for.

This is the rent check I've written that must clear.

No one is challenging me here except for myself. The only one throwing a gauntlet is me. For this book, I see myself in Houston at Ground Control, wearing a handmade vest and a pocket protector, an old-school headset resting on my buzz cut, barking out with the utmost confidence, *Failure is not an option!*

Yet I'm pretty sure Penguin would be happy if I told funny stories about plodding along on the treadmill with a piece of pie tied to a string dangling from a stick on my head.

I'm better than that.

I can do more.

I didn't become a vice president because I followed the rules and met my goals; I pushed myself relentlessly.[85] I was never satisfied with good enough. Now writing is my career, and I can't let myself be lazy.

Plus, there's no way I'm earning myself a seat on Oprah's couch if I don't approach this with one hundred percent intensity.

Now, how the hell do I get started?

---

[85]Again, as described in the bestselling *Bitter Is the New Black*. Have you purchased your copy yet? Makes a great gift!

If I'm going to do this—wait, there's no "if" here—I need a real baseline of how much I weigh. I can't just rely on my inner carnival barker; I actually need to see numbers on a scale. I have too much pride not to do this right, and that means getting an honest assessment of where I'm starting.

Why am I suddenly so afraid?

I strip down to my sensible underpants and utilitarian bra and enter my guest bathroom. This is normally such a happy place; it's where I sit in a tub scented with tea-tree oil and read good books. This is where I do my hair in the giant trifold mirror. Look at the festive plaid shower curtain—bad stuff can't happen in here, right?

I'm confident I already know what number's going to come up. Pretty? No, but probably manageable. And it's nice to know that whatever number it is, it won't be that high again anytime soon. In my proposal, I said I'd like to drop fifty pounds. With this loss, I'll be back at a normal weight, and then, damn, I will really look good.

I take a deep breath and step on the scale. The scale I have is all old school with a spring-loaded dial. I'm greatly dismayed at how fast the needle dives to the right once I step on.

I'm even more dismayed when I see where it lands.

No.

Wrong.

This number is obviously a mistake. I step off so the scale can reset itself, and I hop on again. The same number, the same *awful, horrible, completely devastating number*, comes up again.

I step on and off a third time with the same result.

I don't weigh this much. I can't weigh this much. I'm a cute ex-sorority girl, not some six-foot-four, corn-fed linebacker from Nebraska. I belong in a pedicure chair, not on a football field, trying to keep the quarterback from getting his ass handed to him.

This weight is wrong. *Wrong.* I'm not a professional wrestler. Or a baby beluga. Or a barrel full of butter.

I step on and off a fourth time.

Why? Why is the scale lying to me? And what of my inner carnival barker? She's never off by more than a minute or a dollar or a degree; there's no way she could be off by almost fifty pounds.

Fifth time up to bat and I honestly expect it will be different, but it's not. How am I fifty pounds heavier than I thought? I love me—I would never let myself get this kind of fat. I would never, ever weigh this much. Ridiculous! I'd sooner dye my hair orange with a box of color from the grocery store. I'd sooner wear frosty white eye shadow. I'd sooner sell *s-e-x* stories to *Penthouse Forum*. This is impossible.

A lightbulb goes off and I smack my hand to my head. Of course! The scale is wrong. *That's* what it is. Silly old-school scale! You should be digital and accurate and not *lie* to the pretty, vibrant girls who stand on you. Because telling them they weigh this much is *mean*. Cruel, even. Showing them this kind of wrong number will make them *cry*. Why do you want to make me cry, scale? I've been so good to you, letting you sit in the corner of my bathroom for years, gathering dust and making you work only once or twice a year when a random guest steps on you.

Liar. That's what you are. A terrible, terrible liar. Telling this kind of lie is exactly what's going to get you set out with the next round of trash. Obviously I don't eat like someone who'd weigh this much. I don't drink like a huge, huge person. I move often enough to not weigh this . . . right? I went to the gym three times in a row! People who go to the gym three times in a row can't possibly put up these numbers.

Stupid scale. Stupid, lying, inaccurate scale.

Hate you.

So much.

The only thing to do is to go to Fletch's bathroom, use his digital scale, and figure out what I *really* weigh. Yes, genius!

I trot down the hall—which I can do because I'm *not* completely obese—and try to calm myself down. I'm totally overreacting here. I am fine. I know I'm fine. Whatever I weigh is just a number. I'm fun and smart and I can perfectly blend three shades of eyeliner. I enjoy my own company and I make myself laugh. I dress well, even on a budget while wearing Crocs, and no one makes a banana daiquiri like I can.

I sit on the edge of the bed and take a number of deep breaths, trying to slow my pulse. Ahh, OK. I can do this. Think sand. White sand, warmed by the sun. Palm trees. Trade winds. The scent of Coppertone and coconuts in the air. A tin drum plays in the distance. Relax . . . relax. A shady harbor. Calm blue waters. Gentle waves lightly buffeting the shoreline. Tide comes in, *whoosh*. Tide goes out, *whoosh*. Pretty shells left in the wake of the wave. Sparkly. Calm. Relaxed. Lovely flat sea. A sea in which I would never drown because I'm so fucking buoyant.

Trying to relax isn't helping. The only way I can fix this is by accepting it as reality.

I step on Fletch's scale.

A different number comes up.

It's two pounds more.

I'm not sure if I want to throw up or buy a third scale. I can't believe this is true . . . although it would explain a lot. Possibly this is why I sweat when I eat. Perhaps this is why I don't care to bend. Maybe this is why I can't climb a flight of stairs without sucking wind and why I peter out so easily at the gym. Conceivably this is why my mother clucks about my health whenever she sees me.

Is it possible my raging self-esteem has kept me from confronting this truth? I guess I'll find out in the next six months.

The worst thing is that if this number is accurate—and I'm grudgingly beginning to believe it may be—even when I lose fifty pounds, *I will still be fat*.

Shit.

Dear Ice Cube,

Dude, um . . . what happened? You used to be all scary and badass, singing about how today you didn't even have to use your AK. Like, your life in Compton was so hard-core, you were all surprised you didn't need your AK. And that gave you credibility and made your music so powerful. Yet now I'm seeing movie trailers starring you and a wacky deer and a station wagon full of precocious, scene-stealing kids.

It hurts my heart to think you're all grown up and living in suburbia, minus your AK (because of block association rules). On the other hand, you're probably really rich now, so I guess it's not so bad?

Best,

Jen Lancaster

I Like New York in June; How About You?

I've been to the gym what feels like a thousand times in the past week, although it's really more like four. Now that this is my job, I'm literally and figuratively attempting to work my ass off.[86]

The problem is, the more I do, the more I hear the same damn songs on my iPod, and I'm beginning to tire of my superfantastic treadmill mix. Although it remains superfantastic, I need to add some new superfantastic music because I am superfantastically sick of all its superfantasticness. I've listened to these songs so many times, they're no longer effective at keeping me going. I've gotten so bored with all my favorite tunes that lately when I'm midworkout, I've been making up new lyrics.

---

[86]I don't dare complain to anyone about my new workout schedule because they'd be all, "Oh, poor you, getting paid to do the kind of thing the rest of us have to squeeze into the limited time we have when not at work. We should throw you a parade, for you are a *hero*."

For example, "Straight Outta Compton" now sounds like this on the turntable in my head:

> *Straight outta Bucktown, crazy motherfucker*
> *named Jennifer*
> *This goddamned treadmill gonna be the end of her*
> *Now she's pissed off, she wanna sit down*
> *Eat up the chocolate cake 'til her body is*
> *completely round*

"Faith" has morphed into:

> *Well, I guess it would be nice*
> *If I could thin my body*
> *Too bad not everybody*
> *Metabolizes like you*

"Somebody Told Me" new lyrics:

> *Well somebody told me*
> *That you had some Trimspa*
> *But that would be cheating*
> *And nobody buys books penned by a fibber*
> *Just look at James Frey*
> *He told a fat lie*
> *And enraged Miss Oprah Winfrey*

And my favorite, "Do Me," Jen style:

> *Backstage, overweight, with a cocktail*
> *How ya doin'? "Drunk," I replied*
> *And sighed . . . "I'd like to order pizza*
> *Extra cheese please,*

> *Hot and fresh, and don't forget*
> *The O, the L, the I, the V, the ES*
> *And maybe Diet Coke."*

After yet another yawn of a workout, I go directly upstairs to my computer, not even stopping to reward myself with a little snack, because the best treat in the world would be to never hear Kelly Clarkson again. Seriously, I hit a wall at the gym today, and I cannot listen to this mix one more time. It's hard enough just getting my ass on the treadmill; being bored with what I'm listening to just makes it ten thousand times worse, and I run out of patience before I run out of steam.

I need new music, better music, more stimulating music, or, failing that, possibly just some songs that won't make Fletch laugh at me. I sit down in my sweaty clothing and begin to trawl playlists on iTunes to find more inspiration to supplement my perspiration.

I'm a solid hour into my search when Fletch returns from his new job. I talked him into taking the train today so I could use the car to go to the gym. He comes upstairs looking very professional in his suit. He also looks extraordinarily aggravated. He's scowling and wagging a finger when he enters the guest room.

"New rule," he says, sitting on the bed and loosening his tie. "From now on, I only travel to and from work in vehicles where people can't spit on my shoes."

I consider his statement. "I have no idea what that means."

"It means this morning a homeless lady spat on my foot just as I was getting on the el."

I have yet to come to terms with the el, Chicago's elevated mass-transit system, because it's so badly designed. Our train system operates on a hub-and-spoke system rather than a grid. All trains are routed to one place in the center of the city, and then if you need to go elsewhere, you have to go downtown, ride around the Loop, and switch trains. So, if I want to go to Lincoln Park from my house (a mile away) I have to travel almost seven because the only other crosstown option is the bus, which . . . no.

This is why the city has such a traffic problem. Driving is the least of all evils. But when I drove Fletch the three miles to his job yesterday, it took me forty-five minutes to get there and forty-five minutes to get home. And then when I picked him up, it was the same exact thing. It's a wonder anyone who doesn't telecommute is ever in a good mood. The mayor's solution is to ride a bike to work, but how are you supposed to do that if you have to wear a suit and don't have shower facilities in your office? And yesterday when we were in the car it was a gorgeous early spring day, so there were hundreds of bikes on the road, none of which were obeying basic traffic laws. I was all, *"Where are we? China?"*

Still, I'm sorry Fletch was spat on, and I try to muster appropriate sympathy. "Hmm . . . was it like a loogie or just excess saliva?"

"Does it matter? Her nasty bodily fluids hit my foot just as the door closed, so I couldn't even yell her stupid. I'd rather she tried to pick my pocket to avoid the biohazard."

"Was she aiming for you?"

"Again, you're missing the point. Me. Spit. Foot. Brief stop at the shoeshine place before I hit the office." I look down at his shoes, and they're so shiny they're practically incandescent.

"They look very nice. What did you do to make her spit on you?"

Fletch throws his hands in the air. "I don't know. Maybe it's because I was reading the *Sun Times* and she's more of a *Tribune* fan? Maybe she was mad that I got Starbucks and she'd rather I support local coffee shops. Or maybe it's because she was wearing a garbage bag stuffed with socks and had an aluminum foil cap and her decision-making process is skewed. Kind of hard to tell what was the exacerbating factor."

"That reminds me—one time a guy, um . . . *exacerbated* on my friend's coat on the Red Line. She got to her office and threw up in a trash can. She was traumatized way more than you."

"I should be thankful no one jerked off on me?"

I giggle and blush. "Yeah, I guess so."

"You won't be laughing tomorrow morning at seven o'clock when you drive me to work. That is, if you want to use the car."

"We really need another vehicle, and I don't mean a bike." Although I would be pro-Vespa if I were allowed to drive it on the sidewalk.

"I'm aware of that. When you get your next check, we'll buy a second car. 'Til then, see you at seven a.m."

"Um . . . other than the spitting, how did you enjoy the play, Mrs. Lincoln?"

He shrugs. "I had a good day, but there was nowhere to go but up after that. And what are you doing? Downloading more shit?"

"Don't touch me because I stink. And no, I'm buying really good stuff," I reply.

He guffaws. "I'll bet. What are the damages so far?" He leans over my shoulder to look at what I've purchased and wrinkles his nose. I can't tell if he's more repelled by me or by my choices. "Let's see, first, Asia . . . *Asia*? Why would you buy Asia? Do you have a head injury?"

This is a legitimate question. I accidentally bump my noggin so many times a day, Fletch has suggested a helmet. Last year I was bent over looking in the fridge, and when I stood up I hit the open freezer door so hard, the whole unit lifted off the floor. Everything tasted green for a while, and when Fletch asked me who the president was, I said, *"You?"*

"Because of *The 40-Year-Old Virgin*, of course. The bike scene made me remember how much I liked that song back in high school."

He makes a little disapproving noise. "Yeah, I liked parachute pants in high school, but you don't see me buying them now. What else? Ah . . . *very* nice. Vanilla Ice."

Will everyone's incessant Robert Van Winkle bashing never stop? "Number one, he had fantastic hair, and you can't say he didn't, because I've seen the photos where you tried to copy it. Unsuccessfully, I might add. Number two, the man knew how to groom his eyebrows. And number three, he was rollin'! In his 5.0! He had the top flipped down so his glorious hair could blow! And all the girlies? Were totally on standby and they were waiting just to say hi. Did he stop? *No!* He just kept rollin'. Try to argue with the fine, fine wordsmithery in that song. I dare you."

"Do you even have any clue what a 5.0 is?"

"A car? Of some sort?"

"A Mustang."

"Whatev. That downbeat was groundbreaking."

"Yeah, I imagine that's what David Bowie and Queen thought when they came out with it in the first place."

I look over my shoulder and give Fletch a withering glance. "You're awfully smug for a man who paid to see *Cool as Ice*[87] in the theater."

Fletch clears his throat. "Err, what else do you have? Aqua? Who are Aqua?"

"They sing the 'Barbie Girl' song. Which is thirty-one flavors of awesome."

"Mmm-hmm. Let's see, Ricky Martin . . . ridiculous; Pat Benatar . . ."

I poke him with an accusatory finger. "Do not even start on Pat Benatar. Her stuff is classic, and if you don't believe me, ask anyone on *I Love the '80s*. You want to argue with me about the impact 'Love Is a Battlefield' had on every girl born between 1960 and 1975? No. Because you can't." Every time I hear her I still want to don a skirt made of rags and all the eyeliner in the tristate area.

---

[87] Vanilla Ice's movie that was too cheesy even for my liking.

"Hey, you've got the Mighty Mighty Bosstones. I actually like them."

"And what movie brought them into the mainstream? That's right. *Clueless.* Which you claim—wrongly—was dumb." Oh, Cher Horowitz, your legacy continues to impact my life in so many ways. Thank you again for teaching me the importance of designing a lighting concept.

"The Bosstones. Huh. Maybe there's hope for you ye— Wait . . . did you download *the Spice Girls*?" His lip curls with revulsion.

The Spice Girls . . . my secret shame. Fletch isn't supposed to know I like them. Kind of like how he's not supposed to know I put deodorant on every part of my body that bends, creases, or folds[88] or that I lie when I say I rinsed off the tip of the whipped cream container after I squirted it into the dogs' mouths. Although I'm all for open communication, I feel there's some stuff he'd prefer to be in the dark about. "That was a mistake. I didn't mean to download them."

"You have six of their songs on here. I see 'Wannabe,' 'Spice Up Your Life'—"

"And I made six separate mistakes. My fingers slipped. I was drunk. And distracted. Shut up."

He begins to smirk in earnest as he clicks through my list. "MC Hammer . . . Kriss Kross . . ."

"Stirring tunes and interesting pants. What of it?"

"Smash Mouth . . . Positive K . . . New Edition . . . and Lynyrd Skynyrd? Did you mean to put them on here?"

---

[88]My back fat is April fresh!

"Um, duh? They sing 'Sweet Home Alabama,' do they not?" And possibly when I get bored on the treadmill, "Sweet Home Jennsylvania."

"But Skynyrd had talent."

"Hence my download."

"Five bucks says the only reason you have any idea who they are is because someone sang this song on *American Idol*."

"Ha!" I exclaim. "Shows what you know. I am thoroughly familiar with Skynyrd, thank you." Despite Bo Bice's stirring rendition in season four. And Ruben's in season two.

"Because of the KFC commercial?"

"Yeah, right." *Yes, right.*[89]

"And finally, Lou Bega and Naughty by Nature. Wow. This is a cavalcade of suck."

"Mock me as much as you want, but when all my working out gives me big *strongs*"—I curl my biceps—"we'll see who's laughing."

"I already know who'll be laughing. Me. At your deplorable playlist."

Through clenched lips I ask, "Shouldn't you be changing out of your spitty clothes right about now?"

"On my way." He places a hand on my shoulder before leaving the guest room. I can hear him digging around in his closet, and I recognize the sound of him neatly folding and placing his garments in the dry-cleaning basket and insert-

---

[89]And yes, I became familiar with Gorillaz because of that iPod commercial. Shut up.

ing cedar trees into his shoes. I'm perpetually amused at how careful he is with all of his clothes. If he wears one of his dress shirts for even an hour, it goes right in the basket. He goes through so many outfits each week, for the past four years our dry cleaners have given him a Christmas present.[90] He goes past the guest room wearing a crisp pair of track pants—ironed?—and a starchy white T-shirt on his way down the stairs. "Hey, don't forget to download 'The Macarena,'" he jokes.

Ooh, good call!

The good news is, I'm getting ready to go to New York. The bad news is, I decided to get my roots fixed before I go. In so doing, I've placed myself in the hands of a fresh-from-beauty-school assistant. She's washing my hair, and by washing, I mean banging my skull around like it's a maraca.

"Goddamn it, it's a *head* and not a *coconut*! Will you *please* be more careful?" I shout.

"Oh, sorry; did you say something?" she asks. The assistant is coiffed with two enormous blond pigtails—Hi; you're how old? Thirty?—streaked with an entire spectrum of colors, and she sports six different shades of eye shadow. She's having trouble reaching the shampoo bowl because she's extratall and highly unstable due to her goofy goth moon boots with ridiculous platform heels. Here's a tip, Rainbow

[90] I bet he'd never shove his dirty wedding dress in a garbage bag and stuff it on a shelf in the back of his closet for five years until he just now remembered he should probably get it cleaned.

Brite—start wearing sensible kicks to work. And try to not snap your customers' necks when rinsing out their conditioner.

"I did. I guess you couldn't hear me over the sound of my skull thudding repeatedly against the porcelain," I tell her.

"You're so funny!" she squeals.

"Yeah, hilarious," I agree. "And I've got a great idea. Why don't you bang my head one more time and we can see how hysterical it is when I forget how to drive home?"

She giggles and wrenches my hair, twisting the last bit of water out before throwing a towel in the general direction of my face and leading me to my stylist, Monique. "Here's your next victim!" she exclaims.

I settle into the chair in Monique's station. She secures a plastic gown over me and removes the towel, then begins to comb and assess. "Hey, Jen; how are you? Your color looks great!"

We look at each other in the big mirror as we chat. "Really? I'm surprised there's any hair left. Your assistant yanked the foils off like they were live grenades."

A look of concern crosses Monique's face. "Sorry about that. We've been talking to her about being more gentle with our clients."

"Does she listen, or does she laugh and tell you you're funny?"

Monique blows a thin stream of air out of pursed lips and nods. "The latter."

"Her ponytails are too tight."

She nods. "What are we doing today? Trim?"

"No, I want to go modern. Think more New York and less Junior League of Central Texas. I want smaller hair so everything else looks smaller by comparison." As she artfully snips and shears, I tell her all about how I'm going to New York again and my diet. I explain how I'm rewarding myself with treats like haircuts and pedicures for every ten pounds I lose.

"If you're here, that means you're ten pounds down!" Monique says.

"Right!"

Sort of.

It's more like three. But since I refuse to go to New York with visible roots, split ends, and naked toenails, I bent my own rules. Besides, I've got *plenty* of time to lose my weight before my self-imposed deadline. No need to go whole hog right this minute.

She begins to smooth my hair with a bunch of potions, and then picks up a blow-dryer and a boar-bristle brush, the resultant sound rendering conversation impossible. After she dries the back, she spins my chair around so I can't see her working on the front. Twenty minutes later, she's finished and whirls me back around.

"What do you think?"

I look at my hair, open my mouth—and no sound comes out. Monique hands me a mirror to check out the back. "You love it, right?"

"I . . . I . . . oh." My hair is shorter, shooting up in the front and kind of bent at a ninety-degree angle at the top, hanging down in odd little waves on the sides. It's not *framing* my face so much as *sandwiching* it. Picture a cocker spaniel's ears. On my head.

"It's chic; it's modern; it's just perfect! What a great look! All right. Helena's waiting for you, so I'll see you next time. Have a wonderful trip!"

Dazed, I'm led back to the pedicure area of the salon. While Helena works on my feet, I keep running my fingers through the strands, trying to make the do less *rectangular*. I'm fretting so much over what's happening at the top of my body, I don't notice when Helena accidentally slashes my big toe with the cuticle nippers—until I get up and try to put weight on my foot. I can barely walk out of the salon.

I drive home and go directly to the full-length mirror in the bedroom. I hobble up to it to take a better look at myself, and a grin spreads across my face like an Italian sunrise.

With my hair cut to look exactly like a Russian fur hat with earflaps and my brand new gimp, no one in that city is going to notice the size of my ass.

"I *hate* New York."

Stacey gives me an unblinking stare, looking me up and down as I say this, starting with the Russian earflaps and making her way down to the sweatpants, socks, and floppy green Crocs. "Clearly you are a crazy person, and you should probably leave my home before you soil yourself on my couch." Were it not for her family in Chicago, Stacey would live in New York in a heartbeat.

"Perhaps hate is too strong a word," I concede.

"Your e-mail said you had a fantastic time."

"I did—I had a blast. Nothing *specifically* bad happened, except I figured out I am not and will never be a New Yorker. And I'm secretly disappointed. I've always considered myself kind of New York-y. Upper West Side, bay-bee." I flash her my approximation of a gang sign.

"Meaning what in English?" Stacey asks.

"First of all, everyone there is tiny. Not so much as in 'not fat' but more like they're all built to a two-thirds scale. They're all wee little bird people. Take my publicist, Mary Ann, for example. She's adorable and totally proportionate—she's probably five-two or five-three, but she's really slender. I actually bet her that she weighed less than a hundred pounds. Granted, I lost, but only by six pounds. If she gets the flu really bad, she's going to be down to double digits. Can you imagine being double digits?"

"Yeah . . . in grade school."

"When we said good-night, I hugged her, and I was able to pick her up and swing her around. She told me she could totally do the same to me, and I wouldn't let her try because her spine would snap and then I'd be in trouble. And yet she totally ate and drank everywhere we went. She doesn't have a problem with food; it's just that she walks everywhere and can't put weight on."

"Tragic."

"And that's not even what got me. She and I went out for a late dinner one night down in the West Village, and there must have been a Ford Models party or something in the front of the restaurant. We were in the back on the way to the washrooms, and an entire parade of frigging gazelles loped past us. Seeing them made Mary Ann feel fat because they clocked in at a buck-five and had a good eight to ten inches on her. On what fucking planet is a hundred pounds fat? On planet New York, that's where."

"There are models all over the city. They breed there. Like cockroaches. You can't take a step without bumping into some anorexic Amazon, swinging her ponytail and portfolio. You really want to feel bad, try standing next to one of the fourteen-year-old Brazilian models in an elevator. I'm normally nothing but confident, but when I come face-to-fat with one of them, I wonder if we're even the same species."

"Exactly." Stacey always gets it. "So we're at this restaurant and I'm eating a bowl of pasta. It's a small bowl and I got it with a light garlic sauce and some langoustines, so it was pretty healthy, not to mention totally delish. Yet every single model on her way to the potty gave me a look of horror, like I was supping on live snake or something. Me being me, I started to get mad. Finally, I got all aggressive, like, '*Of course I'm eating. I'm in a fucking restaurant. This place exists solely for the purpose of dining. That's what you do here. You eat. Digestion optional.*'"

"You make friends everywhere, don't you?"

"At that point I was cranky anyway because of all the walking. I limped everywhere because of my stupid pedicure, and I felt like I was being stabbed in the foot. Plus, because I'm vain, I refused to wear sensible shoes and instead wore those cute little black suede Mary Janes I ordered from London, with the pink embroidered flowers on them, and they just made every step ten times more painful. And I ruined them! The constant friction wore all the plastic off the kitten heel, and I ended up wobbling around trying to balance on a tiny peg. Next time, style be damned, I *am* wearing my Crocs."

"OK, fine, frustrating, but that's more your fault than New York's. You can't let your own poor judgment color your opinion of an entire city."

"Here's the crux of it. We went to all kinds of cool places, but every single one of them was just . . . so small. This happened last time I was there, too, but it's only now I'm able to put my finger on what bothered me. Anyway, the tables were wee. The chairs were delicate. The bathrooms were bite-sized. Everyone there is little because there's simply no room for their bodies to expand, kind of like they're all living in an overcrowded fish tank. There was something so Dostoyevsky about the place, like everyone gets their square foot of space, and they can't take up more than that."

"Obviously, Jen, space is at a premium there."

"And I *hate* that. I hate that the only time I was comfortable was when I was in my hotel room or walking down the street. I felt so claustrophobic and, like, even if I wanted to hold my arms out at my shoulders, I couldn't. Much as I enjoy veal, I can't abide a veal pen. I just don't remember everything being so small back when I used to do so much business there."

Stacey stretches, probably subconsciously glad for all the space we're afforded here in Chicago. "How's Fletch doing?"

"Bah, Fletch. He's another issue. I'm away three days, and when I get home, I find that he's gone completely feral."

"He's normally so tidy and put together."

"I know! That's what made it worse. On the plane, I read. my friend Annabelle's[91] book, and she writes about how men have this 'learned helplessness.' I felt slightly superior at having a husband who has never once left the seat up, doesn't watch professional sports, and grudgingly, but fully, participates in all the household chores. Fletch is a whiz at laundry, scrubs a mean toilet, and can always be counted on to whip up something for dinner. Sure, it's usually inedible, but the effort is there, and that's what counts."

"All I ever ask is for effort. Success is a bonus."

"Exactly!" I pause to take a sip of water. After all the drinking and shouting I've done in the past few days, my voice is almost shot. "I've gone away before, and each time I've returned to a clean, orderly house, regardless of how messy it was when I left. Fletch is always neatly shaved and dressed nicely, and there's often something bubbling away on the stove. Granted, it may be purple and gelatinous and not fit for human consumption, but again, it's *effort*. Big snaps for effort," I croak.

"Do you need some tea with honey? Your voice sounds like hell." When I grow up, I want to be the kind of gracious hostess Stacey is.

....

[91]By Annabelle Robertson: *The Southern Girl's Guide to Surviving the New-lywed Years: How to Stay Sane Once You've Caught Your Man.*

"Nah, I'm OK. I'm almost done and we can start the show. I get back on Saturday, and he must have worked from home while I was gone because he's got three days of growth on his face, he's dressed in a filthy Blackhawks jersey, and there are empty pizza boxes and sticky soda and beer cans everywhere. The house wasn't exactly clean when I left because I figured if I died in the air or somehow crash-landed on an uncharted island between here and New York—"

"Excuse me?"

"Not important. But if I didn't come back for some reason, I figured he'd look around at the squalor, and cleaning would take his mind off the fact I didn't make it."

"Except for the island bit, I actually get that."

I smile. "I knew you would."

"Why did he go feral? What was different from your last trip out there? Is this New York's fault?"

"No, he discovered some stupid Chuck Norris Web site, and ever since I got back, he's been strutting around saying stuff like, '*After a night of drinking, I don't throw up—I throw down.*'"

"Lucky you! But you can't blame New York."

"Fair enough. However, this was the first time I didn't come home wanting to move there afterward. Loving New York has been such a constant in my life that the trip was weird. It's like I've had a crush on New York for years, and we finally hook up and I find out he still reads comic books, has skid-marked undies, and smells like summer sausage."

"That makes sense." Stacey aims the remote at the TV. "You ready for Bravo?"

"I am," I say. "One more thing, though. I was the only person I saw in three whole days wearing anything pastel. Even though it's spring, New Yorkers don't wear pink. And that's just fucked up."

Dear Resident at 2337 North x——Street,

Our office has received numerous calls about your vo-
ciferous canine. Some of our residents work from home
and find it difficult to complete their tasks when your
dog barks all day. Please rectify the situation or fines
will be assessed and authorities will be notified.

Best,

Jen Cognito, Association President

Less Talk-y, More Drive-y

"*I* am fucking *losing it*."

It's spring, my windows are open, and Little Dog is up to his old tricks.

"Have you called the city?" Angie asks. "A barking dog is a nuisance, and it's illegal. Slightly different situation, but once I had a neighbor with a bite-y dog who kept getting out through a hole in their fence and snapping at my kids. I called the mayor's office, and the city took care of it."

"I've dialed the Chicago city services line so many times, they answer, '*Hey Jen, who's bothering you now?*' I've filed a stack of complaints and have no doubt the operators at 311[92] make talky-talky hand-puppet gestures and roll their eyes every time they get me on the line. What's ironic is, I look back at what I wrote about my neighbors a year

---

[92]The city's nonemergency line.

ago, and I have to laugh. I was worried about people who didn't mow and had rats thriving in their backyard jungle? Really? That was my problem? At least rodents and ragweed are quiet. I haven't written anything in weeks because of the noise."

"Nothing? Are you worried you won't meet your weight-loss goal?"

"Nah, I've got plenty of time. I still have almost five months to lose the weight and write about it. I could probably even do it in three months if I had to. I'm just annoyed by all the yapping."

"You wonder if you might be overreacting out of hunger?"

"More likely I'm cranky because I'm not drinking. I've been on the wagon ever since I got back from New York."

"You mentioned you were considering it, but I figured it was like my fasting. Good for you!"

"I miss wine. A lot."

"Alcohol doesn't have *that* many calories. You could have a glass of wine if you wanted."

"I can't. Two glasses of wine isn't what gets me. What's made me fat is the loaf of sourdough and pint of spinach dip I'll inhale *after* drinking the wine. Cold turkey's been the only way to go. I'm not allowing myself any liquor until I see you guys this weekend."

"You haven't cheated at all? Doesn't sound like the Jen I know."

"I did kind of snap a couple of weeks ago. We were watching movies all night, and Fletch had a few beers. I could smell them and practically feel the effervescence on my tongue. Torture. He went up to bed, and before I knew what I was doing, I ran to the fridge, stole a beer, and guzzled an entire Miller High Life in one fell swoop while standing in the dark in the living room. Don't know why I felt like I had to sneak it or why I didn't just sip it slowly and enjoy it. We didn't have any temperance-type bet, and he'd probably be happier if I were drinking. He keeps telling me I'm being a pill, which is true."

"How was it?"

"It was the most delicious beer I've ever tasted."[93]

The guest room is getting hot, so I lean over the bed and open the window. Of course the neighbor's dog is outside again. *Yap! Yap! Yap!*

"What is that noise? Is that the dog? Whoa, that *is* loud."

"Welcome to my world." While we chat, I've got MySpace up, and I'm approving friend requests. One requester has a *Leave It to Beaver* family picture up as her member photo, and seeing it makes a little bell go off in my head. "Wait a sec; your neighbors' dog didn't stop escaping through the broken fence because you made a call. Your neighbors fixed the hole because you went over to their house all decked out in June Cleaver's gardening togs. You told his owners you were going to beat their dog with a shovel if he ever bared his teeth at your children again."

She giggles. "Heh. I know, but if I told you to do the same, you'd probably get shot, and then I'd have no place to

---

[93]Jen's Life Lesson #7843: No beer tastes as good as *forbidden* beer.

stay when I come to visit. I'm dying to go thrifting with the girls, so I lied."

In my best DeNiro impersonation I say, "You, you're a giver." I slam the window shut again, deciding I'd rather be hot than annoyed. "Speaking of, am I going to *like* going to thrift shops? It sounds creepy. Do I really need a bunch of people's old shit?"

"Wendy has a bead on where all the nice ones are in the western 'burbs, so that's where we're going. Last time we went, she got a brand-new pair of Dansko clogs for a dollar. *One dollar.* She picked up some awesome fifties tablecloths and Wedgewood plates for fifty cents, and she got an Ellen Tracy skirt with tags still on it."

"Huh . . . would I be able to get Baccarat crystal pieces for next to nothing?"[94]

"If they've got 'em, sure. You'll die when you see what people give away."

"I'm withholding judgment until we get there. If these places smell like feet—which is my fear—I reserve the right to bitch."

"Deal."

Am suffocating again. This room heats up faster than my microwave. I crack the window to a chorus of *Yap! Yap! Yap!* "Great," I say. "Sounds like it's going to be another wasted afternoon."

"Lucky you. Listen, I've got to get James at school—I guess I'll see you Thursday afternoon."

....
[94]I do not have too many Baccarat crystal glasses in my house. Just every other kind.

"Do me a favor?"

"Sure. What do you need?"

"Bring your shovel."

"Ang, it's nine a.m. on the dot. We've got one hour to pick up Carol and get out to the suburbs. Chop-chop; let's go." I bang on the bathroom door.

"Almost ready, I promise! Just finishing up my makeup," Angie replies.

"If we're late, we're not getting coffee *and* I'm telling Wendy it was your fault."

"Shit! No!" Angie practically explodes out of the bathroom, tossing her cosmetic case in her purse. "I'll finish in the car!"

Normally neither of us would care about being on time, but Wendy is waiting, and I have every confidence she'll do us all great bodily harm if we're not there exactly when we're supposed to be. It's not that Wendy is rigid or mean; rather, she's in charge of our shopping expedition today, and everything will have been orchestrated to the minute, and if we're late, there will be consequences. And I'm not anxious to find out what they might be. Wendy learned to be strict when she taught high school LD classes. Had she shown any weakness, the students would have eaten her alive. She stopped teaching when she had kids, but the toughness stuck.[95]

---

[95]My favorite story is when she disciplined her all-male classes by making them watch her wedding video. I can't recall what prompted this punishment, but they never did it again. Apparently it was so effective, Wendy

Wendy's a marvel of organization, so much so that she has a gift-wrap closet in which every scrap of paper and bit of ribbon hangs in color-coordinated ruler-straight little rows. Going to her home is like visiting an efficiency museum. She's not a self-righteous jackass about it, though; she even volunteers to come to friends' houses to help them. This fall she's driving up to Angie's place to help make over her basement with paint and pretty vintage fabric. When I told Fletch about this, he asked if Wendy would paint our basement, but I explained that there's a difference between sewing pillows and slapping a darker coat of beige on paneled walls and fixing up what looks like Saddam Hussein's spider hole.

"Hustle, hustle; down the stairs; let's go!" We dash out the back door and into the garage. I make us both get in the car with the windows up, locks engaged, before I open the automatic garage door. I've forced Angie to participate in my elaborate garage security ritual every time we've gone anywhere in the past few days.

"I thought we were in a hurry," she says.

"We are."

"Then why do we have to go through this ridiculous exercise?"

"Because you never get a second chance for safety first. There's danger everywhere."

"Oh. Danger. All right, then." She nods slowly and hands me my purse. "Want me to have 911 cued up on your cell phone, just in case?"

....

could just open the drawer where she kept the tape and everyone would immediately fall in line.

"Yes, not being robbed and murdered in my garage is simply hilarious," I reply, backing out into the alley. There is nothing wrong with employing a bit of caution. "Won't it be a shame when a bad guy doesn't stab you in the pancreas and you get to go home whole and healthy on Sunday?"

Angie peers out the windows. "Well . . . I don't see any potential robbers or murderers, but there are two boys playing kickball in their side yard. Sure, they're only five years old but they could be packing heat; you never know. Good thing we've got our doors locked."

"Shut it."

"What about that little blond woman over there and her purse-dog? That miniature poodle could totally be rabid. Shall we get a series of inoculations as a preventative measure?"

I press my lips together, saying nothing as I navigate backward and then forward.

"I also see a couple of shifty-looking alley cats. You think they're more likely to rob or murder us? Or maybe just rub up against our ankles?"

"You know who's not funny?" I ask. "You." Angie smiles serenely and flips down the visor so she can finish putting on her mascara. "Keep smirking and I will make you listen to Rush Limbaugh all the way to Wendy's."

She slicks on lipstick. "And I'll tell you exactly why he's wrong."

Check and mate.

"Um . . . are we going to pass any coffee places? I could use some," Angie says. She's been here for less than forty-eight hours and we've stopped to get some variety of coffee-based beverage seven times. She's also pointed out each Starbucks we've passed. Because there's one on every block, the number of times she's shouted, "Look! There's a Star-bucks!" has not been insubstantial.

"Jesus, Angie, we'll be at Jen's place to pick up Carol in about five minutes. You can wait, right? This way Carol can get something to drink and we won't have to make two stops, so we'll be on time and Wendy won't fillet us."

"Look! There's one right there! We could run in if we wanted to."

I glance away from the road and notice she's practically trembling with anticipation. "Five minutes? You can't wait *five minutes*?"

"Come on," she cajoles. "It's right there! And there's an open spot—pull in! *Pull in now, damn it!*"

"Honey," I say gently, patting her on the knee. "Take it down a notch. I think you may have a small caffeine addic-tion."

"Yeah, Jim says that, too. I wonder why."

"Hmm . . . maybe because everyone at the new Starbucks in your town already knows your name and they begin to prepare your drink when they see you pull in?" I ask.

"Maybe. Did I tell you about the ass who works the drive-thru there? His name is Dustin, and I hate him. He needs to learn to keep his piehole closed. Shut up! I don't want to have a conversation; I want to place an order. Every time he wel-comes me, I get a monologue about the day and the weather, and when he's finally done and gets around to asking me how

I am, I tell him, *I'm venti skim vanilla latte, thanks.* My kids are mortified. They think I'm rude."

"Aren't you? Sounds like he's trying to be friendly. I'd kill for a cashier who wasn't openly hostile. Really? I don't know what a cheeseburger served without loogies even tastes like."

"No! *He's* rude because he's wasting my time. I'm in the drive-thru because I'm in a hurry. If I wanted to chat, I'd go inside. The last time I pulled up, he had his big, thick head completely sticking out the window, resting his chin in his hands like he was all smitten with me."

"Maybe he was. You look way younger than you are, your hair is pretty, and you're got nice skin. You're a bit of a MILF. Better yet, you're like Stacy's mom in that song! You've got it goin' on!"

As a mom, Angie's more used to giving out compliments than receiving them. "What*ever.* Anyway, I picked up my Altoids tin and pretended I was talking into it, and I waved him off when he greeted me. Oh, remind me—Wendy said she'd paint little buttons on my tin to make it look more like a cell phone."[96]

Before I can respond, we arrive at Jen's place. "Can you run up and buzz to let them know we're here?"

"Sure! And then we'll get coffee, right? You won't forget?" Fueled by her suddenly remembered need for no less than four shots of espresso, Angie hurls herself out of the car and begins to mash the buzzer repeatedly.

----

[96]Sometimes I worry about my influence leeching into Angie's life.

Carol comes out about a minute later dressed casually and comfortably for a day of thrifting. Angie forbade me to wear Crocs, so I'm stuck in a pair of loafers with zero arch support. I fear I will regret this decision later.

They greet each other, and then Carol hops in the front seat because she's been to Wendy's place more often than I have and she's got the directions. "Good morning! So happy to see you!" After we hug, she jerks a thumb in Angie's direction. "Why aren't you letting her have coffee?"

I suck air in between my gritted teeth. "I didn't forbid her; I even offered to make it at home, but she insisted on Starbucks and I thought stopping on the way would be excessive." I lower my voice and lean in. "I think she has a problem," I say.

Carol replies, "That's what I've been telling her."

"You're both full of shit," Angie shouts from the backseat.

I mouth the word "problem" to Carol and she nods.

Carol asks, "Jen, how's the diet going? You look—"

I stop her. "I look exactly the fucking same. I've only taken off six pounds and I'm really trying; I swear I am. I'm going to the gym,[97] I'm eating right,[98] I'm not drinking alcohol . . ." I throw my hands up. "I'm starting to worry it's not going to happen."

"What about a diet center? I did Weight Watchers after each of my pregnancies and the flab came off. Takes a while to do it their way, but it's not hard," Carol says. At forty,

[97]On the days I get the car.

[98]For the most part, except when I declare myself on vacation from my diet.

Carol looks more like Rene Russo now than she did in high school. Bitch.

"I don't know," I sigh. "Weight loss is a private thing. You're *supposed* do it alone . . . like going to the bathroom. I wouldn't wipe my ass in front of strangers, so I'm not going to sit in a room and discuss how birthday cake makes me *feel*."

"The meetings can be a little too group-therapy for my liking. Sometimes you have to go to a couple to find the right one," Carol admits.

"For a minute, I thought about joining until I stumbled across a Weight Watchers message board. The very first post I read went something like, *'There's a lady in my office who's very skinny and she does not ever eat in her cubicle. She's anorexic if you ask me because she does not like to eat. Many of us on my floor are on diets and each Thursday she brings in Krispy Kreme, even though she knows some of us are trying to lose weight. I hate her because I know she is trying to sabotage all my good work. She's a hypocrite and she is divorced and has a mullet and wears high-waist jeans.'"*

"People like this really exist?" Angie asks.

"Let me guess; she got a dozen sycophantic responses saying *'She's just jealous of you,'* right?" Carol says.

"Ooh, gold star!" I cheer. "How'd you know?"

"I'm a Weight Watchers veteran. I've heard it a hundred times."

Angie shifts in the backseat, craning her neck to spot the nearest Starbucks, just in case I miss it. "That's all they had to say? Pretty shitty advice, if you ask me."

I reply, "Finally, a voice of reason chimes in on the board and suggests maybe Eighties Donut Lady is just trying to be nice? The original poster replied, no, that can't be true because Eighties Donut Lady wants everyone else to be overweight so they all pay attention to her, which . . . of course. There's no other explanation. Eighties Donut Lady gets up early every Thursday, snaps on her high-fastening pants, drives out of the way to Krispy Kreme, picks out a dozen of their best-looking offerings, and hands over her hard-earned dollars to pay for said donuts, but not because she likes her coworkers. And she doesn't commit this thoughtful act for others because it might make her happy or feel good to do something kind."

"Yeah," Angie agrees. "She only takes the time and effort fifty-two times a year *specifically to fuck with you*."

I slow down to stop at a red light. "Honestly, I'd rather be fat and working a temp job than go to a meeting where I'm faced with this kind of logic."

Carol says, "What I've learned is, though people may comment on your appearance, fat, thin, or otherwise, ultimately, no one really cares what you weigh except for *you*." She cocks her head and looks thoughtfully at me for a second before adding, "And possibly your mother."

The day is gorgeous, and I crack my window for fresh air. Unfortunately, as I do so, Angie must catch the scent of coffee brewing somewhere and starts bouncing around the car like Maisy and Loki on the way to the doggie park. She thrusts her head between the two of us in the front seat, exclaiming, "Less talk-y, more drive-y! It's latte time; let's go, let's go, let's go!"

Two minutes later we're at the Starbucks at Diversey and Paulina. Angie streaks out of the car and into the shop, not even bothering to check for oncoming cars. An old Accord screeches to a halt, but Angie is singular in her determination.

Carol turns to me while we wait for a passing Volvo. "Problem."

We place our orders, and they're prepared quickly. Angie gulps a quarter of hers down before she even gets over to the sugar station to add sweetener. She notices how Carol and I are staring at her, mouths agape, and responds, "I don't have a problem."

Riiight, Cornholio.[99]

We get back in the car and I notice the clock on the dashboard. Oh, my God; how is it after nine thirty already? I say, "You guys—look what time it is. Wendy is going to cut off our legs and send us home in organic, recycled paper bags."

"Should we call her and tell her we're going to be late?" Carol asks.

"No—I'll just drive really fast and try to make up time," I respond. "Hey, why are you guys giving each other that face? I *am* capable of driving fast."

"Sure, yeah, of course. I'm curious—have you figured out how to merge?" Carol asks, eyes dancing. She's referring to an incident that happened in 1983. My family was in Boston for the holidays. My brother and I went to visit our cousins a few towns over from my grandparents' house, and my

---

[99]Beavis and Butthead reference. Ten points if you caught it.

brother promptly got drunk, making my fifteen-year-old non-learner's-permit-having ass responsible for driving us back on the Boston turnpike. Tears may have been involved because I wasn't a confident driver, particularly on the rudest road in the country. There might have been some cries of "*I hate to merge!*" And isn't it charming of my brother to trot that story out every single time I see him?

"Like you were both perfect drivers when you were fifteen?" I accuse.

"No . . . but I knew how to merge," Angie replies. Carol and Angie collapse into another set of giggles.

We turn off Diversey and go up the ramp to get onto the Kennedy Expressway. I make my way onto the road seamlessly. "See? I'm a fine driver. And by the way? Fuck you both."

"Hey, look; there's a car from Arizona!" Carol calls and pokes me hard right below my triceps.

"Ow! What are you doing?" I shout.

"The license-plate game. Our family plays it every time we go on a car trip. We just passed a car from Arizona, and I called it," Carol says.

"Jesus, I hope you don't poke your kids so hard; it would be child abuse. You practically broke the skin." I hold on to the steering wheel with one hand and rub my throbbing arm with the other.

"How much fun would that have been if we'd all gone to high school together?" Angie asks.

"Probably not that much," Carol admits. "Jen and I were nerds in high school."

I respond immediately, "What, are you kidding me? We were really popular. We were thin and cute. We weren't nerds; why are you rewriting history?"

Carol pokes me again. "Iowa!" Then she turns to Angie. "I assure you, we were nerds."

"Wrong. We weren't A-listers, but people liked us." Didn't they?

Poke. "Wisconsin!" Carol's head swings from side to side. "And yes, we *were* nerds."

"That really hurts—don't do that, please. Tell me this: how were we nerds? We wore pretty clothes and we were in a ton of clubs."

"What kind of stuff did you do?" Angie asks. "Poms? Dance squad?"

Poke. "Connecticut!"

"*Quit it.* No, the pep steppers were boyfriend-stealing skanks. Also, I can't dance. We were on the newspaper staff, we were in the drama club, I also did radio and yearbook one year, and we, like, practically owned the whole speech team. The team was called the Golden Tongues, and I remember one time I published a headline that read 'Golden Tongues Lick Competitors.' It was hilarious," I tell her.

Angie nods. "Nerds."

Poke. "Illinois!"

"Stop poking me and navigate, please? When do we turn?"

"Lemme check my palm pilot." Carol opens her purse, pulls out a little notepad of paper, and holds it up in her hand. "Get it? Fits in my palm? Heh." She flips through the book. "Take exit 51H. Oh, and by the way?"

"What?" I ask.

Poke. "Montana!"

"That should be right about here." I check out my side mirrors because I need to cut over two lanes, and quick. I try to pull over, but a white contractor van is positioned in my blind spot and keeps speeding up for no reason. "Hey, come on, pal . . . let me in. Ang, move your head; I can't see. . . . No, the other way." The quick influx of caffeine has left her flailing about the backseat and incapable of responding to simple commands. I honk and gesture, but the white van won't move. I try to floor it, but we're in an SUV and it's always been a bit sluggish on the uptake.

"Hey, nerd . . . are there any Starbucks by Wendy's house?"

Poke. "Indiana!"

"*Stop poking me.* Yes, there are Starbucks, but we have to get there before you can have more coffee. Why didn't you just buy two like we suggested?"

"Because I don't have a problem. I'm just thirstier than I thought."

To Angie, Carol says, "You sound like every alcoholic I've ever seen on daytime talk shows." And to me? Poke. "California!"

"Listen, guys, I'm trying to make this exit, but the ass-munch next to us isn't letting me." Our turn comes . . . and goes. "Oh, great, now we've got to turn around in the Loop and go back. Fan-frigging-tastic."

We make our way into the Loop in order to get back onto the Kennedy in order to hit exit 51H again.

Angie asks, "What was Jen like in high school?"

Carol considers for a moment as we cruise down Wacker Drive. "Hmm. Fun. But high-strung. Vapid. Supermodest. If you wanted to make her scream, you just had to say, 'Vagina!'"

"Stop it," I snap, out of reflex. "And don't tell Angie stuff she can use against me."

"I don't understand how you can swear so much, yet you spell out anything vaguely sexual," Angie chimes in. "Hey, Carol, we were on the phone last week and she shouted for no reason. I asked what happened and she told me one of the dogs bit her on the '*n-i-p-p-l-e*.'"

"Um, *hello*? Driving here? Your lives, my hands? Might want to think about that," I remind them.

Carol taps her fingers to her forehead. "Oh, I forgot to tell you the biggest thing. She was really, really vain. Way worse than now. We'd have conversations about why she thought she was pretty. Like, she'd want to discuss every feature.[100] She did have a pool, though. That made up for a lot. Hey, look, Ang; there's a Starbucks."

"Cool! Can we stop? I already finished my latte."

"No. It's Saturday and we're in the middle of the business district. Starbucks is closed and we're so late that Wendy's going to plant her foot firmly in each of our asses." I then address Carol. "I wasn't that vain, and if you only liked

---

[100]I will neither confirm nor deny this nasty rumor.

me for my pool, we wouldn't have been friends in the winter months, too. And I *was* cute. So there." I blow a raspberry at her.

To Angie, Carol says, "That doesn't mean she wasn't a handful. If Jen were over and I needed a minute to get ready, I could just say, *'Hey, Jeni, here's a mirror!'* and she'd amuse herself for half an hour."

"It was an act. I was trying to make you laugh." We're back on the expressway and should be able to take our exit any second now.

"Of course you were."

It *was* an act. I think.

"I can see you mouthing the word 'no' to Angie in the mirror," I growl. As I take in the signs, I realize I got on the expressway too far south and we've completely missed our exit again. "Oh, fuck me! I did it again!"

"Did you mean that in a sexual sense? If so, wouldn't you have had to say *f-u-c-k* me?" Carol asks.

Angie adds, "Distracted by your own reflection?"

Naturally, this is very, very funny to everyone in the car.

Except me.

Poke. "Florida!"

We turn around again and drive back on the same road we just traveled. Before Tweedledum or Tweedledee can say a word, I tersely explain, "Yes, it's the same Starbucks, and yes, it's still closed!" Their amusement isn't making me like them more.

We're back on the expressway. "FYI, if I don't make the turn this time, I am dropping you two off at the train station and you can locomote your asses out to Wheaton to buy up other people's old crap without me. Now, I am going to try to get in the right lane and you both are going to be quiet."

"OK, OK; sorry," they both mutter.

Poke. "Illinois!"

Urge to kill rising.

We're almost at the exit, and *another* white contractor's van is the only thing standing between me and safe passage to Wendy's house. I turn on my signal, honk, and try to nudge my way over, to no avail. "Help! Motion to him he needs to move, please!"

Poke. "Another Illinois!"

"Less poking and more motioning, please! Do you want to get to Wendy's or not?"

Trying to merge . . . trying to merge . . . unsuccessful . . . unsuccessful . . .

Poke. "A third Illinois!"

And that's the final straw.

"Of course it's an Illinois plate! They're all fucking Illinois plates because we're in fucking Illinois, which as of now shall be known as 'the fucking Starbucks state.' " I lay on my horn, slam on the brakes, and wrench the steering wheel, miraculously squeezing into the gap between the contractor's van and the Toyota behind it with maybe a millimeter between bumpers.

The car is completely silent for the next five minutes.

Carol speaks first. "She still hates to merge."

Angie adds, "And she's probably had too much coffee. Or

maybe she just needs a good *f-u-c-k*." Slowly but surely, their little gasps of suppressed glee turn into gale-force laughter.

"Yuck it up all you want. When you're finished, you guys can call Wendy and tell her why we're late."

A frisson of fear shoots through the passenger seats. Finally satisfied, I give Carol's arm a solid poke.

"Illinois."

Jen's Life Lessons, Thrifting Edition

- I am not a good thrifter. At all.
- The western suburbs in DuPage County are gorgeous, but I'd still rather have a honey enema at the Country Bear Jamboree than live there.
- In the nice thrift shops, the Real Housewives of DuPage County will cut you for looking at the Baccarat crystal.
- In the shitty ones in Cook County, patrons will cut you just for being there.[101]
- There are six Starbucks on Wendy's top secret thrifting route.
- We hit all of them.
- Angie has *a problem*.
- The troops will mutiny and demand Wendy

---

[101] Also, many people do not wash their plates and silverware before donating them. To say I was appalled at the idea of being stabbed with a dirty steak knife would be an understatement.

commandeer my car when I jump the curb trying to parallel park in front of her house. Joke's on them because I'd rather be a passenger.

- Thrifting involves walking. A lot.
- Apparently the amount of walking I am forced to do in stupid loafers is directly proportional to the amount of complaining I do.
- Which is why none of my companions told me about the possibility of thrift-store hats harboring *lice* before I put the cute straw cowboy one on my head.
- Am still itchy.
- And next time, I wear Crocs.
- In an effort to make my friends like me again, I will grudgingly agree to participate when Jen offers to teach us belly dancing six hours[102] later.
- I am spectacularly, embarrassingly good at belly dancing due to the laws of physics as they relate to the size of my ass.
- Which reminds me; I really have to get serious about this diet, or I'm not going to achieve my goal.

---

[102] And seventeen sangrias.

Dear Mom,

I accept your apology. (Was that really so hard?) Let us never speak of this again.

Looking forward to seeing you in New York next month! I'm attaching my hotel information so you guys can all coordinate.

Love,
Jen

Reaching Critical (M)ass

"Did anyone ever die from nerves? I might be dying. Do you think I'm dying?"

"Um . . . probably?"

"Wrong answer!" I swat Fletch on the arm. He's seated at the computer, and I pace back and forth behind him, scowling at myself in the big mirror on the wall. Every article of clothing I own is currently piled up on the bed, and the dogs are cowering in the bathroom because they don't understand why the Feeder is suddenly all shout-y. "Nothing! I have nothing!"

"Why didn't you buy some clothes when you went shopping with Angie and Carol?"

"Like I'm going on TV in a shirt I got for a nickel? Riiight." *Bright Lights, Big Ass* comes out tomorrow, and my publicist booked me on a local news segment in the morning. Earlier today I was all freaked out because there was confusion and the show thought I was coming to talk about dating in the city. Dating? *Moi*? The last time I dated was in 1994, and I managed to snare Fletch by saying the words guaranteed to drive all men wild:

"There's gin at my house!"

All day I panicked about going on TV to waggle a bottle of Tanqueray.

Fortunately, we got it straightened out and now I'm having stress-kittens over my appearance. I'm down almost ten pounds, but the camera's going to put those right back on me. I should be bouncing off the walls with excitement over Mary Ann scoring such a coup, because I've wanted to be on TV my whole life. And I'm mentally prepared, as I've practiced interviewing myself in the bathroom mirror for years. Yet I can't get past the thought of my blubber being broadcast across the Greater Chicago area. I'm proud to have claimed a spot on the show without having done something spectacularly stupid—always a possibility—but my elaborate bathroom broadcast fantasies never entailed me wearing a girdle.

I'm so mad at myself—I've known for a year I'd have a bunch of events in May; why didn't I try harder sooner? Why didn't I do crunches all those times I parked myself in front of *Idol* and *Veronica Mars* and *Lost*? If I couldn't get to the gym, why didn't I just take the dogs out for vigorous strolls? Why did I let myself "celebrate" with cake, wine, and Whoppers whenever I went off my diet?[103] And why is it that anytime something good *or* bad happens, I

---

[103] Which was more often than not.

gravitate toward anything fried, breaded, or *con queso*? I'd be much better off if I trained myself to celebrate or lament with an apple.

Generally I'm pretty happy with how I look, and there are only a handful of instances over the course of a year where I actively wish I were thinner. Tomorrow is one of those days. I'd kill for some sort of drug that would give me the illusion of being a size eight for a few hours. Like, I'd take it, and poof! Ten percent body fat! The weight would come back once I ate or drank something, and that's totally fair. The Insti-Slim[104] would work just like those dinosaur sponges that expand to four times their size when you drop them in water, only in reverse.

I glower at the pile of stuff on the bed. There is nothing here I want to wear unless it's a size small. Chances are, the Nutty Professor won't miracle up a batch of Insti-Slim for public consumption between now and seven a.m. tomorrow, so whatever I choose will have to hide four layers of girdle.

The TV studio isn't far from our house. I'm supposed to be there at 7:15 a.m. for an appearance at 7:48 a.m., and we're en route. I'm presently wedged in the front seat like a surfboard because I have so much spandex on, I've lost the ability to bend. I've built quite the house of cards with my foundation garments—if one layer blows, they're all going down. I finally settled on a black V-neck and gold wide-legged capris, and I resurrected my London shoes. I'm tidy and nondescript; no one's putting me on Mr. Blackwell's list, but it's TV appropriate.

Since I resolved the what-to-wear dilemma, I've begun to ruminate on the interview itself. I hate going into any situation where I don't already know the outcome, and today is a massive unknown. What if the anchorwoman goes all investigative reporter on me and grills me about sending my neighbors anonymous letters from a fictitious homeowners' association?[105] And I accidentally start spewing obscenities and get a million-dollar fine from the FCC? Or what if I turn into Cindy Brady and freeze on camera like on the "You Can't Win 'Em All" episode? And Cindy wasn't even wearing restrictive Lycra underwear.

The second we arrive at the studio, I break into a terror sweat. Completely dripping, I check in, and an assistant escorts us to the green room.[106] There are bagels and donuts and bottles of Fiji water sitting out, but I don't take anything because of the Girdle Rodeo going on in my pants. Everything's so tightly bound, I can't breathe, let alone imbibe. Anyway, even if I were clad in my most forgiving jammie pants, I couldn't eat because I'm too nervous to swallow. I practice easing myself into a chair—unsuccessfully—and Fletch documents my shame via camera phone.

A producer comes in and explains how everything will

---

[105]Shit; what if they're watching?

[106]Which, disappointingly, is not green.

shake out on set. She covers the questions I'll be asked and tells me where to look when we're rolling.[107] She gives me a once-over and proclaims me styled nicely and says there's no need for me to go to hair and makeup. I'm not sure whether to be flattered or disappointed. A tech guy enters and clips a battery pack on my waistband, slipping a cord up the back of my sweater. I bet he wonders why I've got a sweaty swimsuit on under my top.

The producer leads both Fletch and me to the set. I'm sent to a small love seat across from the anchor desk, and Fletch is allowed to stand behind the cameraman to watch. While they're showing the weather forecast, I meet the anchorwoman. Robin introduces herself like the consummate professional she is. As for me, the combination of circulation-cutting underpants and nervous energy proves to be too much. Instead of saying, *Hi, I'm Jen; thanks for having me on*, I glance down, notice she's wearing the most adorable Mary Janes with big buckles, and begin *to point and squeal*.

Something tells me Condoleezza Rice's interviews do not start like this.

I pull myself together somewhat by the time the weather is over and we cut to a commercial. My face was already sweaty, and now it's beet red, too.[108] I perch on the edge of the couch, trying to remember how I sat when I practiced in front of the mirror last night. I discovered there's a distinct way I should position myself to camouflage the fat rolls . . .

---

[107]Hint—talk to the person talking to you.

[108]How glad am I to have set both our TiVos for this auspicious occasion?

and the way escapes me. Something to do with my posture? More slouchy? Less slouchy? Shoulders akimbo? Shit; I can't remember now. The producer tells us we'll be on in less than thirty seconds and encourages me to get comfortable, so I propel myself into the seat with such force, I end up arching slightly, leaning backward, chin pointed toward the ceiling, and clutching pillows on either side—exactly the way I'd sit if I were having a cavity filled. The show cuts to our segment, and Robin begins to talk to me, or possibly my neck.

The next four and a half minutes are almost completely blank. I'm vaguely aware of participating in a conversation and am pretty sure I smile, laugh, and nod in the right places, but I could not tell you what I say for a million dollars.

When it's over, I say thank you to everyone[109] and practically run off set to Fletch. As we head to the parking lot, he tells me I did a good job. However, we took vows in front of God and the Nevada State Gaming Commission, so I'm pretty sure he's got no choice but to be supportive. We stop for breakfast at Burger King,[110] and I've inhaled my order of Cheesy Tots before we even pull into the garage.

I eat my Croissan'wich, then go upstairs to peel off my clothes. Released from its Lycra prison cell, my body goes *whoompfh* like a tube of Pillsbury biscuits being cracked against the counter. At this moment, I decide not to watch myself on TiVo because I'm sure I won't like what I see.

Instead, I opt to go back to bed because I've got to do the

---

[109] I think. I hope?

[110] Why, self? Why?

whole angling-dressing-nervous-talking thing over again to-night at my book signing.[111]

"These next two weeks will be like fat camp, except I'll be the counselor *and* the camper," I tell Fletch as we wend our way to the airport through rush-hour traffic. He's off to Denver for a couple weeks of intensive training.

"Fat camp for schizophrenics," he muses.

I'm trying to convince myself I won't miss Fletch while he's away. "I'm glad you're going to be gone. I'll be able to work out for as long as I like without having to stop and pick you up, and I won't be tempted to eat the fattening dinners I make for you."

"Ultimately you'll be more successful if you learn to eat what I'm having in more sensible portions."

"Keep saying stuff like that, and I won't miss you. And I'm not *asking* your opinion. I'm *telling* you how I'm going to run the next two weeks. Since I'm going to New York again and Philly next month for tour dates, I want to demonstrate some progress to my publisher. I want them to be proud of me. I've got to build on my momentum. I've lost ten pounds, but I can do better."

"Don't you *have* to do better?"

I'm not going to let myself rest until I've lost forty more pounds by the end of August. I figure if people on *The Biggest*

---

[111]Both my book signings go well this week. I'd like to say it's because the more I have, the better I get, and this is the job I'm really meant to do. The more likely explanation is that I drank wine beforehand.

Loser can dump eight to ten pounds a week, surely if I put my mind to it, I can easily hit my number. Doing it in a month would be awesome, but if I go too quickly, I fear I'll get saggy skin like a shar-pei. "*As I was saying*, the next two weeks are going to be my boot camp. Here's what I'm going to do—I'll be up at eight a.m. every day—"

"And you'll *stay* up?" Fletch interrupts.

"Just because I drive you to the office in my pajamas doesn't mean I always go back to bed.[112] Oh, I'm sorry, are you having a seizure? Because I know you didn't just roll your eyes at me. Anyway, I'll have a healthy breakfast, hit the gym for a couple of hours of cardio, maybe do some housework, and possibly double back to the gym in the afternoon for weight training. That way I'll be extratired when it's time for bed and I won't stay awake all night worrying someone will break in."

Fletch flips on his blinker and merges to the left. Even though I'm technically taking him to the airport, he's driving due to my penchant for going forty-five miles per hour in the fast lane.[113] "Glad you have a plan. Usually you go a little *Home Alone* when I'm gone."

"*Pfft*, what are you talking about? I'm almost forty years old. I can certainly stay by myself without incident. I don't know why you exaggerate. I'm not a cartoon character."

....

[112]Only most of the time. Seriously, sometimes we leave at six thirty a.m. What are we, farmers?

[113]Used to laugh at my mom for doing this before I realized it was hereditary.

"How about the time I had to go to Ohio and you did nothing but eat Lucky Charms and watch TV, and you almost stabbed your coat because you thought it was an intruder? Or when I came back from New Jersey and found your 'arsenal' under the covers on my side of the bed? The machete and BB gun I understand, the crab mallet less so. And what was the deal with the duct tape?"

"If I was going to catch someone breaking in, how was I going to hold them after I stabbed them and before the police came? Duct tape. Duh."

"And the Benadryl?"

I fold my arms across my chest and glower out the window, saying nothing.

He gives me a sideways glance. "Well?"

I mumble something Fletch can't hear.

He puts a finger to his ear. "What was that?"

"Benadryl would make them sleepy so they'd put up less of a fight. It always knocks me out when I take it." I glance over at him, and his mouth is all scrunched like he just took a bite of a lemon. I can see he's fighting the urge to burst into laughter. "You promised not to tease me about that again."

He wipes away a stray tear and attempts to put on a serious face. "You're right. I'm sorry. Jack Bauer and the Navy SEALS would give you a merit badge for your resourcefulness with antihistamines."

"Exactly."

"And . . ." He begins to choke and sputter a little bit. "And . . . and . . . they'd truly appreciate the homemade blowtorch you tried to create with compressed air and matches."

He howls in earnest now. How was I supposed to know the air would blow out the flame? The warning label said it would potentially ignite. Stupid misleading warning label.

"Listen up; I'll do so well on my own while you're gone, you won't even recognize me when you get back. And you know what? The house will be, like, ten thousand percent cleaner than when I came home from New York last time and found you and the dogs wandering around in your own filth."

"Okay," he agrees. "While you're cleaning, see what you can do with the basement. Maisy's been peeing on the rug down there, and we're at a full red alert on the Homeland Stink Advisory System."

We ease into the curbside check-in area for American Airlines, and I hop out of the car to give him a hug and a kiss. "You just worry about you, because I? Will be *outstanding*."

"Outstanding, eh?" He hoists his bags out of the back of our car and then closes the hatch. "I look forward to it. Love you—see you in two weeks!" We say good-bye, and as I pull away, I see he's still giggling and shaking his head. Jackass.

Oh, I will show him exactly what I can accomplish. Just wait. In two weeks, I'll be a whole new me.

The first thing I do when I get home is fix myself a big salad with fat-free dressing. Look at me! Eating vegetables! Not Lucky Charms! Ha. And I'm going to clean this house like it's never been cleaned before.

I start on the top floor, dusting every surface and storing

or disposing of anything on the floors or in garbage cans. I make the bed and sort laundry and run the Dyson over the hardwood, sucking up enough fur to create two new dogs, perhaps of the non-basement-peeing variety. Then I attack the bathrooms with enough chemicals and paper towels to make Al Gore cry. I even take down the curtains and run them through the wash.

On the first floor, I vacuum and mop some more, slay dust bunnies, and haul out Great Garbage Bag Mountain, which I wouldn't have had to do if *someone* had disposed of the trash before we left like he promised.

Then I take the show outdoors, hauling our little push mower through the house to get to our eight-by-ten patch of grass in front. I'd planned on getting a string trimmer to hit the edging, but when I priced them at Home Depot they were $169. For $169, I will fucking bend over with hand clippers. I weed and neaten my flower beds and survey my work—fabulous!

Accomplishing everything takes the better part of the day, and when I finish I still have energy. Hey, how about that? I guess working out has given me some endurance.

Delighted with my newfound strength, I go to the basement for litter-box maintenance. Fletch was right; it reeks down here. Stockyards and leather tanneries smell better than this. An oil refinery or a tire fire would be pleasant by comparison. How can such sweet and benign little kitties excrete so much . . . *horrible*? I crack open the windows and cellar door, placing a box fan in the center of the room to move the thick, fetid air around. Blech.

Breathing through only my mouth, I scour boxes and put in fresh clay. I expect this to clear the air significantly, but the basement's still redolent of Eau de Doody. Then I remember what Fletch said about the rug. Maisy has been using it as a toilet because she doesn't like the backyard.[114] I bend to take a whiff to see if it's the offender, and the smell hits me in the face before I even get a chance to double over. Wow. The rug isn't stinky—it's downright *stanky*. I've got to haul this out pronto.

I move the futon, coffee table, chairs, and TV stand off the rug. I'd helped Fletch set up the basement as kind of a man lair about six months ago, but so far the only residents who've availed themselves of it are the dogs. I guess my sparkling personality is too much of a draw on the first floor.[115]

Drawing the deepest breath I can muster, I squat and begin to roll up the rug. Argh, it's *sticky*. I try really hard to keep my salad down. After I get it all rolled, I begin to navigate it through the basement and to the cellar door. The rug is way heavier than it was six months ago when we brought it down here, and it's entirely Maisy's fault. I get to the screen door, flip up both the locks, and rear back to toss the whole lot out the door. And then a funny thing happens.

I hear a rip.

I check out the door frame to see if the rug got caught on something sharp. Nope; it made it out with no problems. Then I realize the sound came from behind me.

. . . .

[114]What kind of dog hates her yard? A very, very spoiled one.

[115]Or possibly because the big TV's up there.

More specifically, it came from my back. Something in my back *ripped*.

Further, I realize I can no longer stand upright.

Uh-oh.

There's a hairline crack running the length of my ceiling over the couch. I'm aware of this because I've been lying on this couch for a week and a half, looking at it. I've replastered it a million times in my head because that's about the only thing I can do other than watch television and fend off dog nudges.

I've injured my back before—once in college I had to have physical therapy and I missed weeks and weeks of work. And class. Technically I was allowed to go to class, but I wanted to be extrasure. Who knows what negative impact a boring eight thirty a.m. French 201 lab may have had on my strained sacroiliac?

This time I'm taking pain meds and muscle relaxants by the handful. At first I tried to down them with the salads and other low-cal items I'd stocked the fridge with, but I kept getting lightheaded and nauseous. I finally broke out an emergency portion of macaroni and cheese to coat my stomach so the pills wouldn't make me sick, and I've been eating much heavier items ever since.

Normally I'd be delighted to have a back injury—it's a lot like a personal snow day. I'm permitted, no, *required* to lie around and watch daytime court shows and drink cocoa, and no smart-assed husband will mock me, because I'm legitimately out of commission. However, this time is different.

I honestly wanted to step it up in regards to exercise and diet. Instead, I'm prone on this couch, being prodded by wet noses, and feeling like a complete washout because I've gained back every pound I fought to lose in the past few months.

A major part of my ridiculously inflated self-esteem comes from having done what others said was impossible, e.g., becoming the first female executive officer at the investment relations firm where I used to work, or making a living as an author. The whole less-food / more-activity paradigm seems so easy, it's like something I should be able to do in my sleep . . . yet it's been a constant struggle. My failure to excel here makes me question all my past successes; was I really talented, or did I just get lucky? Is my rosy self-concept based on nothing but a fluke?

This time if I can't lose the weight, not only am I going to be jeopardizing my health, but I feel like it will be a big career misstep. Sure, it's OK with my "people" if I give them a lighthearted book about unsuccessful dieting. Or I could write something more serious about learning to live with my body image. But my friend already wrote a really poignant book on this topic,[116] and it was so good, I know I'd never do the subject the same kind of justice. The bottom line is, I said I'd lose this weight, and I want to lose it just as much as I don't want to go back on my word. And I've thought about nothing else for the past week and a half.

....

[116] *I'm Not the New Me* by the lovely and talented Wendy (not my thrift buddy) McClure. Buy now!

Since we're on speaking terms again, I want to call my mother and have her tell me what to do. I've always gone to her when things have gotten too tough, and this is why I've been stuck in a perpetual adolescence. Until we stopped speaking, I never completely resolved issues on my own before. This is the problem with our relationship and the root of why we end up fighting—I'm almost forty, and I've been forcing my mother to actively parent me far past the point when she should have to worry about me. And then after she's helped me and gotten enmeshed in whatever my problems are, I get defensive when it feels like she's overstepping her bounds. I realize now that I've put her in a lot of unwinnable situations, and I am sorry.

So I can't ask her help, for both our sakes. I've got to figure this out on my own. Maybe that's the whole point of this exercise? And maybe my weight isn't only because I eat too much and don't move enough—maybe I'm heavy because I just haven't been ready to act like an adult? I see plenty of people my age buying fat-free cheese and jogging along the lakeshore in the morning. I wonder how many of them do these sorts of things not because they want to, but because they have to. Many? Most?

To protect my health and, by extension, my career, I need to actively start making decisions like a grown-up, but I don't know how to be an adult.

I *do* have experience being a professional, though, and that's a reasonable facsimile. How would a professional handle my situation? If I break things down into business terms, perhaps the answer will present itself?

Say I owned a coffee shop—how would I handle it if my espresso maker broke? The wrong thing would be to ignore it and attempt to convince my customers they'd rather have tea, although that's exactly what I've done with my body. No, if I had a broken machine, I might give it a once-over to see if there were any glaring items I could fix myself. But I'd understand that the espresso maker was a central part of my business and I'd call a professional to fix it as soon as possible.

Bingo.

I need a professional.

Correction: I need professional diet help.

But from where?

If I've learned anything in the past few months, it's that I'm ultimately going to gravitate toward whatever is easiest and most convenient. While I'm deep in thought and staring at the ceiling, a Jenny Craig commercial comes on, so here we go. Cordless in hand, I dial.

Kirstie Alley answers and shrieks, "*Yay!* Where else can you lose weight *and* eat fettuccini?"

I shriek, too, hanging up the phone.

Five tries later, I finally get through her whole recorded greeting without exploding into laughter. I make an appointment with a local center for later this morning.

As I slowly drag my stiff, sore body up the stairs to get ready, I refrain from my usual inner dialogue, which generally sounds like, *Yay, me, for trying! Let's have a cookie!* I've let myself get away with far too much stupid, self-destructive behavior over the years because I gave myself mad props for effort, not success. The endeavor doesn't count in this situation. There's no more partial credit; I have to win the game.

I undress for the shower and glance at myself in the bathroom mirror. There's much work to be done here. Right before he left for Denver, Fletch said, "Do, or do not. There is no try." I thought it the most profound statement he'd ever uttered . . . even after I found out Yoda said it in *The Empire Strikes Back*.

Today I choose *do*.

TO: fletch@work
FROM: jen@jenlancaster.com
SUBJECT: Am. Not. Kidding.

Hey, Fletch,

A couple of favors—one, can you please pick up a bag of dog food on your way home from work? I'd get it, but it's too heavy for me to manage.

Two, please, please, please stop sending me links to the watch you want. Buy it, don't buy it; either way is just fine. But I swear if you mention this damn watch once more, you will have to bend over to tell what time it is.

Love you,

Jen

Baby Steps

"Welcome to Jenny Craig! Is this your first time here?"

My sarcasm gene kicks into overdrive and I bite back a dozen different snappy retorts, such as *Do I look like I've been a longtime client?* Alienating the staff with a smart-ass remark seems like the wrong move, so I return the perky receptionist's pleasant greeting sans snark. She tells me someone will be right with me and to please make myself comfortable in the lobby.

Located in a storefront not far from my house, the Jenny Craig lobby is quite clean and sunny, and it's decorated with big pictures of Jenny Craig's menu items. The food pictured seems appetizing, but there's a quite a dichotomy between what a food stylist can do in a professional photo shoot and what a freezer-burnt box of diet food looks like after it's been nuked. This is one of those makes-you-buy-the-food plans. I don't see photos of powdered soup or oatmeal, which is a relief.

Kirstie Alley looms (less) large behind the counter in a Plexiglas frame holding an old-fashioned phone. Secretly I'm kind of disappointed that Kirstie Alley called Jenny. A couple of years ago she had the best sitcom on cable, called *Fat Actress*. She played the role of herself, and the show was about her unsuccessful bids to lose weight following the advice of a deranged diet guru who had her eating cigarettes and ordering tapeworms off the Internet. I guess I'm glad she found a way in real life to slim down, but I wish she'd have waited one more season to get all sensible.

I sit in my chair, studying life-sized Kirstie's highly animated face. The more I stare at her picture, the more it looks like her eyes are following me. Yikes. I wonder if the staff here ever gets creeped out by Kirstie hovering in the background all the time. Before I get a chance to ask, the receptionist leads me back to an office to meet with a counselor.

A trim brunette in her midthirties leaps out of her chair to greet me before I take the seat across from her desk. The receptionist leapt when I came in, too. And walking down the hall, I saw another counselor leap up from her desk when her client entered. Awful lot of leaping going on here. I'm sure that's not going to be annoying *at all*.

"Welcome, Jen! Glad to have you! I'm Maggie!"[117]

Even though the jury's still out, I tell her I'm happy to meet her.

Maggie beams at me and leans across her desk. "Jen, what brings you in?"

---

[117]And they speak with a lot of exclamation points, too.

Old Jen would quip *I'm here because I beat anorexia!* but New Jen is desperately trying to behave like an adult. "I'm interested in losing weight, and Kirstie Alley says you can help."[118] I don't mention I'm here because I'm trying to lose weight for a book. I consider my project to be on a need-to-know basis. And they? Don't need to know.

Maggie gets right into the pitch, telling me how the program works. I'll start off following a weekly planned menu consisting of breakfast, lunch, dinner, and two snacks. Having damaged my metabolism time and again by not eating at regular intervals, I acknowledge that this makes sense. Maggie says because I'll be eating all the time, there's no chance I'll feel hungry. But if I am, I can choose from plenty of "free" foods—mostly vegetables—which I can consume anytime.

Once a week I'll come in to meet with a counselor[119] and weigh in. They offer twenty-four-hour phone support, an idea that cracks me up. I imagine this phone center being a cross between a suicide-prevention hotline and a 911 dispatch, doing triage when there's an accidental inhalation of meatballs. Can't you picture it?

Jenny Craig; what's your situation?

I've had a bad day and I am going to eat this whole bag of Oreos.

Noooooooooooo! You have too much to live for! Put the cookies down!

As Maggie talks about their Web site, where clients can

---

[118] Fine; Old Jen isn't quite dead yet.

[119] Alone; no groups of angry chicks crying about birthday cake here.

access message boards, chat rooms, journals, and menu planners, I sort of zone out, imaging all sorts of food-based emergencies and giggling to myself. But she gets my attention again when she sums up the Jenny Craig experience—they tell me what to eat and I lose weight.

I'm not in love with the idea of sticking to a menu of boxed food every day, but I've been spectacularly unsuccessful planning meals on my own. And I realize they didn't become a multimillion-dollar business by not fulfilling their promises. Despite my aversion to frozen meatloaf, this is the best option for me right now. So when Maggie asks me if I have any questions, I say, "Yes—how do I get started?"

I review the contract before I sign it, making sure there's no what-happens-in-Jenny-Craig-Fight-Club-stays-in-Jenny-Craig-Fight-Club language. I opt for the monthly payment plan, with an initial down payment of $174. I'll be billed $75 for the next three months, before the cost of food. Meals should run me between $11 and $15 per day, not including fresh fruits, vegetables, and dairy products, which I'm to provide myself.

I don't mention that being fat is cheaper.

Doesn't mean that I don't think it.

Maggie brings me to get weighed in a private enclave in the back. I step on the scale and there are no surprises. Or miracles. She records the number and then takes my measurements. Finally, she snaps a Polaroid of me standing by a pole that reads I CAN DO IT and clips it into my file.

After I pay for everything, Maggie collects my purchases from the cooler. She returns with three big grocery bags, and before I go, I schedule an appointment for next week. I leave laden with food and spiral-bound pamphlets.

More important, I leave with hope.

My first official Jenny meal consists of a salad, an orange, and a turkey burger. I stopped at the fancy organic supermarket on the way home to pick up the fruit and dairy items, figuring if I'm allotted such a limited amount of food, I'll be damned if what I get isn't the very best quality. For example, a couple of times this week, I'm supposed to eat olives. Given the choice, I'd rather indulge in the plump, delicious ones found on Whole Foods' fresh olive bar for $8.99 a pound than in a few pale, shriveled ones from a can costing ninety-nine cents. I bet this is why all the gourmands on *Top Chef* are thin—they don't eat quantity; they eat quality.

I have my salad with Jenny dressing—ranch, but not homemade or chock-full of mayo and buttermilk—and open my turkey-burger package. Including the bun, my "lunch" is the size of a tin of tuna. This isn't lunch—this is an amuse-bouche.[120] I heat it up and top it with a packet of Jenny-approved mustard sauce. There's nothing special or dietetic about the mustard, so next time I'll probably substitute one of the gourmet brown mustards Fletch is so adamant we stock. Lean and light, the turkey burger is fairly tasty, but I have only three bites in which to determine this. I gobble

---

[120]Wikipedia defines these as tiny bite-sized morsels served before the hors d'oeuvres or first course. And yes, I've watched way too much *Top Chef*.

down my orange and toss back two bottles of water to quell the hunger I still feel.

I take my pain meds and retreat to the couch. Snack time can't come fast enough today.

I'm still ravenous after my snack of vegetable sticks and ounce of low-fat cheese. And I formally want to apologize to low-fat cheese—the Babybel round I just ate was delicious, and I wish I was allowed to have fifteen more.

By five p.m., the sofas are starting to look tasty. Being leather, they're part of the beef family, right? A crown roast of love seat doesn't sound terrible right now, especially if it's all browned nicely and served with little paper booties on its square legs. I'm famished and want dinner *right this second.* Normally I don't eat this early, as I'm often awake for another seven hours. I want to hold out for a while, but I can't take these hunger pangs anymore. And Fletch will be pissed if he comes home and finds I've flame-broiled the ottoman and dunked it in barbecue sauce. Reluctantly, I open the freezer and remove tonight's repast.

Aha! So *this* is the fettuccini of which Kirstie Alley speaks. I boil my fresh side of baby carrots while I microwave the tiny black plastic tub containing my dinner. Tonight I also get a teaspoon of margarine and two tablespoons of the most expensive Parmigiano Reggiano available in Whole Foods' cheese cooler. No Kraft in a shaker for me, thanks.[121] Again, the portions are ridiculously small, but at least with the accoutrement of freshly cracked black pepper and good cheese, it should be palatable.

The microwave dings and I pull out my dinner. The plastic over the tub was covered in frost when I put it in, and I couldn't tell the portion size. Now that it's cooked, I see that my dinner is equal to the amount of meat, pasta, and sauce normally stuck to the side of the pan when I craft my own Alfredo out of fresh cheese, butter, and heavy cream.

I take my feast into the other room to watch a TiVoed episode of *King of the Hill*. I press PLAY and catch the end of a commercial for upscale floor coverings, idly wondering whether bamboo is tasty. If it weren't, panda bears wouldn't be fat, right? I devour my frozen meal, and I finish as the opening credits stop rolling. Nice. Way to savor, self. For dessert I wolf down my wee chocolate Bundt cake and glass of organic skim milk.

It's five fifteen and I'm still famished. This does not bode well.

"Are you hungry? There's a pizza for you in the kitchen."

"Great! I'm starving. I only had a sandwich in the airport, and that was hours ago," Fletch says.

He's home from Denver, just in time for me to be completely ambulatory again. I went to the gym this morning

---

[121]Even though I'd happily suck down a whole canister with a straw at the moment.

and spent an unpleasant half hour on the treadmill. I swear every muscle in my body atrophied in the past two weeks. However, movement must have been what I needed because, after I got home, I felt something in my back pop and the pain's been gone since then.

I hear him banging around in the kitchen. "Where is it?"

"In the fridge."

"Oh, I thought it'd be sitting out. You didn't just order it?"

Truth? I made it until 8:47 last night, until my stomach began to growl so loudly, I couldn't hear the TV. I'd been snacking on free foods for an hour and chugging water to no avail. So at 8:48, I picked up the phone and dialed Philly's Best.

I got a plain cheese, I had only one piece, and I blotted the oil and tossed the crust to the dogs. I didn't expect to start Jenny on the spot, so there was no transition period where I went from having whatever I wanted to eat[122] to being restricted to seventeen hundred calories a day. Maggie told me that when she started Jenny, she was eating two or three frozen meals at a time, so it sounds like I'm not the only person who didn't ease into the diet seamlessly.

I haven't been able to stop obsessing over what I'm allowed to eat, so I consider having just one piece a victory. If it sounds like I'm giving myself yet another A for effort, I'm not. My punishment was going to the gym this morning, even though I didn't feel up to it.

....

[122]In unlimited amounts.

Baby steps.
Baby bell.
Babybel.
Is it time for cheese yet?

I've been on Jenny a solid week, and I can account for about four minutes when I wasn't dreaming about food. I've been to Whole Foods at least five times because buying groceries makes me so damn happy. I enjoy examining all the oranges to get the biggest ones, and I delight doing a side-by-side comparison of calorie counts on the low-fat yogurts. I'm limited in what I'm allowed to eat but am confident that my careful shopping means my choices are the freshest, juiciest, and most flavorful.

In terms of taste, the Jenny meals range anywhere from blandly inoffensive to crave worthy. There's a pot-sticker entrée made with tofu and chicken that made me lick my plate (much to the dogs' dismay). And the iced lemon cake is something I'd buy even if I weren't dieting. I'm not sure if this is because these products are truly tasty, or if at seventeen hundred calories a day, everything's a palate pleaser. I've disliked only one item—a tuna salad redolent of cat food mixed with pickle relish and dirty feet. After I had the first bite, I had to plug my nose and down it like a Jäger shot.

I haven't eaten this light in years, so I just know I'm going to chart a huge loss on the scale this week.

At least I'd better.

Happy Weigh-in Day! Today I get tangible proof of just how hard I've worked this week. I was antsy the whole drive over here, and now as I pull up to the storefront, I'm full of nervous energy. I park and leap out of my car. You know what? That should be their slogan—*Jenny Craig. We Will Make You Leap.*

I wonder how much I'm down. Six pounds, easily. After a few days of so many fruits and vegetables, I probably peed out that much. I would not be surprised if I've lost more like eight. And I'd be over the moon if I hit double digits! I (almost) leap into the lobby to check in with the receptionist.

I want my weigh-ins to be as consistent as possible, so today I'm wearing the same outfit I wore last week: a Lacoste shirt—pink this time—khaki shorts, and a pair of Crocs; jewelry on, sunglasses off. (Essentially this is my summer uniform, so it's not like getting dressed today required a lot of extra planning.)

Maggie meets me up at the front desk. Before we sit down to chat, we go back to the scale. I step on, and the digital display climbs and finally settles. And because I am *brave*, I watch the entire time.

"You lost 2.2 pounds! Nicely done!" Maggie congratulates me.

Excuse me?

"Are you joking?" I am incredulous. Why? Why so little? How come I can be good all week—fucking saintly, really—and lose only two pounds, but anytime I have one freaking dessert, boom! Five pounds, no problem. It's not fair.

Except for one slice of pizza, I've followed this diet to the letter. I even turned down an opportunity to go for gelato, damn it. That alone should count for three solid pounds.

"What am I doing wrong?" I ask Maggie once we're back in her office. Since I was here last, Maggie replaced her desk chair with one of those big, plastic exercise balls just like Dwight Schrute did on that episode of *The Office*.[123] Listen; work your glutes on your own time, all right?

"Why do you feel you've done anything wrong? Two point two pounds is great! Be happy!" *Boing, boing!*

"I wanted to do better."

Touching my arm gently, Maggie asks, "Jen, may I ask, how long did it take you to gain all your weight?"

"Um . . . maybe about eleven years?"

"Eleven years is a long time." *Boing!*

"And?" I archly respond, withdrawing my arm from her touch. Possibly this would be a profound conversation were she not *fucking bouncing all over the place.* I mean, would anyone have taken the Gettysburg Address seriously had Lincoln given it from atop a trampoline?

Boing! "And, if you lost 2.2 pounds every week, you'd be down 114 pounds in a year."

OK, bouncing be damned, that's actually pretty cool. If I lost 114 pounds, I'd be beyond-Miss-America skinny. Hell, I'd look like a supermodel. Correction: an older, mean, leathery supermodel. Oh, my God; I'd look just like Janice Dickinson!

----

[123]Too bad I can't go all Jim Halpert on her and pop the damn thing with some scissors.

"Give yourself a break. You're doing very well. Now, let's talk about motivation. What'd you think of the disc I gave you?" *Boing!*

Last time I was here I received Jenny Craig's *28 to Motivate* CD. According to the attached literature, it's a month's worth of affirmations and strategies meant to help keep me on track. Unfortunately, it was also the perfect size to fix the wobbly bookcase in my guest room. "Useful!" I exclaim. "I find the CD very useful."

We talk about motivation a while longer, and I'm crabby from hunger and distracted by Maggie's big, stupid ball. "Let's talk about your eating style. How would you say you eat?"

"I guess I chew and swallow, attempting to do so with a closed mouth? And I try not to drip butter on my shirt."

Maggie's curls bounce up and down as she rephrases her question. "What I mean is, are you an uninformed eater? An emotional one? An unconscious one?" *Boing!*

"I'm the kind of eater who eats too much and exercises too little. That's why I'm here."

Boing, boing! "To be successful long term, we have to get to the root of *why* you eat."

I try hard not to grit my teeth. "I eat because it's the first tier of Maslow's hierarchy of human needs. FYI, this is also why I wear pants and live indoors." Hey, no one said teaching me to be healthier was going to be fun. Plus, I refuse to entertain this line of questioning, as I'm not about to enter into the Therapy Zone with a noncredentialed individual. I've *decided* to lose weight, and that's the key. No need to go dredging up my past when I'm specifically paying to fix my present.

"What has your relationship with food been—"

I hold up my hand. *"Bup, bup, bup;* let's stop right there. I'm not here to talk about my *feeelings*." Real mental health professionals have advanced degrees and years and years of professional training. Maybe this is why bus people call me a bitch, but I'm not about to solicit counseling from someone with a high school diploma, particularly when she's speaking to me while flailing about on a stability ball. "Listen, I'm here so you can tell me how many Jenny Craig turkey burgers and slices of Jenny Craig lemon cake I can eat a week in order to lose weight. If you're concerned about my emotional well-being, give me specific steps to follow to make numbers on the scale descend more quickly, and I assure you the emotion I feel will be happy."

Maggie ends our session pretty quickly after that. I get my food and walk out to the parking lot. I stand there for a moment with an idiotic grin on my face, looking at Fletch's new car. By the way? A big, shiny German automobile paid for with book money is *way* more motivational than any Jenny Craig–branded faux therapy.

The car is much nicer than I'd planned on it being. I was dead set against anything European or flashy because Fletch and I already lived a life where our sole purpose was to impress people and it *did not end well*. I wanted something safe, boring, and reliable that wouldn't cost us any money in maintenance or interest. We were paying cash for a used Honda. Period.

In lieu of getting gelato earlier this week, Fletch and I walked the lot of a fancy car dealership, full of vehicles I'd deemed too excessive. As we strolled, touching glossy paint jobs and peering in at pristine leather interiors, Fletch talked me through all the safety features on his dream car, using comforting words like "side curtain airbags," "panic buttons," "sensors," "dual thresholds," and "stability tracking." Then he explained how every single bit of maintenance on Dream Car would be covered for the next three years, even oil changes, and we'd get a free loaner Dream Car any time ours needed service. We'd have to pay only for gas and the occasional air freshener.

I began to show signs of cracking.

He then whipped out a spreadsheet and demonstrated the positive impact financing a small portion of the car[124] would have on our credit rating as opposed to paying cash. I felt my resolve evaporating. Then he delivered the punishing blow—he got my dad to tell me it was a wise decision.

So we're a two-car family. And if Fletch ever gets laid off again, he'll have a job at Perillo Pre-Owned Outlet selling snappy luxury cars to reluctant wives.

What sucks is I'm allowing myself to drive the new car only to the gym and Jenny Craig.

---

[124]After a hefty down payment.

Dear Mom,

Attached you'll find some clippings I thought you'd enjoy. Also, can you please reconfirm with Auntie Ann where you're staying? I'm pretty sure the Woo Hoo hotel doesn't exist—when I Googled it, the only entries were from blogs and people saying, "I'm in New York at the hotel, woo-hoo!"

My concern is that you and the aunties will get to the city and climb into some poor Pakistani guy's cab, and when he says, "Where to?" you all start shouting, "Woo Hoo! Woo Hoo!" and he won't understand, and then your group of aggressive Italian relatives will beat the cab driver with umbrellas in an effort to *make* him understand.

Just trying to avoid an international incident,

Jen

C·H·A·P·T·E·R F·I·F·T·E·E·N

Metamorpha-Sissy

*I*f I keep doing Jenny Craig and my usual workout, I can count on losing only about two pounds per week. If I don't step it up, I won't reach my goal by the end of the summer, and that motivates me to buy a big package of personal-training sessions at the gym. I've done better by being accountable to someone else each week with the diet, and I'm sure the same holds true for exercise.

The trainer I worked with a few times a couple of years ago isn't at my gym anymore. Which is fine. She scared me more than anything and had no sense of humor.[125] She worked me out hard, but I didn't enjoy her company. Stacey says the key is finding a trainer with whom you have good chemistry. Having no clue how to determine who might be my chemistry buddy by looking at their framed photos on the wall by

[125]Meaning she didn't find me funny.

the locker room, I simply tell Mike, the gym's manager, to assign someone. If he or she and I don't gel, I can go with a different trainer.

But I'm not thinking about tomorrow's training session. Right now, I'm at a party. A bunch of fun people came to my signing at the beginning of the month, and during Q and A, a girl named Kristin raised her hand and asked me if I'd attend their book club. My response? "Sure! What are you guys reading?" The whole audience laughed at me.

Oh. That's right. They're reading *my* book.

So I'm here, and I'm trying not to eat, and it's hard, especially because these guys have put out quite a spread, with so many treats I love, like toffee cookies and guacamole. One of the girls, Jessica, makes the group's signature dish—a creamy, cheesy corn dip with diced jalapeños. Gesturing toward the big, gelatinous bowl of yellow lumps, she says, "Disgusting, right? But try it; I promise you'll love it." I take a bite. And I do.

I'm frustrated because I told my Jenny counselor I was coming to this party tonight and I wasn't sure how to handle myself when faced with a buffet. I didn't catch the counselor's name today[126] because I was too focused on her ginormous, Guinness-book-esque birthmark. I felt like an asshole for staring, but I was trying to ascertain if she could even rest her chin in her hand because of it, and it was all I could do not to urge her to get a biopsy on that thing, like, yesterday, and I kept wondering if people always tell her

---

[126] I suspect Maggie may be avoiding me.

she should see the movie *Uncle Buck* by way of broad hint, and—

Ahem.

Anyway, I assumed the counselor would suggest I graze on crudités if available, which is logical . . . yet doesn't reflect reality. I didn't want to be all *Hey, thanks for spending a hundred dollars on groceries and three hours cooking and assembling, but I'm just going to eat this here carrot, alrighty?* So I asked how I could go about skipping dinner and picking at the appetizers so I wouldn't feel like I was being rude, turning my nose up at their extensive preparations. Birthmarkie Mark's response? "You should eat your Jenny Craig meal and have club soda at the party."

OK, then.

I've been nursing the same glass of wine since I got here because the girls literally put it in my hand when I walked in the door. And how much of an asshole would I have been to say, "Oh, no; club soda for me, thanks!" I mean, there's diet and there's real life, and to be successful, there's got to be some middle ground. Tonight my middle ground is slightly oaky with notes of pear and apple. Because I have been dry since I started on Jenny, the wine is a huge treat.

We're outside on the hostess's deck when it starts to drizzle, so we bring the party inside. While we're sitting around the dining room table, we hear the opening strains of "Back in Black." We're all confused where the AC/DC is coming from until I realize it's my phone. Because I never use it, I've heard it ring only a couple of times. I scramble to snap it open before the call goes to voice mail and Fletch is forced to show me how to retrieve the message.

I step into the hallway to take the call.

When I return, I'm ashen. Kristin asks, "Is everything all right?"

I slowly reply, "Yes. Or no. I'm not . . . I'm not sure."

"What happened?" Jessica asks.

Shell-shocked, I begin to explain. "The call . . . that was my trainer; my new trainer. At my gym. We start tomorrow. And . . . and . . . and her name is *Barbie* and she sounds fifteen. I'm training with a little girl named *Barbie*." I sit down heavily in my chair.

Kristin pats me on the shoulder and snatches up my empty glass. "Sounds like you're going to need a refill."

Three hours later, Fletch comes to get me in the new car. My shirt and shorts are soaked because at some point while telling a story, I gestured too dramatically and threw an entire glass of red wine all over myself and my handbag. Everyone gasped and tried to help me, but I was *fine*. "This is the kind of bag you can wash in the sink!" I exclaimed before dousing it under the tap.[127]

I pour myself into the car idling at the curb. "Hi! My bra is wet!" I tell him.

"What happened to you?" he asks.

I shrug. "I forgot to not drink."

Later, as I run my shirt through the washer for the thirty-

-----

[127]FYI? It's not.

sixth time in an attempt to remove the Cabernet stains, I have to laugh.

Because club soda would have really been useful.

❧

It occurs to me that if I'm going to do a book about the weight-loss process, I should probably start taking notes. I begin today, documenting my first training session.

God help me.

Personal Training, Session One

I'm standing at the front desk, waiting for the mythical "Barbie" to appear. While I was sucking down water and aspirin earlier today, trying to shed my hangover, I started thinking about how judgmental I can be. I mean, why should I have instantly freaked out when I heard someone named *Barbie* was going to be my trainer? Sure, the name brings up images of gorgeous girls with long blond hair, shiny white teeth, deep tans, and impossible-to-achieve, completely enviable figures, but maybe this Barbie is different. Maybe Trainer Barbie is a dark, homely girl with an overbite and she took up fitness to feel better about her hump and her skin condition.

Yes, *that's* it. Barbie is all hideous and disfigured and she will have a heart of gold, and because of this, she'll be devoted to nothing but making me lose weight.

While I wait for my Troll Barbie to appear, I walk over to the wall of framed trainers' photographs. Hers isn't posted yet, so I can't confirm her cleft lip and club foot, but I'm sure it's coming.

I stand by the magazine rack, and I'm about to pull out this week's *In Touch* when I hear my name being called. I turn around and look for my gargoyle of a trainer.

But I don't see any monsters.

All I see is a gorgeous girl with long blond hair, shiny white teeth, a deep tan, and an impossible-to-achieve, completely enviable figure standing there. "Hey, are you Jen?" she asks. "I'm Barbie!"

Of course you are.

Of course you fucking are.

I get home from my first session and head directly to the shower. I have to sit on the small stool I use as a ledge when shaving my legs because I'm too sore to stand. I practically crawl out of the bathroom and throw on pajamas, proceeding to cry briefly before falling asleep for the next six hours.

Hate Barbie.

Hate training.

Hate everything.

Princess Big Birthmark and I are in her office. I just weighed in and lost only a pound this week. I'm not happy, but after swallowing a barrel full of wine at the book club, I realize that it could be a lot worse.

"Are you doing any exercise?" she asks.

"I am. I've started personal training, and I had my first session yesterday. God, I worked so freaking hard. The trainer made me do this one move where I held on to heavy weights and kept stepping up and down on this platform that was easily twenty-four inches high. I had to cut my very last set of reps short because I literally thought I'd burst a valve. My heart rate was over 175 beats per minute."

Nodding, she tells me, "You should just try walking."

Um . . . what?

"Walking burns about seven hundred less calories per hour," I argue.

"You should get one of our pedometers and track how many steps you take in a day, because walking is a really good exercise."

"Yeah, totally! Why bother pushing myself to burn twelve hundred calories when I can burn five hundred instead?"

"Right!" she agrees. Arrggh. "Have you got anything coming up this week that you're concerned about?"

Seething, I reply, "Actually, I do. I'm traveling to Philadelphia and New York for work.[128] I'll be going to a couple of big events and I'm going to need some help planning for them. What do I do? How do I handle eating there?"

"Bring your Jenny Craig meals with you!" she says with great conviction.

"Yeah, that's not going to work. I'm not dragging a bunch of frozen food on a plane. What am I supposed to do, pack a cooler? And a microwave?"

"Take the ones that don't need to be refrigerated," she counters.

----

[128]Also known as book signings.

"Perhaps I'm not making myself clear. I'm going to be in a couple of huge cities, staying in hotels, and going out for meals. One of the places I'm eating is a Mario Batali restaurant. Pretty sure he'd have my ankles broken if I whipped out a plate of Jenny Craig fettuccini."

Concern flashes across her features. "I guess . . . um . . . order some fish or something? Or, like, a salad?"

This is the advice I spent five hundred dollars to solicit?

"Great; sure; I'll do just that," I snap.

While Miss Melanoma goes off to the cooler to get my food, I notice there's quite a crowd of clients in here today. One of them is talking to Maggie and saying how she has only five more pounds to go before her bridesmaid dress looks awesome. Up and down I inspect her, taking in her pointy clavicles, her knobby elbows and knees, and her visible hip bones. The client is maybe a size six, bordering on a size four. The only way she's losing five pounds is via an amputation.

And that's when I really become aware of what the other people here weigh. Everyone is small, and I don't mean in-comparison-to-me small. I mean low-BMI small. Falls-within-the-normal-range-on-the-weight-chart small. I don't understand—why are all these healthy people at a weight-loss center?

It's possible they're all Jenny success stories.

But I doubt it.

There's a stack of magazines on the table next to me. The one on top is a *Star* with Nicole Richie on the cover. She really didn't get famous until she got pin thin. Ditto Kate Bosworth and Lindsay Lohan. And no one would have even remembered Mary Kate Olsen if she'd just eaten a sandwich once in while. This makes me wonder how much the media plays into the self-image of the other people in this room. Did they call Jenny because fashion and gossip magazines force photos of hungry women down our throats and try to make us believe their boyish bodies are the ideal? If so, we're all destined to fail.

Personally, I never want to be as thin as most of the women in this magazine; they look gross to me. The only ribs I want to see are covered in barbecue sauce. If I could choose whom I looked like, it would be Barbie from my session yesterday. In the few minutes I wasn't busy plotting her untimely death, I really admired how toned she was. She's not thin because she exists on a diet of Red Bull and blow; she's fit because she teaches ten exercise classes a week when she's not busy training. And although it made me want to disembowel her when she told me, she can eat and drink what she wants because she's active. I think I'd rather work harder and get the chance to enjoy food, too.

"Are you ready?" Gorbachev asks, returning with a couple of baskets of frozen meals. To ensure that all my items are enclosed, I have to read the pick list back to her while she places my items in grocery bags. I walk over to her[129] and we begin the count.

When the job is complete, she tells me to have a good day. And I will.

Because I don't have to see her again for a whole week.

---

[129] That's six steps on the pedometer I'm not going to purchase.

Session Two

Today I try to beg off on finishing my squats because my (mythological) doctor told me to take it easy. Also? I inform Barbie my blood pressure's kind of a problem so we can't do that many moves where my head dips below my heart.

Barbie smiles and chats with me about Hollywood gossip, barely changing our pacing.

Hate her. So much.

Session Three

Today at exactly sixty grueling minutes after we started, Barbie says, "We can get in one more set!"

"We've already gone an hour!" I protest.

"I don't mind; we can go a little longer—I don't have another appointment this afternoon."

I'm so spent, I don't even have the strength to curse her out properly. Instead, I moan, "You are a very bad girl!"

To which she replies, "Three more; let's go!"

I wonder how much it would cost to have her killed.

Session Four

OW! OW! OW! HATE! OW! OW! SUCKS! OW! OW! OW! OW! HATE! OW! OW! SUCKS! NO MORE SETS! OW! NO MORE SETS! OW! YOU MUST DIE! YOU MUST DIE! OW! OW! OW! WOULD PUT THIS BITCH IN

THE GROUND BUT CAN'T PICK UP A SHOVEL! OW!
OW! OW!

Session Five

There's such pain and exertion involved in these sessions,
my body hijacks my brain and continues to invent entirely
new problems in an attempt to get Barbie to take it easy on
me, e.g., "These lunges just sprained my prostate, so let's not
finish the set, OK?"

Sadly, I've cried wolf one too many times, and now unless we can see bone sticking out, she doesn't even pretend to
listen when I beg for a moment to tend to all my "injuries."
She just smiles and tells me how many more I need to do.

I am *so* going to buy her a pony when we reach my goal.

That is, if she doesn't kill me first.

Or vice versa.

"I owe the entire city of Philadelphia a huge apology."

I started my book tour yesterday, and now I'm standing at
the cash register of a shoe store off South Street in Philly,
talking to the clerk who's ringing up my black Croc flip-
flops. Angie told me she wouldn't consider me her style icon
anymore if I dared bring my goofy clown shoes on this trip. I
acquiesced, packing three gorgeous pairs of thong sandals
instead. There's a silver jeweled pair of Beverly Feldmans,
and I love them even more than the Chanel sling-backs Maisy
ate. The second is a pair of Jessica Bennetts in brown suede

with pink mother-of-pearl discs attached with brown strings and amber beads. They clatter delightfully with each step I take, like my feet are belly dancing. Completing my shoe arsenal is a black patent-leather stack-heeled pair of Donald J. Pliners.

I'm not sure which hurt most.

So, I'm walking around the most historic parts of the city in the sneakers I threw in the bag at the last minute. The only outfit I have to go with them is some ugly sweatpants and a too-big T-shirt I brought in case the hotel rooms were too cold. All I need right now to look like the consummate tourist is a fanny pack. This is not the style splash I'd hoped to make on my East Coast debut. I'm buying the Crocs because at least they'll be cute with the other stuff I packed.

As he works the register, the shoe salesman says, "Why do you need to apologize to Philadelphia?"

"Like ten years ago I had to come out here in the winter, and I didn't get a very good impression of the city." It was my first business trip and I was stuck in a crappy hotel in the suburbs for an entire month, learning a job I had no clue if I'd ever master. "But now with everything green and blooming and so clean? I can't get over how beautiful it is here."

"Thanks! The city's done a lot by means of urban renewal over the past few years."

"It shows." He begins to pack up my shoes, but I stop him. "Do you mind if I just wear them?"

He hands them over, and I'm on my way.

I'm out on this walk sort of by accident. I meant to go out for a Philly cheesesteak, but right as I was leaving the hotel, I got a text message from Barbie, detailing all the exercises I could do in my hotel room.

"Oh, Barbie," I texted back. "You are ADORABLE if you think I'm working out on this trip."

"U CAN DO IT!! ☺" was her enthusiastic reply.

I walked out the door, fuming to myself. *Right. I'm on a book tour. I'm allowed to do what I want. This is my week! Who does she think she is texting me when I'm not even in town, giving me instructions on what I'm supposed to do? Tell you what; she's allowed to train me when I am in the gym. Her dominion over me does not extend to fucking Pennsylvania. This is my personal time right now, and I do not need some Barbie doll telling me what to do. For Christ's sake, how often am I going to be in Philadelphia with the opportunity to buy an authentic cheesesteak? This is a once-in-a-lifetime experience, and that little girl is out of her goddamned mind if she thinks I'm going to—*

At this point I realized I'd been stomping around on the cobbled streets of Philadelphia, not only for forty-five minutes, but also past a dozen different shops selling cheesesteaks. And I was hot and sweaty, and the idea of greasy meat swimming in cheese didn't sound that great anymore.

After getting the shoes, I walk some more and I pick up a big salad and an apple at a Cosi on my way back to the hotel. When I get to my room, I pick up my cell phone and text, "I walked for 1.5 hours, so get off my shit."

Her reply? "WOO-HOO, GOOD JOB! HOW ABOUT SOME CRUNCHES NOW? ☺"

I still hate her.

I'm also beginning to respect her.

I leave Philadelphia with my lips having never touched a cheesesteak. I'm not sure if this makes me angry or happy.

Now I'm off to New York . . . again.

I have nine thousand key lime martinis with a group of fans after my book event at the Astor Place Barnes & Noble.[130] Fletch thinks it's odd that I like to try to connect with people who read my books, but how could I resist hanging out with a group of funny, smart, tan people wearing pearls and looking to share stories with me over cocktails? What's not to like?

At some point in the evening, I lose my voice (and part of my mind) when I can't stop loudly exclaiming over how one of the women never saw the movie *Footloose*. Seriously, how do you make it to 2007 without your RDA of Kevin Bacon? It's practically criminal.

Most of the evening is a pink-plaid, jeweled-sandaled, vodka-soaked blur, and it goes by way too fast. I end up passed out on my hotel bed, face-first in the club sandwich and French fries my agent bought me right before she deposited my drunk ass in a cab.

I did get to see my family, though, and that was great, too. Turns out they were staying at the Milford Plaza. Woo-hoo?

------

[130]I don't mean to get all religious here, but I'm pretty sure key lime martinis (with a graham-cracker-and-sugar rim) are proof that Jesus loves us.

I didn't hate New York this time: I didn't feel quite so claustrophobic. We either went to restaurants with bigger chairs or else I'm a little bit smaller. Either way, it was a pleasant change.

I know my book tour is truly over when the plane comes alive with the happy noise of 164 cell phones springing to life at the same time. I quickly dial Fletch. "The eagle has landed. The eagle, of course, being me." Fletch is hovering around the periphery of the airport somewhere. Although we're well past the pick-you-up-at-the-airport phase, he's still very much in the will-drive-the-new-car-to-hell-and-back stage and thus volunteered to collect me. "Great! Call me when you have your bags and tell me what door you exit."

I snap my phone shut and retrieve my carry-on, and within five minutes I'm out of the plane and back in O'Hare. I make my way to baggage claim, ignoring how my pretty silver thong sandals fail to absorb any sort of shock from walking. I was going to wear my Crocs, but I figured these are the kind of shoes that get you an upgrade . . . except they didn't. I briefly consider explaining my dilemma to one of those red-vested golf-cart guys in the airport to see if he'll drive me to baggage claim, but decide doing so will probably put me on a terrorist watch list.

As I clomp along, pain shooting up my spine with every (adorable!) step I take, I think about how this is the first time in days I've laid a paw on my own luggage, instead choosing to pass out five-dollar bills[131] like Halloween candy. New York and Philly were nothing but skycaps, bellmen, and taxis, and it was heavenly. I don't care how fit I get; I will always delight in someone else carrying the heavy stuff.

My easily spotted pewter suitcase is among the first off the conveyor. I notice that at some point between New York and here, someone slapped a HEAVY sticker on it. For a second I panic and assume American Airlines is passing judgment on me and not my bag, and then I remember I've stuffed it full of the free books I begged for when I visited the Take Room at my publisher. Stuffed to bursting, the bag easily weighs seventy-five pounds.

I quickly dial Fletch and take myself out to the curb. Within moments, Fletch pulls up and pops the trunk.

"Hello!" I call, waving furiously. Fletch waves back, gesturing to his BlackBerry. Looks like he's wrapping up a call.

I stand on the curb and wait with my bag.

Waiting.

Waiting.

Waiting.

Oh, boy, Fletch is going to really struggle getting this puppy into the trunk! AA was right—it *is* heavy.

Waiting.

While I wait, I examine the damage this week's done to my manicure. My coral-colored polish has held up nicely, and I'm pleased. I got the bottle free with a coupon because I

---

[131]Tax deductible, of course.

spent more than $100 at Ulta3 last quarter. I congratulate myself on my ability to be thrifty.

Waiting.

I wonder whom he's talking to.

Waiting.

I take a closer look at the HEAVY sticker on my bag. The airline has kindly informed anyone who comes near it to lift with her knees and not her back. Or, in this case, Fletch should lift with his knees.

Waiting.

Isn't that nice of American Airlines? Certainly I don't want Fletch throwing out his back because of me and my free-book habit.

Waiting.

I glance down at my traveling outfit. My black Lacoste and green cargo capris have survived the journey well.

Waiting.

Waiting.

Horns honking.

Waiting.

I again admire my shiny silver thong sandals. Even though they hurt, I really dig the practically flat stacked heel, and the shiny baubles and attached pearls are just too cute.

Waiting.

Shiny!

Waiting.

Sparkly!

Waiting.

Honking?

Waiting.

Honking with a side of mild profanity.

Fletch really must be on an important call.

Waiting.

At this point, an airport security guard approaches and very loudly tells me to, "Stop fucking standing there looking at your feet, lady. Get in the car or move on!"

Ahh! I can't wait for Fletch! Damn it; I knew I'd somehow end up at Gitmo because of this trip! And I even wore sandals so no one would think I was a shoe bomber! Shit!

I grab my heavy, heavy suitcase filled with all my hoarded books and attempt to jam it in this very small trunk.

There's sweating, swearing, shoving with a side of nail breaking, shoe scuffing, and pants smearing.

I finally stuff it in and am far worse for the wear when I get in the car. I yell, "Hey, asshole! You made me load my bag myself!" We quickly pull away from the curb . . . and angry security guard.

I continue. "And it was *heavy*!"

"Uh-huh," Fletch replies.

"And I scuffed my beautiful shoes!"

"Uh-huh."

"I am *so* not giving you five dollars!"

Fletch nods. "I'll get over it. Oh, and by the way? There's a mountain of dog shit in the backyard with your name on it. You might want to change your shoes before you attack it."

Dog shit? *Moi*? With these hands and this manicure? I sputter, "But, no . . . but . . . I'm . . . I'm an author. . . . I went on tour. . . . I sign autographs . . . and have fans . . . and . . ."

Fletch pats my now-filthy knee and smiles. "Welcome back to reality, Princess."

You know what? Even without professional luggage management and with a husband who makes me touch doody, it's still damn good to be home. Now's there's nothing between me and my goal until the end of the summer.

TO: order_fulfillment
FROM: jen@jenlancaster.com
SUBJECT: Quality Control

Dear JustMySize.com Order Fulfillment,

I'm not telling you how to do your job; I'm simply asking you to exercise a little bit of common sense.

When your plus-sized customer orders three pairs of extra-extra-large gym shorts online, do you really think two pairs of XXL shorts and one 32 Barely A training bra is the most appropriate substitution?

Attached you will find a photograph of me wearing this bra on my head because it is the only part of my body that it fits.

Please fix,

Jen Lancaster

Gym Dandy

*H*ere I am, firmly residing in reality again. Last week was a total blast, with cocktails and club sandwiches and cabbies who'd happily haul my bags. Somehow I forgot I'd be coming back to my regular life (and my real-life baggage), which is why I'm in the lobby of Jenny Craig, debating whether I should take off my underpants and bra before I hop on the scale. I'm desperately afraid to see the damages last week wrought.

While I was away, I tried to fill up on vegetables and fruit when I could,[132] and I got a handle on portion control. When I was at the airport, I got a low-fat yogurt parfait with strawberries and granola and threw it away when I'd finished only half. I hated wasting the food, but better in the trash than on my ass, right? Plus, I did have Barbie's annoying little voice

---

[132] Key lime martinis are a fruit, yes?

in my head, so I probably exercised more than I normally would have done. However, I scarfed down everything on the table at Mario's, and each time I ordered room service, I requested two glasses of wine because, really? Wine pairs perfectly with French fries.

I'm aggravated with myself for not having better control, and I will be blissfully happy today if I haven't gained more than two pounds. Fortunately, I'm confident I can shake off any book-tour gain by doing time on the elliptical trainer after my session with Barbie. Whatever the news is, I'll simply deal with it by exercising harder.

An entirely new counselor named Veronica comes to get me before I have the chance to ditch my foundation garments. We go directly to the scale, and I step on, shut my eyes, and hold my breath.

"Ohhhh-kay! Looks like four point five pounds," she says cheerfully.

"Damn. I didn't think I gained that much," I say, stepping off the scale with a heavy heart.

"You didn't gain four point five pounds. You *lost* it."

"*What*? No, I didn't. Your scale is wrong. Weigh me again." This time I hop back on the platform. I watch as the loss registers, and I can't stop myself from shouting, "*Now, that's what I'm talking about!*"

I'm elated, and I float back into Veronica's office to discuss my week.

Yet I can't help but wonder how I lost the most weight during the week I was responsible for choosing my own food.

I've been to the gym often enough to notice some stuff I don't like about the other patrons' gym etiquette. From now on, I would like everyone to please abide by the following principles.

Jen's Life Lessons, Gym Edition

Think CSI: West Loop Gym—The towels here are free and plentiful. Please use them to clean up all the DNA you've left on the equipment. When I put my shoulders in the squat machine and the bar slips off because you left it sweaty, I will scream, *"Gross!"* And you will be ashamed.

It's a Locker Room, Not Your Bedroom—Hey, I love the feeling of community and personal service at this gym, too. But that doesn't mean I'm *so* comfortable here that I'm happy to simply drop my clothing all over the bench and floor before toddling off naked into the shower. Also, please never leave your dirty underpants sunny-side up again.

Shut the Fuck Up—People are here lifting heavy things. Not me, of course, but others, and that requires concentration. When you squawk about your mother-in-law loud enough for others to hear it in the Spinning room, we have a problem. Inside voices, people. Inside voices.

Mind Your Funk—No one's saying you have to come to the gym showered, shaved, and sparkle powdered. But a little Speed Stick never hurt anyone.

Really? Spitting? Really?—The fact that you belong to an urban gym tells me you don't live in a barn. Start acting like it.

Keep the Tunes Low—If I can hear Coldplay coming out your nose, your iPod is *too goddamned loud*. And how do you work out to Coldplay, anyway? They make me want to lie on a fainting couch, discussing how very gauche Americans are. What's up with that?

Stop Marking Your Territory—The nice thing about this gym is that it's never, ever crowded. So there's no need for you to drape your towel on one machine, then place your water on another and your magazine on a third. Jesus, why not just pee on everything?

Thanks in advance for your participation.

Session Seven
This is the first day I don't have to nap after a session.

Session Eight

Barbie asks me if the weight is too heavy and I say, "No, it's actually a little too light," so she adds five pounds.

How did *that* happen?

Session Ten and a Half

"Barbie promised it would be fun," I say, pulling on my pale blue Nikes with the electric lime swoosh, neatly mirroring the acid green of my baggy V-neck. Someday I'll have a whole wardrobe of those superfitted moisture-wicking Lycra work-out tops, but not until I have considerably fewer rolls. Tight gym shirts are a privilege to be earned, and I haven't yet. Until then, I suffer in a variety of thick pastel cotton T-shirts that nicely conceal the lumps in my topography yet feel like a sweaty bedsheet by the time I finish a workout.

"Explain to me again what it entails," says Fletch. He sifts through the baskets of clothing on the bed. I should probably admit here that I have a bit of a laundry problem. I will sort, wash, and dry all day long, but when it comes to folding, I lose steam. You could ski down the massive slopes of clean socks and towels stacked up in our bedroom most days. Fletch hates having full baskets of clean, unfolded clothes, but I've yet to come up with the proper motivation to spend an afternoon turning someone else's underpants into origami. If I hold out long enough, he'll eventually tackle the folding himself.[133] Fletch continues to paw through reams of sheets and pillowcases, and he

---

[133] Obviously my preferred plan.

bypasses the attractive moisture-wicking tops I got for him. He finally opts for a grungy old concert T-shirt with cutoff sleeves.[134]

I yank my hair back into a ponytail and adjust my madras do-rag, smoothing it and securing it in place with a couple of bobby pins. I love this particular bandana because it serves a dual purpose: not only does it keep my bangs from falling in my eyes when I'm huffing away on the treadmill, but also all the pretty colors in the plaid tie the various hues of my shorts, shirts, and shoes together.[135]

"I don't know exactly; I've never been to one, either. But Barbie told me it's strength training and we'll do resistance-based exercises with bands, barbells, and stuff. That doesn't sound bad, right?" I catch the furrow in Fletch's brow and cut him off before he can complain. "For God's sake, I promise it's not a ballet class. We're going to be working with weights, not disco dancing, OK?"

Fletch has a bizarre phobia about people thinking he's gay, which is way more ridiculous than my finding-a-severed-head-in-the-toilet fear. If you find a severed head, that's patently terrifying. What's the worst that would happen if someone thought he was playing for the home team? He might get a free drink? Or have a conversation about some shoes? He loves drinks and shoes! I guarantee no one's first thought when they see the guy with a military-grade hair cut

---

[134]Sexy! As in "not."

[135]I may not be athletically coordinated, but I'm certainly a gold medalist when it comes to color coordination.

in the Metallica T-shirt—especially *with his wife*—is going to be, "Oh, yeah, total flamer."[136]

Fletch begins to waver. "Jen, I'm kind of tired, and this doesn't—"

"No! You have to come! I can't go without you because I'm afraid I won't be able to keep up, and if I'm the only fat, lazy person in the class *and* I'm alone, then I will die of shame and you will be forced to wash your own damn drawers."

Fletch considers this. "You want me there not because you're concerned about my health, but because you don't want to be alone?"

"Exactly. Also, I'm banking on your lack of endurance. You never do cardio, so there's a good chance I'll last longer than you because I've been training. You'll make me look better by comparison. Wait, I said that out loud, didn't I? What I meant to say was *pleeeeease*?"

Frowning, Fletch walks over to his closet and pulls out a pair of slick silver and black running shoes and locates an extra-squashy pair of white socks from the mass tangle of clean duds. "You realize you'll owe me after this."

"Name your price."

He cuts his eyes over to the piles and says, "Mount Polyester is gone before bedtime tonight."

"Done." I walk over to inspect myself in the full-length mirror and notice a splotch right where an embroidered

---

[136]This is also why he won't order chicken in a restaurant or buy his own hair gel.

alligator or pledge pin would go. "Aw, shit; there's a big butter stain on my shirt. Or maybe it's olive oil?" I glance over at Fletch. "Oh, stop smirking. At least it's not chocolate or red wine."

"Mmm. Thank God," he concurs.

"Hey, can you grab my New Balance sneaks out of the guest room closet while I search for a different top? I have to change shoes so they match."

I dig through the piles and toss on a plain white T and my brand-new red mesh shorts. They are both sparkling clean and will do nicely, except now I'll have to find a different bandana, too. I locate a white one locked in mortal static-cling combat with a fuzzy pair of pajama bottoms. I remove the plaid one and redo the pins just as Fletch returns with my shoes. "Here you go," he says. "Hey, you've got a couple of stickers on your butt. Here, I'll get them." He leans down behind me and pulls them off.

"Stickers? What do they say?"

He squints. "*2XL* and *Made in Vietnam*." He folds the papers tacky-side down and flicks them into the garbage can.

"Huh," I muse. "I didn't know Vietnam manufactured clothes. Then again, almost all my knowledge of Vietnam comes from a single film I saw in a History of War class in college. Basically all I remember is how wee all the Vietnamese were compared to the American GIs."[137]

"Asians are significantly smaller than us. During the last

---

[137] Also, the Viet Cong were the bad guys. Yay me and my poli sci degree!

Olympics in Japan, they had to rip out all the seats so they could accommodate our expansive Western asses." He pumps his fists in the air, "USA! USA!"

I look at myself in the mirror, turning from side to side. "I wonder what those lithe little Vietnamese thought as they were sewing up my big red shorts. They must feel we're so overindulged and decadent here."

"Nah." Fletch giggles. "I bet they waved them over their heads and ran around the factory shouting, *'Gojira, Gojira!'* and then stomped up and down the aisle between the sewing machines, pretending they were crushing cars and fighting Mothra." He collapses into a pile of laundry, clutching his sides.

"Nice," I say. "What an excellent support system you are. You can fold your own damn laundry, mister." I hear him call out an apology as I clamor down the stairs, but he's still laughing, so it doesn't count. "Oh, and by the way, Fletch? If some guy wants to touch your winky at the gym? I'm going to let him."

I step over the yoga mat where Fletch lies clutching his sides for a second time today. I think Barbie's free-motion fitness class may well have killed him.

Barbie points at me as I walk up to her. "You've been holding out on me, girl! I figured you'd have to modify some of the moves, but you did them all! I'm so proud of you!"

"I know!" I exclaim. "I can't believe I kept up!"

Barbie glances at Fletch's prone form. "Is he going to be OK?"

"He's fine, just settling a little karmic debt. Anyway, that was kind of fun. I liked working out with the sound system—really got me motivated."

"This is the first time we've been together and I didn't hear you complaining," she tells me with a big grin.

"Probably a pleasant change for you, right? Frankly, I would have started to whine, but I was too busy trying not to attract attention from the fit people during class."

"Can I expect this new and improved attitude during our session tomorrow?"

"Oh, Christ, no."

"Good. Because that would be boring!" We walk out to the reception desk so she can grab her calendar. We confirm our time for tomorrow and she gives me a little hug even though I'm gross. She heads into the office, and I go back to the group fitness room to stand over Fletch, who's quietly whimpering.

"Hey, sweetie? If you can get up, I can take you home."

I'm upstairs in the bedroom trying on my new dress, which is *sleeveless*. I can't believe I bought a sleeveless dress. For me, sleeveless is the new *n-a-k-e-d*. But this was on major markdown, and it was so pretty that I couldn't help but try it on. I was attracted to it because it's deep purple, and it's printed with designs in teals and golds, and there are sparkly beads all over it. Empire waisted, it falls to the perfect midcalf length, but it's cut conservatively enough to be appropriate on any veranda on Martha's Vineyard.[138] I was shocked when I looked at myself in the trifold mirror—where'd all my back fat go?

While I'm busy admiring myself, the phone rings. "Hello?"

"Jen, it's Kate—I've got good news! We got a bid for *Bitter* rights in Korea!" What my agent means is, someone in Korea wants to publish my first book. Foreign rights sales are the best because as a writer you don't have to do *anything* except sign a contract.

"Really? Wow!" Then I remember something. "But aren't they communists? Why do they want to publish a book about my rampant consumerism?"

I hear Kate take a deep breath, like she often does when we chat. "Ah, no. We're talking about *South* Korea. Kim Jong Il did not make the offer, Jen."

"Oh. Well, that's good, right?"

"Of course! Congratulations!"

"One question, though."

"What's that?"

"How are they going to translate 'asshat' into Korean?"

After I finally stop modeling my new dress for myself, I e-mail my mother with the news of the Korean sale, relaying the conversation I had with Kate. My mother's response?

....

[138]Not that I've been invited to any Edgartown soirees. But if I am, I will be ready.

They read right to left in Korea, so "asshat" is going to be translated backwards. Thousands of Koreans will be trying to picture what a hat for the ass looks like.

Seriously, how do I ever fight with this woman?

Session Seventeen

All of my regular bras are too big—not only are they loose in the band, but I could totally stow a pair of socks in each cup. I'm delighted at this development, but I don't like how everything clatters around up there now when I'm at the gym. Before I leave for my session today, I dig out an old bra from the bag I've yet to remember to bring to Goodwill.

I pull out a nice white racer-back. Why was I giving this one away? Since I'm the perpetual optimist, I never get rid of stuff when it gets too small, although I donate what I'm tired of seeing or don't use anymore. Last charity go-round, I did a huge suit purge. I had really nice pieces, too, but I haven't needed anything business-y for years. These suits are going to get a second life somewhere in the corporate world, and that makes me happy.

As I dress, I notice that this bra is snug in all the right places, and I like how much support it has. Plus, I love having a front hook—none of that upside-down-and-around-the-waist business here![139] What was my problem?

....

[139] Wait; am I the only person not in a training bra who still has to do this?

Why would I dump something with such a great fit? I turn and look at myself sideways in the mirror. Very nice!

I'm not more than thirty seconds into the warm-up matrix Barbie has me do prior to each of our sessions when I remember why this bra was in the donation bin. In the middle of my set of weighted uppercuts, *bing!* My bra flies open. Oh, yeah. . . . It has a faulty hook. The slightest lateral movement and the clasp pops.

"Why did you stop?" Barbie asks.

"My bra came undone," I reply. "I'm going to duck into the yoga room to rehook it. Stand by." I've developed quite the comfort level around Barbie, so this does not cause the earth to open up and swallow me whole. After all, she witnessed my attempts at squats and lunges on my first day, and nothing could be any more graceless or ungainly than that.

After the minor adjustment, I pick up my weights and continue. "We left off at ten, so there's nine, eight, seven, six . . . again?"

I have to dash into the yoga room a second time.

This happens four more times in as many minutes, and now it's just funny. "Can you check the office for some duct tape?" I ask.

"Good call." Barbie bounds across the gym and returns a few minutes later with a safety pin and some Scotch tape.

"No duct tape?" I ask.

"This is all I could find."

I MacGyver my bra closed and continue our session. The pin and the tape hold together so well, I decide to walk on the treadmill afterward. I started doing extra cardio a while back when an older gentleman was training at the same time as me. After he finished his grueling session, I watched as he hopped on the treadmill for a quick jog. I figured if a man in his seventies could do it, damn it, so could I.

Other than the exploding underwear, I'm pleased about the work I did today. I'm starting to feel really energized during my sessions, and I daresay I might even be enjoying them. This is *entirely* Barbie's doing. It took me weeks to realize that during the hardest parts of whatever we were into, she'd start talking about either celebrity gossip or my writing. Until she finally admitted it, I had no clue she was intentionally distracting me with my favorite topics.

Strong is the force in this one.

I'm down another five pounds this week, exactly the amount I'd hoped for. However, I've been conducting an experiment with my eating. This week I ate Jenny Craig meals only about half the time. The other half, I ate whatever I fixed for Fletch, portioning out smaller servings of meat, pasta, and fats, and loading up on vegetables.

Jenny Craig has a formula I'm supposed to follow when preparing meals on my own, but it's confusing and entails math, so I based my decisions on a straight calorie count.

My intention is to go off the Jenny meals because they're kind of a crutch and they aren't meant to be a long-term solution. Besides, I'm really, really sick of the food. The more I eat it, the more I find fault. At this point I'm getting the same four lunches, four dinners, and three breakfasts each week, and my palate is about to go on strike. Boredom is exactly why so many diets are unsuccessful, and I don't want monotony to tempt me back into my old way of eating. I feel too good.

I'm in my regular meeting at Jenny with Little Miss Birthmark and I mention for the third week running that I'd really like to transition onto nonfrozen, nonboxed food. I don't tell her how much menu planning I've already been doing on my own.

"Sure, we'll talk about that next time. For now, you should appreciate what great results you're getting on the Jenny Craig meals," she says.

Wrong answer, Señorita Carcinoma. Wrong answer.

Session Twenty

Today's my third training session in as many days because Barbie's going out of town for the Fourth of July. The more I do, the better I get at this, and the last sixty minutes have been grueling. I pushed myself so hard this afternoon, there's barely a dry spot on my T-shirt. Funny, but I used to base my self-esteem on nothing but designer labels and fancy handbags, yet now I'm positively beaming over a saturated gray T-shirt.

"Check me out!" I exclaim. "There's even a big line of sweat where my fat roll is!"

"Don't call it a fat roll," Barbie scolds. "Let's call it a two-pack. You only have four to go to make it a six pack! And you did so good today! You going to hit the treadmill now?"

"I am."

"Way to go! Listen, I'm out of here—I'll see you next week, all right?" She bounces off, hair swinging, and it makes me smile. How is it I ever contemplated cutting off her pony-tail and stuffing it in her mouth so she wouldn't be able to say, "Four more! Let's go!"?

I hop on the treadmill, and as I move forward, my steps begin to feel lighter and lighter. I keep walking, but my usual 3.0 mph speed seems like a turtle crawl. I bump it up to 3.2, and that's still really poky. I add another .4 and I'm up to 3.6, barely breaking my stride. Then I really dial it up, selecting 4.5. The conveyor belt springs to life under my feet, and I have to stand on the rails to keep from shooting off the back of it. OK, *that's* fast enough.

Gingerly I step back on and begin to power walk in a most unbecoming fashion, so I jump on the rails again. I want to go this speed, but I can't walk that fast.

What if I were to run?

No. I can't *run*. I mean, I run to the store. I'll run for the phone. I run out for ice cream. I run my mouth. When I accidentally kicked myself with my London shoes, I put a run in my trouser socks. But I can't *run* run. I tried to run once with the dogs about five years ago, but I was too out of shape and they kept tripping me with their leashes.

I can't run. I have bad knees. A weak back. And I'm totally fat. And I just can't do it. I'm not a run-away person. I'm a stand-and-fight person.

But what if I were to try anyway?

I can't run.

I am wearing running shoes.

No. I'm not a runner.

I bet running would burn a shitload of calories. Maybe if I ran, I could have a banana daiquiri over the holiday.

Running . . . ridiculous!

How will I know for sure I'm not a runner if I don't try it, at least once?

But I'll look like an ass.

Then again, since when has that stopped me from doing anything?

Running . . . that's crazy talk!

You know what else is crazy? Standing here on the rails, the treadmill zipping away underneath me, having an argument with myself.

I take a deep breath. Do or do not.

Again, I choose do.

Every single bone in my body is jarred. My knees in particular are screaming and need to be iced, like, right this second.

I don't even want to think about how my back is going to feel tomorrow.

Yet I don't care.

Because I *ran*.

TO: angie_at_home
FROM: jen@jenlancaster.com
SUBJECT: Jen-Point Quiz

Imagine you're in your basement sorting your work clothes so you can take them to the dry cleaner. While sorting, you run across your wife's favorite bathing suit drying on a rack.

What do you do next?

A) You put it right back where you found it because your wife expressly instructed you to only grab your work clothes. And as this is plus-sized women's swimwear, you're pretty sure you've never worn this piece to the office. Also, she yelled at you the seventeen times you accidentally washed and dried it last year.

B) You put it right back where you found it because your wife expressly instructed you to stay the hell away from her laundry as she's still pissed off you shrunk most of her polo shirts when you washed them in boiling water and dried them within an inch of their lives last week and thank fucking God she's a little thinner and can fit into them because otherwise they'd be ruined.

C) You put it right back where you found it because your wife begged you to please, please, *please* ask her if you ever have any laundry-based questions. And, really? Since you work hard, maybe just leave everything for her because she promises you she doesn't mind washing all the clothes, especially since nothing gets ruined that way.

D) You take the bathing suit directly to the dry cleaner.

Try to guess how Fletch answered this question.

Here's a hint—it involves a sheet of clear plastic and a hanger.

Arrggh.

Et Tu, Valerie Bertinelli?

When I get back from the store, there's a message on my voice mail. I drop my shopping bags and punch in the access code, and Angie's voice comes across the speakerphone. *"Hey, it's Ang. You're not home, so possibly that means you found somewhere to wallow. Hope that improved your mood. Call me when you're dry."* I quickly stow the light rum and banana daiquiri mix and dash upstairs to return her call. She answers on the second ring.

"Yo, Happy Fourth of July!" I shout.

"Your spirits have improved considerably," she replies. "Did your plotting work out? Did you get yourself invited to a pool party?"

I spent an hour last night complaining to her that this was the first Fourth of July in decades I wouldn't spend submerged, as my parents sold their home with its in-ground pool last summer. I hate that they no longer have a body of water in their backyard.

Technically, they have a lake, but it's a nonswimming lake, and please don't even get me started on how you can have a lake and not be able to swim in it because it's a freaking lake and that's *madness*, I tell you.[140]

I'd have other stuff to do and wouldn't be so fixated on swimming if Fletch were home, but he's in Texas. During our millionth we-should-move-to-the-suburbs argument, he brought up the idea of moving to a smaller city since we both can do our jobs anywhere.[141] We did a ton of research and decided Austin could be ideal for a variety of factors, not the least of which is how many people we know down there. Fletch is currently a guest at his best friend's house, and he's having a blast running recon missions. He's already done the most important legwork—checking out the grocery stores. Two thumbs up for Central Market!

When he gets back, I'm sure we'll go to Oak Street beach. For now, I'm fixated on my old pool. It's not just the loss of a place to swim that had me so wound up when I talked to Angie last night. There was always something magical about this time of year at my parents' house. Somehow the Fourth was the one time my brother and I could declare a détente. Regardless of how much we fought the rest of the year,[142] we always put our differences aside enough to have fun for a couple of steamy midsummer days.

-----

[140]Although it may have something to do with all the snakes.

[141]I told him if we got a suburban home with a game room, the only game I'd play would be Russian roulette.

[142]What with my parents' children's propensity for being assholes and all.

Except for the addition of a wife, a husband, and three grandchildren over the years, our holiday was always exactly the same. We'd get out of bed and change directly from pajamas to swimsuits and have breakfast on the patio, finding common ground in ridiculing my mother's terrible coffee and burnt toast. (Perhaps those days weren't quite so magic for my mom? Regardless, after sixty-plus years you'd think she'd know not to put the bagels in the oven on high for thirty minutes.)

After breakfast we'd jump in the water, which had finally grown warm in the July sun, to rinse off the bits of bagel carbon, and we'd have our first Funnoodle battle of the day. Todd could hit much harder, but I was better at treading water, so we often ended in a draw. Then, working together, we'd take the metal table and umbrella off the patio and place it in the shallow end, complete with all the matching metal chairs, and we'd spend the rest of the day using it as a swim-up bar, never once leaving for biology breaks.[143]

During the course of the afternoon, we'd have daiquiri-making contests—mine were always the sweetest, and Dad's tended to be so booze laden they'd tear all the skin off our lips. There'd be naps in the sun and trashy books read while sitting on the pool's wide, smooth cement steps or balanced on one of the many air mattresses from the pool house. Later, there'd be another Funnoodle battle royale and grilled meats, and my mom would serve her red, white, and blue Jell-O flag

---

[143]Shut up. That's why we chlorinated the water.

cake that no one liked, except we'd always demand she make it because it was tradition. We'd cap off the evening with fireworks, and eventually we'd all pass out, still feeling the rippling of the water underneath the floats we'd lounged on during the day. Yet now some random family is enjoying my pool.[144]

Anyway, this year I figured I had two choices. Plan A, I could go down to my parents' house with a backhoe, some cement, and a better attitude, or, Plan B, I wangle an invitation to someone else's pool because I like wallowing and reading and drinking daiquiris a lot more than trying to dig a big hole. I made a concerted effort to charm everyone I know with access to water and . . . nothing. Either no one got the hint, or they assumed I'd go to their house and mock their bagels.

For the moment I'm happy because I came up with Plan C. I just picked up a copy of Will Smith's *Independence Day* at Target, and I have banana daiquiri fixings.[145]

But if I don't get access to a pool soon, something very bad is going to happen.

Fletch is back from Austin, and turns out what sounded great on paper didn't match up to reality. He says it's so hot down

---

[144] I take some comfort in knowing I left enough of myself in that water for my legacy to swim on forever. Or until they drain it.

[145] And I will tear up when Bill Pullman does his speech at the airfield, like I do every single time.

there, I'd spontaneously combust the second I stepped off the plane. Plus with humidity turning the air as thick as oatmeal, my hair would always be a disaster.

So Austin's out.

Save for two daiquiris, this week I follow the Jenny Craig plan to the letter. I'm rewarded with a .2-pound weight loss. Which means if I hadn't peed before I left the house, I'd be at scratch. After three training sessions, four additional cardio hours, including *running*, I'm down .2 pounds? What are those, ounces? Percentages of a pound? No one even knows because the sum is so negligible. We'd have to send it off to NASA for them to figure it out. And Gorbachev wrote the number down on my chart like I'd done something great.

This is *bullshit*.

I'm aware that muscle weighs more than fat, so I ask them to take my measurements. I want tangible proof of my efforts. I'm confident that what I'm doing is working because when I woke up today, I had only one chin, and my knees don't have fat buttresses on either side of them anymore. Yet it would be nice to see some numbers side by side so I can have my *yay, me, three inches!* moment. But according to Betty Birthmark, they do the tape measure only once a month, and today's not my day.

While I was waiting to go into my session and find out about my whopping .2 pounds, I browsed the celebrity magazines in the lobby. A *People* magazine was marked, and I opened it to read about Valerie Bertinelli's success on Jenny

Craig. Turns out she celebrated her son's big day not with triple-layer fudge cake and thick mocha icing, but with a plate of Jenny mac 'n' cheese, which only highlighted how rigid I find the eating plan. Why would I want to continue with a diet that doesn't take real life into account? I understand birthday cake every day is a bad idea, but birthday cake *never*? That's not a world I want to live in.

I am surly and withdrawn for the course of our post-weigh-in pep talk, and by the time I'm halfway home with my hateful groceries, I make my decision.

"Fletch . . . Fletch? Where are you?" I call, dropping my bags on the counter.

He pops into the kitchen. "I'm here. Do you need some help?"

"No, not with carrying stuff. I need an opinion. I look different, right? Thinner? I feel good on the inside, but can you see a difference from the outside?"

"Yes! Absolutely! You're much more"—he makes a packing motion with his hands—"compact. Streamlined. Why do you ask?"

"I'm considering quitting Jenny and doing something else, like Weight Watchers' online program."

"How come?"

"Because I read an article where Valerie Bertinelli couldn't eat a piece of cake at her son's birthday party."

"OK, then." Sometimes he doesn't even want the backstory.

"Yeah. I'm quitting. I'm not eating this stuff anymore." I motion to the boxes splayed all over the table, slowly defrosting. "Again, I look good, right? You'd be honest with me?"

"You look great. But to confirm, you're done? No more boxed food?"

"I am." I take an orange out of the fruit bowl, wash it, and begin to peel.

He raises a lascivious eyebrow. "All right. Then there's been something I've really wanted."

What? There's daylight! And we're in the kitchen! And there's no wine! But I am thinner, and I do look good. . . .

Fletch begins to reach. His arm encircles me . . . before he plunges it into one of my bags of food. He digs around and fishes out a box of silver dollar pancakes and veggie sausage.

"Mmm," he says. "Breakfast!"[146]

"Wouldja look at these morose motherfuckers?[147] Have they been like this all day?" Fletch gestures to the dogs, draped on either side of the couch, heads resting on paws, staring despondently out the window.

"Probably. They're bored and they've been alone most of the day. I was at the gym early this afternoon and then I came back to shower before going out again to the nail salon. See? Look." I waggle my fingers at Fletch, proudly displaying my fresh manicure in Lippman's Dark Side of the Moon.

....

[146]You were expecting a love scene? From me, who wears a bathing suit in a hotel bathroom Jacuzzi and from the man who thinks a pooper-scooper is a romantic birthday present? Your breath? Don't hold it.

[147]Jen-point quiz: Guess what movie this line comes from.

"Yikes. What to you call that color? Black? Muffy Goes Goth?" Fletch asks.

"They aren't black; they're a deep, deep wine, and this is a very stylish color." I hold my foot up to the light coming in from the window and admire. Oh, so cute! If you ask me, this shade of near black is so much prettier than OPI's Lincoln Park After Dark or Chanel's Vamp.[148]

"Didn't you just get your nails done last week?"

"Yeah, *dad*, but the place is supercheap, and it just opened so they've got brand-new equipment. They have massage chairs that punch you so hard you're practically tossed out of them, and they totally work out all the knots. My back is really sore from running, so I figured I could either go the chiropractor and fork over a twenty-dollar copay, or I could go to the nail salon, pay ten dollars more to sit in the punch-y chairs, *and* save myself the time and effort of having to do my nails myself. Genius, right?"

"I guess, except now that the dogs were alone all day, they look about ready to commit suicide." Big sad eyes look up at us. Loki sighs and blinks while Maisy gives her tail a wan little wag, thumping quietly against the leather of the couch. "Should we take them out for a *w-a-l-k*?"

"I don't know—why don't you ask them if they want one? Hey, dogs? Do you . . . *wanna go for a walkies*?" Suddenly the world's most despondent creatures rocket off the couch. Loki spins around in circles, howling with joy, and Maisy

---

[148]And yet if you asked me who the Illinois state senators are, I would have no idea.

tears up and down the hallway, banking off the ottoman every time she hits the living room.

"I'm going to take that as a yes." Fletch attempts to leash the beasts while I go to the kitchen to collect small plastic grocery bags to scoop poop. We used to keep a cool little holder snapped to each of their leashes that came with its own special bags, but we finally figured out that the bags cost fifty cents apiece. Maisy always gets so excited during walks that she'll go three or four times, and I told Fletch we may as well be wiping her ass with dollar bills.

Five minutes later, the dogs are finally corralled and double collared. We lock the front door and trot down the stairs. Fletch asks, "Where to?"

"Why don't we walk by that little playground park? Other dog owners hang out there, and it might be nice for these two to socialize," I suggest. We take off down the street, practically waterskiing behind our respective mutts. Loki stops to lift his leg on every pole, post, and tree for the next four blocks. Maisy won't go until we get to a grassy area, so she chugs ahead like a stinky little steam engine.

We arrive at the park in a few minutes and it's almost exactly like that Chicago song, except the man selling ice cream is actually hawking churros and *elotes*.[149] It's twilight, so the heat of the day is finally starting to dissipate and the whole neighborhood seems to be out here enjoying the evening. Kids climb the jungle gyms, and old men decked out in straw

---

[149]A roasted ear of corn on the cob, covered in mayo, lemon juice, and spices. Used to think they were disgusting . . . until I had one.

hats and guayaberas play chess on stone benches with transistor radios softly playing mariachi music beside them. And our dogs, being the social creatures they are, lose their minds at the site of so many people they've yet to lick. Seriously, who would want to live in the suburbs when there's so much interesting stuff going on here?

We let the neighborhood children pet the dogs until one of them starts to yank on Loki's ears and tail. Whereas Maisy would take this kind of abuse all day, Loki gives us a look that says, "You've got exactly five seconds to make this stop before I do." We quickly say good-bye to the kids and hustle the dogs along.

When we reach the end of the playground, we walk past a giant public pool. I've known it was here for years but always assumed it was all squalid and awful. I wrote it off as being like Caddy Day at Bushwood, with floating Baby Ruth bars and stray scabby Band-Aids and grody kids leaking sewage out the sides of their rubber swim pants. No, thanks.

Right now this place doesn't look at all like the fetid cesspool I'd always assumed it was; rather, it's a big, sparkly, cerulean gem, its calm waters reflecting the halogen lights around it. I turn to Fletch and say, "I just found the solution to my pool lust."

"Very nice," he agrees. "I didn't expect it to be so clean. I figured it would be all broken bottles and stray newspapers."

"Let's see if we can find a schedule," I say, and we navigate the dogs around the large Tudor-style field house. We quickly locate a bulletin board with pool information on it, and it's full of times to come and swim for free.

Jen's Life Lesson #1287: Even if your parents move, it's possible to get your wallow on.

Fletch and I are on one of our daily Target jaunts. We keep a permanent list of what's running low on the fridge, yet we always seem to need something here. I suspect we're not really out of stuff; rather, these constant errand runs are Fletch's excuse to drive the new car. Even though we've had it a couple of months now, I'll often catch him in the garage, gazing at it for no reason.[150]

We're here for dog food, and when we get to the pet aisle, I'm closer to the Iams display, so I grab a huge bag of their lower-calorie[151] formula and toss it in the cart, "Hey! Look at me with all my *strongs*!" I exclaim, curling my bicep so Fletch can get a front-row seat at the gun show.

My arms are *magnificent*.

OK, fine.

My arms are magnificent by no one's standards but my own. They're still bat-wing-y underneath. They could be a lot more solid. But my shoulders square off at the end instead of gently sloping into the beef of my upper arms, and I can clearly see the outlines of my triceps. When I wave, the whole thing is less jiggly. Plus, I can throw around forty pounds of kibble now, as opposed to nothing, and that's a huge victory. I'm as proud of these little mounds of submerged

---

[150]Cute for the first month. Now it's getting on my nerves.

[151]If I'm dieting, *every* creature in this house is dieting.

strength as any Brazilian supermodel would be of her Lloyd's of London–insured multimillion-dollar gams, and at some point this summer, I'm going to go sleeveless in my new dress for the first time this century. I have earned it.

As we pass the liquor aisle,[152] a huge grin spreads across my face. I don't need any wine, but now that I'm doing Weight Watchers online, it's nice to know I could get it if I wanted it. I tell Fletch, "I feel like I've got a piece of my life back because this plan has me making my own food choices."

"Didn't you have a decent amount of freedom of choice with Jenny Craig? There was a bunch of stuff on the menus you had."

"Yes and no. On Jenny, I ate my choice of A, then B, then C, with snacks of D and E, and that was it. I only really liked about fifteen items, so by the time I quit, I never wanted to see another mock-McMuffin, meatloaf, or lemon cake again."

We stroll through the fabric softener aisle and I start unscrewing caps so I can pick the best scent. The first two I sniff are cloying and artificial, but the third is fresh and delightful. Fletch's masculinity won't be compromised if his undershirts smell like wild orchids, right? I toss the bottle in the basket.

Fletch checks fabric softener off the list and we proceed to the soap aisle, where he selects a bottle of unscented bodywash. I guess he doesn't want the smell of his soap clashing with the orchids?

---

[152]Yes! My Target stocks booze! How great is that?

"What's weird is, my eating has been regimented for what feels like so long now, it kind of blows my mind that I can have anything I want, as long as I account for the fat and calories and fiber. Take gelato, for example. I could eat it right now."

Fletch goes all Homer Simpson on me for a moment. "Mmm . . . ge-la-to."

"I've kept my POINTS[153] low today, and I trained with Barbie. I've already more than made up for it if I decide to splurge. I could have gelato, and it won't be served with a side of guilt. Not freaking out over every single calorie going in my mouth feels liberating. And weird."

"Ever since you started Weight Watchers, you're a lot less fixated on what you can't have. There were a few times on Jenny Craig I feared you'd cut me for a bite of my meat." He laughs.

"If you knew how close you were to the business end of my steak knife, you wouldn't be laughing. That night I had two ounces of soggy fish stick and you had a beautifully charred rib eye that covered your entire plate? And while you chewed, you inadvertently made little *yum-yum* noises? Had I stabbed you, no female jury would have convicted me."

"You told me it didn't bother you if I had a steak."

"I lied." We wander through the garden section, and I'm deeply disappointed to see that the four-foot-tall wire rooster has finally sold. Angie and I have been watching this item from our respective Targets all summer. We pledged that the

---

[153]Weight Watchers' numerical system of factoring in fat, calories, and fiber.

minute it was marked down, we'd buy it, even though neither of us had an idea of what we'd do with it. I gesture toward the empty shelf. "It's gone."

"I'm sure the dogs will sleep easier tonight knowing you won't be chasing them around with a giant metal bird," he replies. Right, like *I'm* the one who found his father's old bear rug in a box in the basement and put it on his head to "see how the dogs will react."[154] It took me a week to scrub off the putrescent fluid that shot out of Loki's bunghole and onto the cabinet when he caught site of a bear in his kitchen. To this day I can't go to the basement to wash a load of socks without Loki barking his face off to let me know there might be bears downstairs.

Again, this is why we aren't having children.

"Anyway," Fletch continues, "how does Weight Watchers give you back your life?"

I stop to run my hands over a display of beach towels while I gather my thoughts. I'm going swimming tomorrow and I don't want to have to use a towel from our bathroom. These are all stripe-y and cute, so I toss a couple in the cart. "OK, here's an example: One of our favorite things to do in the summer is go to Caffe Gelato on Division, right?"

"We haven't been there in forever," Fletch says.

"Right. And we used to go all the time last year. In the winter when we'd drive past, I'd be happy remembering how much we enjoy that place. But this year, every time we'd go down Division, I'd get depressed."

---

[154]Target liquor may have been involved.

"I know."

"Really? How?" I love how perceptive Fletch is. Some-times it's like we have this whole unspoken bond and he just senses my feelings.

"You've yelled, *'I want some goddamned gelato!'* every time we've driven by it this summer."

Oh, right.

I continue, "I wasn't just mad about the ice cream. Think about it—what do we do when we go to Caffe Gelato?"

"Have dessert?" Fletch takes a sleeveless gray shirt off the rack and holds it up. He does not share my fear of bare arms and seems to enjoy exposing his pits at the gym. He checks the price—$3.99; score!—and tosses it in the cart.

"Yes, but we do more than that. Since you don't let me eat ice cream in the car—"

"If you could keep all the 'sticky' in the cup, I would."

I can't help but roll my eyes. From how he talks, you'd think I was Pigpen, leaving a viscous cloud of filth behind me every time I enter a vehicle. "I was saying, because you're a car Nazi, we have to eat it there, so we station ourselves at one of the little metal tables. It's always a gorgeous night, and we sit at the table, eat gelato, and laugh the whole time."

"Can't help it. That spot is the epicenter of all the hip-sters in the entire city—and thus hilarious to me."

At this point we've wandered into housewares. Target has this whole tiki-bar line of indoor-outdoor entertaining pieces with monkeys on them, and I'm totally enamored. Because you know what my house needs? Plastic cups adorned with cartoon monkeys.

I continue, "See, getting gelato isn't just about eating something sweet; it's a whole ritual. If we were to simply have a Jenny Craig dessert in our house, we'd miss out on the experience of giggling at Wicker Park residents sauntering by with their skinny jeans and random facial hair. And how would they know they're ridiculous if we weren't there to laugh at them? Getting gelato is a fun summer habit, and I've really missed not being able to do so this year. But now that I'm on Weight Watchers, we can go." I inspect all sides of the glass—looks like it would hold a whole can of soda plus ice and—

"Then why are we screwing around at Target? Let's check out and get gelato." We start to walk away from the tiki display. "Take those out of the cart—we're not getting them. We have ten thousand drink containers because you buy glasses everywhere we go."

Huh. I guess that's one mystery solved.

We proceed to the checkout, pushing our cart as fast as its wobbly little wheels will allow us. We pay for our purchases and I'm so excited about the prospect of my first cup of ice cream this whole summer that I don't even correct the cashier for saying neither "hello" nor "thank you."[155]

We load up the car and we're at Caffe Gelato within minutes. Looks like everyone else in Wicker Park had the same idea as us, and we join a line that's a good ten-people deep, all of them doing the inadvertent (and inevitable) side-to-side ice cream shuffle that happens when confronted with a case full of different flavors.

---

[155]Next time, jackass. Next time.

The wait gives me plenty of time to people watch and to pick the perfect combination of gelato flavors. Normally I'm a big fan of coconut and banana, but I figure if I'm indulging, I'm going whole hog. Nothing fruit-based for me today! I choose a small cup of hazelnut and mocha, and Fletch gets a chocolate chip–tiramisu swirl combination. While we wait for the cashier to ring us up, I contemplate bringing some home for the dogs.

"Thanks! That'll be nine seventy-five, please," says the girl working the register. I pay and drop a couple of bucks in her tip jar. "I was going to say we should get some vanilla for Maisy and Loki, but for ten bucks, the dogs can buy their own goddamned gelato." We head for the cluster of tables out on the sidewalk. "Ten dollars! For a tiny cup! Ridiculous! Why would anyone pay that much for four stupid ounces of . . ." I take my first bite, and the creamy hazelnut flavor assaults every single taste bud. Bliss! "Um, never mind."

We begin to eat, and as we talk I notice I'm not making much of a dent in the gelato. I chalk this up to my fantastic new ability to control myself, but then I realize the problem is the spoon. Or, rather, the wee spatula masquerading as a spoon. Measuring in at two inches long and half an inch wide, this flat piece of plastic is practically useless, especially since the heat of the evening is making everything melt quickly.

"You know what they ought to serve this with to make it more convenient? Chopsticks," I say.

Fletch is already covered with a dozen tiny chocolate

drips from his own dish. "A fork would be more effective right now."

"Or a slotted spoon."

"Or a spork!"

"Nah, a spork has a small basin at the end that holds liquid. This holds no liquid; it's more like trying to eat with a matchbox."

"Maybe a stick would be better? Or nothing. Nothing would be great. If they'd given us nothing I would be more able to get this gelato from my cup to my mouth."

Our game is interrupted when a hipster crosses in front of our table. He's wearing the trademark anachronistic T-shirt (this one bearing a *Charles in Charge* logo), stovepipe jeans, tattooed sleeves, Magnum PI moustache, and a messenger bag full of vinyl. He's got coffee in his left hand and smokes in his right, and naturally, he's wearing an iPod with the big stereophonic earphones. We've just seen twenty of his clones wander by in the past few minutes. How exactly is your look supposed to be considered edgy and ironic when everyone else in the neighborhood looks exactly the same? Christ; I've seen cheerleading uniforms with more individuality. Wearing my pink polo and green capris, I'm about the only one who doesn't appear to have been plucked straight from central casting.[156]

This guy's only saving grace is his do. His head is shaved except for a strip in the middle sticking straight up, and there

---

[156] At least not in this decade. Recently we were invited to a party and the invitation said we should dress like we did in the eighties. But that would imply I ever stopped.

are curling tendrils of hair hanging from his temples on either side of his face, like he's a Hasidic student on spring break.

"Haven't seen that before," I muse.

Fletch says, "I bet he went in to his stylist and goes, 'One Jew-hawk, please,'" causing me to choke on my ice cream.

Once I catch my breath, I survey my surroundings and have to smile. A beautiful night, a little gelato, newfound strongs, a smug feeling of self-satisfaction, and a whole lot of snark—my life suddenly makes sense again.

TO: angie_at_home
FROM: jen@jenlancaster.com
SUBJECT: Jealous?

Yo, yo, yo,

You know how on *America's Next Top Model* they show those Cover-Girl infomercials with the previous season's winners? And the girls go on and on about how glamorous their lives are now that they're top models, while conspicuously applying a thick coating of lip gloss?

Today my infomercial would go something like this:

"Hi, I'm Jen Lancaster and this is my life as a best-selling author. Earlier today I put socks on the dogs and watched them slide around on the wood floors. Then I looked at cat pictures with funny captions for about an hour. And when I got dressed, I had to fix my only clean bra with duct tape."

Jealous?

Jen

P.S. I have a dollar in my wallet.

P.P.S. And I got into a fight at Weight Watchers.

Enough with the Cake Already; God!

"*I* just hope it's not incredibly queer."

I'm standing by the mirror in the entry hall, putting on a coat of lipstick. I press my lips together to even out the matte Bobbi Brown Plumberry and I can't help grinning back at my reflection. There are contours under my cheekbones now and they've been carved out by exercise and not three cleverly applied shades of blush. My chin is singular, not plural, and there's jaw, not jowls, before my face merges into my neck. No more Mrs. Potato Head impersonations for me! A few new lines are evident around my eyes, but only when I smile, which seems to happen a lot lately. I look healthy and happy, but more important, I *feel* healthy and happy.

"Why do you think it will be 'queer'?" Fletch asks. He's working from home today and has a Circuit City's worth of electronics spread out in front of him. Everything's blinking either red or blue. His ad hoc desk is our snappy new leather ottoman, which Maisy has already punctured with her dew-claw.[157] He'd look like the consummate professional were he not wearing a T-shirt that says DONKEY PUNCH with a picture of a grinning mule on it.

While he works, I've been standing here by the mirror for the past ten minutes trying to muster the motivation to attend my first Weight Watchers meeting. I've been following the plan online for a few weeks, and I'm delighted with the results. The online applications make it incredibly easy to map out meals, track progress, and, really, live a life that doesn't feel like I'm constantly on a diet.

I particularly like the recipe planner because it lets me cook our favorite dinners. All I do is put in each ingredient, and the tool will tell me how many points a serving is worth. This way I can choose to adjust my portion size and supplement my meal with a big salad, or if I want to go whole hog, I'm able to know in advance how much extra time I should spend on the treadmill if I want an entire plateful. The very worst thing about dieting is feeling like everyone else is having something you can't eat. Being able to have the same dinner as Fletch, even with a vastly smaller portion, has gotten me over a large psychological hurdle; thus, this online tool has been a godsend.

I'd be very content to continue to just use WeightWatchers .com because it's so helpful. However, the site prominently

---

[157]The only constant in our world is, the dogs will always be slightly naughty and we can't have nice things.

features a message that those who attend meetings lose up to three times as much weight as those who do it on their own. With those kinds of stats, I can't *not* give the meetings a try.

Yet I'm still hesitant. I hated the one meeting I attended ten years ago. The whole room was full of angry, bitter women. One gal—a plus-sized, emerald-eyed redhead with skin like a pitcher of cream—claimed her weight problem began when her company started to recognize birthdays. And ever since she'd been on Weight Watchers, she'd been campaigning to stop these celebrations. At that point, she'd only convinced her employers to supplement the parties with a side of fresh fruit, but she was confident if she kept it up, she'd bring an end to serving cake all together.

Yes. *That* must have made her the most popular girl on the thirty-ninth floor. Can't you picture the conference room at her workplace now?

Happy retirement, Jerry! We'd like to celebrate your achievement by sharing a fruit plate with you.

An apple? Really? After thirty-seven years with this company? Fuck all of you.

I felt bad for the redhead because she seemed so unhappy. I bet everyone at work hated her for being the Cake Police, but she probably figured they didn't like her because of her weight. I wondered if she could see how gorgeous she was. Based on her tirade about cake and coworkers, I doubted it. Still, everyone cheered for her because she was brave enough to take a stand against the military-industrial-cake complex.

The redhead wasn't the only one there who turned me

off. Apparently work cake is a much larger problem than I ever imagined. A teacher described an issue she'd had when a colleague of hers was retiring. The home economics instructor baked a huge going-away cake, and Weight Watchers Teacher threw such a fit over it that the principal took her aside and begged her to calm down. The principal asked her if she wouldn't please just hold a slice of the cake for a few minutes in order not to offend its baker or make the retiree feel bad. She refused, and with victory etched all over her face, the teacher explained how she was in the process of consulting an attorney, citing workplace harassment.

Fortunately everyone's applause drowned out my snickering.

A third woman chimed in with her strategy on how to deal with the whole cake issue. She said she'd stay at her desk during the festivities (the first rational course of action I'd heard) and then as soon as they were over, she'd run to the cafeteria, toss the remains in the trash, and squeeze dish soap over the leftovers so she wouldn't be tempted. *Of course,* I thought. *You should definitely punish everyone because of your own lack of self-control.* And when the group applauded again, I considered never returning.

During "sharing time" there was a lot of wailing and gnashing of teeth over the evils of food—even from the group's leader—and I didn't like it. I knew then and I've since relearned that food isn't inherently evil. We need calories to stay alive. Food is fuel. Food gives us the energy to hug our husbands and chase after our kids and pets and rearrange all the furniture in our living rooms.

Food isn't bad; food is *life*.

Hating the very thing that sustains us seemed like a recipe for failure, and I thought maybe what we should have been discussing was finding a sensible way to live with food and to love and appreciate food, but to not let food rule our lives. Ruining birthday cake for everyone else didn't seem like the most effective strategy to make this happen . . . so I raised my hand and made this point.

Let's just say the applause was not forthcoming.

I was the only one not to be invited to the postmeeting dinner. I never went back, mostly because I knew I wouldn't be welcome.

I take a final look at myself, pick a few stray bits of fur off my pink polo, and sigh. "All right, I'm going to go do this thing. Let's just hope this meeting is less birthday-cake centric."

One of Fletch's multiple devices begins to ring. "I'm sure that was an anomaly. Good luck and have fun!" he says, placing his Bluetooth back in his ear to take the call.

According to the Weight Watchers Web site, I'm supposed to arrive at the meeting half an hour early to register. Since I became a member online when I registered to use their e-tools, I have a pass to attend as many meetings as I want.[158] I arrive at the right building and park in the garage. The meeting is a couple of floors up, and locating an elevator

---

[158] That number currently being zero.

seems like a pain, so I just run up the two flights to get to my destination. How about that? I'm not even winded.

I enter the office, and it's not nearly as nice as the Jenny Craig place. The lighting is bad, the carpet is worn, and the furniture is out of date. Oh, well; I'm not here for the aesthetics, right? Plus, I was always vaguely aware of being a customer at Jenny Craig, not a member, and the shoddy look of this place doesn't make me feel like I should whip out my wallet. There are various Weight Watchers snack foods displayed on the walls, but I don't pay much attention to them. The whole beauty of the plan is that I can make my own choices, so I don't need to fill my cabinets with their food. Going straight from packages of Jenny food to packages of WW meals would teach me nothing.

I introduce myself to the woman behind the counter, asking if this is where the new campers check in. She introduces herself as Pat. I show Pat my all-access pass and she seems slightly disappointed for some reason. Um . . . OK? Should I be fatter to join? Or thinner? I don't quite understand what's up with her heavy sigh.

I fill out a form, and my next task is a weigh-in. I step on the scale without hesitation. Is that progress or what? Weight Watchers' weigh-ins are confidential, so the display is behind the counter. I'm somewhat disappointed that I don't get to see the numbers come up myself. I sort of dug when Jenny counselors shouted out how much I'd lost, because everyone up and down the hallway would cheer. A silent weigh-in feels like expectations are lower, somehow.

Pat records my weight and writes it down on a trifold

piece of thick paper. "This is your membership book," she says. "Be sure to bring it back every time you come." She folds the book up and stuffs it in a little plastic sleeve, palming it to me like you might a tampon to your friend at a party.

Impatient, I tear the booklet out of the wrapper. Ha! I'm down six pounds since I quit Jenny and started using the online tools. I attribute this progress to my double workouts more than anything else.

Pat has recorded my goal weight, which is what I weigh now minus ten percent. Seems like I should have had a say in the goal setting, but sure, OK, ten percent is as good as anything else to aim for. Honestly, I stopped thinking in terms of numbers a while back. My real goal is to be able to have the strength and endurance to take the dogs on a run. Also, I'd like my arms to be toned enough that I can go sleeveless with confidence, but if we need a number, fine; ten percent will do nicely.

Pat takes me into the meeting room and explains that she and I will spend some time together in an orientation after the main meeting. I say hello to the two women already in the room and we all just sort of look at each other. Feels like we should have some sort of conversation, but I don't know what to say, like, *Hey, let's all be less fat together!* or *Is it just me or is Pat kind of a bitch?* so I start to read my brochures instead.

A welcome packet explains WW's origins and outlines how their various plans work. I've been following the Flex plan, which is based on an algorithm. Essentially, calories are factored with fat and fiber grams to come up with a POINTS equivalent. I'm allowed so many POINTS per day, but I can consume them however I'd like. I try to eat lower-POINTS-valued food so I can have more, but this particular plan also allows me the occasional gelato. For those who don't want to record everything they eat, there's the Core plan. There's a select variety of low-fat, nutritious foods to choose from, and you can eat whatever you want from the list without tracking.

There's also a quick reference guide called Weight Loss on the Go, and it looks pretty handy. Clear instructions are included on what to order when I find myself in a restaurant for a regular meal and not one that's a special occasion. For example, if a drive-thru is the only breakfast alternative, I should opt for a McMuffin-type sandwich minus the cheese. The booklet gives an estimated POINTS value, and the cheeseless McMuffin is totally reasonable. Even with cheese, it's not ridiculous when other meals consumed that day are lower in points. Who knew?[159]

Five minutes with this guidebook and I already have more information about eating out than any of my Jenny Craig counselors could impart in two months.

The literature also includes a number of menus and all sorts of advice on how to add fitness to one's daily routine. I've got my *strongs* covered already, so I skim over that part. Sprinkled throughout the booklets are a couple of reminders that the monthly pass works out to less than ten dollars a week, but they're not overt or obnoxious. People make themselves

---

[159]Fine; maybe it's common sense. But if it were so common, would the diet industry gross billions each year?

vulnerable when they walk into a weight-loss center, and I'm pleased WW doesn't take advantage of their lowered defenses with a lot of in-your-face sales pitches.

A few more members shuffle in, and I try to look at all of them without being obvious, but most of them are sitting behind me, and I catch only little glimpses. There are ten of us in the meeting, spanning the scale from why-are-you-even-here size to oh-bless-your-heart size. I fall somewhere in the middle, although I appear to be the only one with any muscle tone. Most of the members are women, but I think I spotted a couple of men, too.

Pat opens the session by introducing herself and saying we're all here because we love food but we recognize food is bad.

Uh-oh.

Pat tells us how one of her friends is going backpacking in the Grand Canyon soon and how she's struggling to pack efficiently because everything she carries down will have to be carried back up. Pat says her friend finally had her "aha" moment when she realized if she lost ten pounds then she'd have ten pounds less to carry. Then Pat asks us how long *we've* been carrying around our weight burdens. Pat explained she carried around an extra seventy-five pounds for five years after she had a baby. But thanks to WW, she lost the weight and kept it off, and she's now been a WW leader for fifteen years.

OK, not to be the biggest cynic in the world, but I'm guessing Pat's "friend" has been packing for this Grand Canyon trip for about as long as Pat's been leading WW sessions.

Pat moves on to having everyone discuss their week, and she hands out little star stickers that say BRAVO when someone has "good sharing." (This is what I meant by "queer.") Apparently these stickers go on a Weight Watchers bookmark that you receive once you've come to two consecutive meetings . . . and that I'm pretty sure I'm going to throw away the minute I get it. (If I want a touchstone of how far I've come, I'll simply look at my triceps.) You get a snappy bronze key ring when you hit the ten percent goal, but if the annoyance level of the first five minutes of this meeting is any indication, I'll be long gone before that ever happens.

Pat pulls out an easel and starts discussing how we need to "clean" our lives of temptation. She has a huge list of rooms in our home and places we go every day where we run into food. One of the areas on the sheet is "the closet."

The day I take a meal in the linen closet is the day I sign up for gastric bypass.

Pat starts with the first item, which is "work." "So," she asks, "who can tell me what temptations you run into at work?"

I look back on the various places I've been employed and can't remember a lot of temptations, though I can recall a number of days I was so busy that I didn't have time to eat. Skipping meals did a number on my metabolism, but except for the unbelievable onion rings in the Hyatt-building cafeteria where I temped for a while, I can't think of a lot of times—

"Birthday cake!" shouts the woman sitting directly behind me.

Good ganache-coated Christ; in ten years, has *no one* figured out how to deal with cake in the office? Or has my life become one elaborate setup, à la *The Truman Show*, with Ed Harris orchestrating my every move from the top of a giant bubble in the sky? Is this place a set? These walls covered with Weight Watchers' product displays—are they real? Or are there a bunch of gaffers and grips behind them, drinking coffee and trying to perpetrate my "reality"? Are people in bars all around the world watching me on TV, and betting five bucks that I'd charge like a bull when I heard the words "birthday cake"? We gloss over the work-cake bit rather quickly, so it's probably too soon to tell either way. (But if a can light falls from the sky next time I'm outside, I will totally be on to you people.)

Next up, Pat talks about the temptation of what we eat in our automobiles. I do not raise my hand and suggest that everyone marry Fletch and thus be forbidden to eat in the new car, even though this method is one hundred percent effective in preventing the accidental inhalation of the Burger King Texas Whopper. Seriously, I spilled a splash of skim iced coffee in there last week and I thought he was going to divorce me.

After mentioning hiding food in the closet (again? WTF?), she moves on to discuss the big kahuna, the refrigerator. She stresses again how we have to clean out what's bad for us, and I assume she doesn't mean the hairy kiwis I found rolling around the vegetable crisper earlier today.

"What are your triggers with the fridge?" she asks. "For me, if I open the door and see peanut butter, I throw it away and I don't allow my children to have it for a couple of months. Yes, sir, I clean it out!"

Huh?

Pat continues, "I can't know there's peanut butter in my house. If I see peanut butter, I will eat the whole jar, so either my family has to keep it in a special cabinet that I don't open or my husband has to take it to his office. As a matter of fact, he has his own closet[160] where he keeps the food I don't want to touch, so my kitchen is clean, clean, clean."

All right, I understand temptation. This body is a living monument to the joys of excess and a lack of willpower. And even with my newfound *strongs*, at the moment there's a real possibility that a pie in my home would have a short life expectancy. But I've been dieting in earnest for only about three months. I would hope that after fifteen goddamned years on Weight Watchers I'd somehow get my shit together enough to peaceably coexist with a slice of key lime pie. This leads me to believe that either Pat has Scary Food Issues, which would be better addressed in therapy, or she's putting on a show for us fatties. Either way, I find myself disliking her more and more.

A well-put-together blond woman in her early fifties raises her hand. Today's her first day, too, and she looks as though she has maybe fifteen pounds to lose. Pat calls on her and the woman begins to speak with what sounds like a German accent. "Wiz ze peanut butter, could you not just have ze tablespoon on maybe heavy dark bread wiz ze multigrains? You

---

[160]So that's where the closet business comes from.

could top wiz fresh-cut strawberries. Is delicious and would be low on ze POINTS, yah?"

Oh, honey, I giggle to myself, *you just lost yourself an invitation to the group dinner afterwards.*

I can almost see Pat's head exploding, but surprisingly, a lot of the group nods and agrees. I suspect they aren't drinking Pat's sugar-free Kool-Aid, either.

Pat moves on to discuss how we should clean our relationships. The burly, tattooed, leather-clad biker-type guy who came in late raises his hand and complains that his roommate is a skinny little girl and he's having a lot of problems because she's an "emotional baker" and he doesn't know if he can "clean" her out of the kitchen.

I'm not sure if it's the phrase "emotional baker" or if it's because when he opened his mouth his *t-i-t-s* fell out, but I accidentally bark with laughter and have to cover it up with a coughing fit.

A girl one row over named Rachel tells the group how she's taken control of her relationships. "My sister says she hates the fake sugar I keep in the house we share, but I don't care. She can have Splenda or nothing. I've lost eighty-four pounds and I am not going to let her junk influence my diet." Rachel beams, and it's all I can do not to go over and hug her. She's still a really big girl, but she radiates such confidence in her success that I choke up a bit. Whereas I'd like Pat to kiss the fattest part of my ass, I find Rachel to be an inspiration.

As I look around the room again and listen to everyone's stories, it occurs to me that most of them aren't different from me, Pat and Birthday Cake Girl notwithstanding. They seem pretty sensible and have rolled their eyes, too, whenever Pat's gone off on a tangent. I get the feeling they're here for the collective support and inspiration they get from one another and not for Pat's minisermons. There's a really cute girl two seats over with perfect blond highlights and big sapphire earrings. She looks an awful lot like me, and when she talks about starting to cook and learning to fill up on fruit and vegetables instead of always ordering takeout, she sounds exactly like me. And when Pat hands out little packets of alcohol prep swabs to keep on our persons as a visual reminder to "keep it clean," Ponytail Girl catches my eye and mouths, "Are you fucking kidding me?"

I totally want to be this girl's friend.

Unfortunately, the meeting ends, and before I can firmly establish a relationship with my new bestie, I have to move up front to "get orientated" with Pat. I situate myself in the first row.

I tell Pat a bit about my weight-loss experience and explain how I'm down six pounds on the plan so far, and more than thirty overall. I mention how much I like the POINTS system and eating real food, and then I tell her exactly how helpful I've found the online portion of the plan. In response, Pat hands me a little blue lunch bag.

"Here," she says. "This is your official Weight Watchers starter kit."

Yay, free swag! I love free swag!

"For only twenty-four ninety-nine," she continues.

Oh. No free swag for me.

"It's optional, of course," she says, but I get the feeling it's anything but. "This kit contains all the essential tools you'll require to lose weight." Hold on a second; didn't I just mention how I'd already been losing weight without these "essential" tools?

Pat takes out each item one by one. "This is a complete guide to finding POINTS values, and here are fifty fast and easy recipes. Here's a coupon book worth ten dollars off Weight Watchers products and a three-month journal where you can track your daily food consumption. You need these."

She spends the next ten minutes pitching me not only on the packet, but also on the wide variety of Weight Watchers treats sold in this facility. I'm told the grocery store doesn't sell what they carry in this retail outlet, and vice versa. "Thank God we don't have to compete with the Jewel!" she exclaims.

Argh! Argh! Argh![161]

Number one, I don't *need* any of this stuff. I already paid for the comprehensive suite of online tools, and I made that quite clear. As for the journal, um, hi, but I'm sort of already obligated to record my thoughts and feelings on weight loss in a memoir. I don't want to fill my pantry with a bunch of WW treats because if I wanted to eat packaged food, I'd have stayed on Jenny Craig. Packaged treats teach me nothing about making choices, and it's simply swapping one crutch for another.

I particularly don't like the comment on "competing" with the grocery store because that makes me very aware that

---

[161]Oh, great. Now I'm so aggravated I've turned into a freaking pirate.

this is a business, and I feel like my best interests are not being looked out for when the bottom line is so obviously involved. I was always aware of Jenny Craig being a business, and ultimately, that's why I quit. Although had they been a tad more forthcoming about how I could supplement their food with my own, I'd still be with them.

The Weight Watchers Web site and supporting literature are pretty innocuous, so I'm wondering if this particular place isn't a franchise, hence the blatant emphasis on sales. I quickly review the session in my head and note how Pat mentioned specific products at least a dozen times. Why would I be encouraged to opt for Weight Watchers Fruities rather than a piece of fruit when I want a sweet?

Why didn't Pat talk about exercise *at all*? My God, movement is the key to everything. My life and body have been completely changed because I can sprint up a flight of stairs now, and not because I eat dietetic candy. And shoot, there's a Bally's right across the hall from here. Were I running this session, I'd encourage members to hit the gym afterward, and not inquire about where we'd all be going for our post-weigh-in splurge. I'm willing to wager that after a few more sessions with Barbie, even pie will be safe in my house because I won't want to wreck all the progress I've made.

I am not giving this woman one penny. "I'm pretty happy with the online tools, but thanks anyway."

Suddenly Pat's attitude changes and the rest of my orientation is painfully condescending and full of clichéd advice such as "the plan works if you work the plan." Twenty insufferable minutes later, I finally escape to the parking garage, sans swag bag, as Pat reminds my retreating form that the pretzels are buy one, get one free and this deal won't last!

"You can tell me all about it next time," I say.

But there will be no next time. I'll not be back.

As I drive home, I try to formulate how I'd create a Weight Watchers–approved birthday cake. If I could, I'd make a fucking fortune.

Perhaps I should get in touch with the emotional baker to see what she suggests.

TO: stacey_at_home
FROM: jen@jenlancaster.com
SUBJECT: Tonight

I might be late for *Top Chef* tonight—I'm going to be doing laps at the pool and there's a good chance I'll be slow to shower afterward since it's a double-workout day. Is that cool?

Oh, since you asked, yes, the pool is very nice. But the patrons? Wow. So. Many. Tattoos. When did everyone start getting their resumes permanently inked on their bodies?

Judgmentally yours.

Jen

Swim It Out, Bitch

Session Twenty-six

I threw out my back again because while I'm apparently mentally prepared for running, I'm not quite there physically. I was still able to go to the gym a couple of times last week, but today's the first day my doctor has allowed me to train with Barbie again.

Well, sort of, anyway.

Technically *a week* from today is the first day I'm allowed to work out with Barbie, but I'm desperate to stay on track. I have not enjoyed lying around my house, nursing the injury, watching shitty TV on TiVo. Weird, right? Since I'm really not supposed to be here, Barbie and I decided we'd split the difference—we're going to work only arms and abs this session, and we'll start in on legs next week.

"Sad about not doing lunges today?" Barbie asks. "They're your favorites!"

"Honestly? A little bit," I reply. "I even kind of miss that horrible thing you make me do when I put the resistance band around my ankles and scuttle sideways back and forth between the cones." That move is So. Damn. Hard. By the time I'm finished, I feel like I'm being stabbed both in the lungs and in the butt cheeks. And yet my whole backside is becoming decidedly more round and less rectangular, so I appreciate the efficacy, if not the action.

Barbie giggles. "What is it you call the laterals again?" When Barbie uses the technical terms for exercises, I can't keep them straight, so I often substitute my own terms. For example, there's a move I do where I make a fist and twist downward, which I call "punching the dog." The shoulder press where I take a weight and go from opposite hip to above my head is the "John Travolta," and any crunch done on the stability ball is known as "the wedgie-maker." I also do the "hello, yoga," a balancing exercise, and my favorite, the "thanks for not cutting your grass, asshole." This last one involves using one of those Reebok fitness bars, and Barbie and I push at each other from either side. Last time we did it, I kept thinking of the idiots next door, and I shoved so hard I accidentally knocked her into the Spinning room. We don't do that one a lot anymore.

"The crabby patty," I reply as I finish up my set of "the luggage grab."

"Nice. OK, that's three . . . two . . . one . . . and you're good. We're going to move into the weight room now."

"Really? We never go in there." I'm excited for the change of scenery. Almost everything we do is in one of two training rooms, or on occasion, the cardio room. We went into the weight room during my second training session, and Barbie tried to get me to do this step-on-a-box-while-holding-a-heavy-ass-bar dealie (since dubbed the "no fucking way") and we haven't been in there since.

"We're going to do some moves with free weights, and I want you to be able to sit on a bench to support your back." She grabs her clipboard and I take a swig of my energy drink before trotting along after her. The weight room is different from the rest of the gym because it's not on an exterior wall. All the other rooms are bright and open, but this one's dark because the ceiling in here isn't vaulted. Although everything is nice and still quite new, between the din, the brick walls, and all the free weights, it reminds me of a prison gym.

Barbie demonstrates the exercise—she sits on a bench and, holding a couple of good-sized weights at shoulder level, lifts them up over her head before returning them to the starting position. "Shoulder presses," she tells me. "Make sure you're pinching your shoulder blades the whole time, and exhale on the way up. Slow and controlled, so let's go!"

"Are these the reason my shoulders are kind of square now and my bra straps don't slip anymore?"

"Exactly! Let's go for fifteen, but tell me if the weights are too heavy."

I do one rep and they're heavy, but I can handle it. "No worries," I tell her. I start to do the presses. The whole wall is mirrored, so I have no choice but to look at myself when I do them. As much as I normally like to preen and admire myself in any shiny surface, I don't like to watch myself work out, but I don't have a lot of choice here. As I continue to cycle through the reps, I watch myself strain and sweat. Today I've got on a black T-shirt, a black do-rag, and old gray shorts, since all my pretty gym clothes have been buried at the bottom of the laundry for the past few weeks. "Check out our reflection," I tell Barbie. "Do we not look like we're working out in a women's penitentiary?"

"Oh, shut up!" She laughs and swats in my direction with the clipboard.

"No, seriously, between my outfit, the low lighting, and all the bricks, this totally looks like a prison, and this is the exercise the convicts are always doing right before they get shanked. And look how much larger I am than you. If we were in lockup, I'd probably be in charge. And you're little and you're standing next to me helping me, so I'm pretty sure that would make you my bitch." Barbie smiles and shakes her head at me in the mirror. "Admit it; you missed me last week. None of your other clients would call you their prison bitch, would they?"

"They wouldn't, and I did miss you."

"But I'm probably in big trouble when we start working out my whole body again next week, aren't I?"

Barbie nods earnestly. "Definitely."

I'm OK with that. Every time we work out, Barbie pushes me further and further outside of my comfort zone . . . despite my cries to please, please, make it stop. At this point I'm doing stuff I never thought I'd even be capable of doing, as evidenced by when I ran on the treadmill a couple of weeks ago. Granted, that didn't work out so well, but that I'd even attempt it is huge.

Because of this newfound confidence in fitness, I'm going to go swim laps at the pool tonight. I've been to a couple of the open swims during the day, but so far I've done nothing but float and sunbathe. I've always been a strong swimmer, but over the years my endurance dwindled to nothing, so I've never taken advantage of the lap pool even though I've lived within a mile of it for years. I feared I'd dive in and make it only one Olympic-sized length before collapsing. It's possible I have such muscle memory from years of swimming in my parents' pool that I'd be fine, but until recently I always quit the second anything became too physically demanding. Now that I have both confidence and commitment, I feel like I've become—pardon the pun—unsinkable.

"That's four . . . three . . . two . . . and . . . one. Let's start that round from the beginning again. Tell me what else is new," Barbie says. "How's the diet?"

"Right now I'm on WeightWatchers.com, and I'm using their electronic tools to plan meals and track everything I eat."

"Do you go to meetings?"

"Went to one and I hated it. I'm not sure if I'll go back."

"If you do, maybe I'll go with you."

No one I've ever met has been in better shape than Barbie. She's thin, but that's not why she looks good. Each of her muscles is perfectly defined without being all ridiculous and bodybuilderlike. She's constantly in motion because of her profession, and she pursues fitness in her off time by biking, wake boarding, and playing beach volleyball. She's an athlete and always has been, so I don't even think she fully appreciates exactly what kind of shape she's in.

"Oh, honey, no," I tell her. "No, no, no. You can't go to a Weight Watchers meeting."

Barbie looks puzzled. "Why not?"

"Because they'll *kill* you."

"Really?"

See? Clueless.

"Yeah, I'm pretty sure they would. How about I just tell you what I learn?"

"Deal."

We move on to abs work, and I grunt and complain the entire time. After a week off, I've lost some abdominal strength, and the exercises seem more difficult than usual. She's got me doing push-ups with one hand on the floor and another on a medicine ball, aka the "Jack Palances." Barbie sees I'm struggling, so she tries to distract me. "What are your plans for later?"

"*Ungh* . . . I'm going to go swim laps at *ungh* . . . Holstein Pool." Every time I push myself up, a bead of sweat falls on the floor. I can actually keep track of how many Palances I've done by counting them.

"Really? Double-workout day, huh? Good for you. Swimming sounds like fun. Will Fletch go with you?"

"*Ungh* . . . no, probably not. He's not a great swimmer. *Ungh*. He's more of a *ungh* . . . cocktail-by-the-pool guy."

"Truthfully I'm not great in the water, either. I tried to

swim laps when I was in Miami, and I practically drowned. I had to grab one of those kickboards to hold myself up."

"That's kind of *ungh* . . . surprising. You're so athletic, I assumed you'd be good at any sport."

"Not swimming. And that's two . . . one . . . and you're finished."

I take a second to catch my breath before telling her, "That's because you're not naturally buoyant. Like with me, I can be motionless in the water for hours without any effort. My brother says it's because I'm built like a manatee."

"Your brother sounds like an ass."

"He absolutely is!" I agree. I take another deep breath and stretch my arms over my head. Wow and *ow*. I can already tell my everything is going to hurt tomorrow.

"You're all done."

"Nuh-uh! That was not an hour!"

"We did three sets of every circuit. You were just talking and didn't notice. Check out the clock—it's three p.m. Nice job! Glad to have you back!"

"I'm going to run out of here before you change your mind and try to make me do one more set. See you Wednesday, two o'clock?"

"Yep, see ya then! Have a great swim tonight! Let me know how it goes!"

Fifteen minutes before the lap-swim session begins, I take out my contacts and change into a bathing suit. I have a number of suits, but most of them are cut lower to accommodate proper tanning and wouldn't work for lap swimming. The last thing I want to do is stroke, adjust, stroke, tug, so I put on a ratty old blue tank suit with extragrippy straps and support. I've worn it so many summers that the Lycra has been eaten away in a couple of parts, although it's well lined, so nothing shows. Plus I'm going to be in the water the whole time, and who's going to see me?

I yank my hair back into two rather high pigtails—again, not a look I'd ever, *ever* advocate, but it's the only way I can keep my bangs off my face. I'm about to wash the rest of my eye makeup off, then realize I've spent too much time screwing around with my hair. I figure what didn't already melt off at the gym earlier will rinse clean the second I dive in, so I leave for the pool.

I get to the field house and place everything but my towel and flip-flops in a locker, blindly heading out to the pool. I'd wear my new glasses out there, but I don't want to leave them unattended. They're a gorgeous horn-rim and have little diamonds on the arms, and I'm afraid someone will swipe them. I particularly don't trust the lifeguards who work here, since I've yet to see them guard lives *or* order. They allow way too much horseplay during the open-swim period. Yesterday I saw a group of teenagers trying to drown one another, and the thuggy lifeguard just watched and laughed.

I'm curious; do lifeguards really need to wear cell phones when there's a field-house phone ten paces away? How are any of them going to have time to remove all that stuff if a person needs saving? Aren't they supposed to be in a constant state of readiness? A lifeguard needs a Speedo, whistle, and zinc oxide. (And maybe one of those little orange foot-balls.) They do *not* need a do-rag, elaborately laced basket-ball shoes, multiple necklaces, three layered shirts, and a *pager.* I'm going to be one unhappy camper if I get a cramp and drown because these jokers need to stay in constant touch with their baby-mamas.[162]

I'm waiting at one of the picnic tables for lap swim to begin. A couple of the lifeguards belly flop into the pool. Even with my diminished vision, I can see them thrashing and sputtering along in the water as they stretch the lane dividers from end to end. Wow, we've really got the junior varsity squad playing tonight. I suspect all the good life-guards work the lakefront and these people are just a bunch of guys the parks department found hanging out at a gas sta-tion. Possibly they got hired because they had their own or-ange tank tops embossed with a big white plus sign on the front?

I notice a couple of women sitting at the table next to me, and I see they've got kickboards. "Hi!" I call. "Can you guys tell me where you got those?"

"Ahh, they're right next to you," the younger one says with more than a trace of sarcasm.

Bristling, I look down at my foot, and I'm practically touching a whole bin of them. I'm not even sure how I sat down without tripping over them. Oh. Perhaps the sarcasm was merited.

---

[162]I am sorely tempted to get my own whistle so I can start beaching other patrons. If my hair gets splashed one more time, fists will be thrown.

One of the lifeguards—or possibly the leader of the Crips; who can tell?—blows his whistle, and people begin to jump in. I don't know the protocol for lap swimming, but I assume it's kind of like driving, that being the slower-moving vehicles stay to the right. I imagine I'll be the cement truck on the road, at least at first, so I swan dive at the very far end of the pool.

Hot and muggy, the night is perfect for a swim. The water isn't so cold that it's unpleasant, but it's not so warm that I feel sluggish; I couldn't ask for a more ideal situation. I swim underwater for about fifteen feet and surface. I notice that everyone else is doing the crawl stroke. I much prefer the backstroke because it's easier, but when in Rome . . .

Stroke, stroke, stroke, breathe!

Stroke, stroke, stroke, breathe!

I paddle gracefully, my limbs constantly lengthening. As I kick, I can feel the water ripple from my toes all the way up my thighs, and I know I'm getting more and more toned with every motion. My shoulders, my back, my arms—everything's firming up.

Stroke, stroke, stroke, breathe!

Stroke, stroke, stroke, breathe!

This is glorious! Look at me! I'm a fitness queen! I am inordinately proud of myself. If you'd have told me last winter when I couldn't even climb the stairs without getting winded that I'd easily complete a couple of hours of strenuous activity, I'd have never believed you.

Stroke, stroke, stroke, breathe!

Stroke, stroke, stroke, breathe!

I'm humming along in my lane with my eyes shut, deep in the zone. I feel incredible!

Well, mostly incredible, anyway. My long, firm limbs aren't quite used to this motion yet, but I'm sure it's just a matter of warming up. I'm probably using different muscles than the ones Barbie and I worked on today, so they likely aren't quite as up to speed as the other ones.

Stroke, stroke, stroke, breathe!

Hmm. I extend my legs a bit farther. Shouldn't I be touching the bottom of the pool in the shallow end by now? I've been on this lap quite a while. I've got to be pretty close to the wall on the other side, and honestly, I could use a second or two to catch my breath.

Stroke, stroke, stroke, breathe, pant, breathe, pant.

Oh, my. My muscles are getting a bit *too* toned right now. As a matter of fact, one could say they are . . . tight.

One could also say they are getting warmed up.

To the point of burning.

Stroke, stroke, pant, pant, stroke, burn, gasp.

Shallow end . . . where are you?

I finally leave the zone and open my eyes. I'm a solid mile and a half away from the other side. Wait a minute; those aren't lifeguards stationed around the edges of the pool—they're sorcerers! And they're pissed off that I mocked them, so now they've magically, exponentially lengthened the pool in order to make me have a heart attack and die.

Or maybe I'm not quite as fit as I thought.

I try to take a huge breath and continue, but I end up swallowing a mouthful. I choke and wheeze and try to dig in to no avail. I'm barely moving forward with the crawl stroke. Finally, I flip over and begin to do the backstroke. At least I know I won't sink doing it.

I've huffed and puffed about halfway down the pool when an old man buzzes past me like a speedboat . . . *vroom*! Nice. Now your grandfather moves faster than me.

Since I'm on my back, I can see a whole parade of swimmers cruising past me. This is terrific! What fun! Maybe tomorrow I can go to the prom with my brother. The day after, perhaps I can wear white pants and unexpectedly get my period.

I finally get to the other end and double over trying to catch my breath. This is ridiculous—I already worked out today. There's no reason for me to embarrass myself in this pool. I should just go home now.

But if I get out now, that means I'll have been gone from my house for ten whole minutes. Although Fletch is quite nice to me, there's no way he wouldn't tease me, particularly after the grilling I gave him for pooping out during the group class.

You know what? I've probably got another lap or two in me. I'll swim down and back once or twice more, and then I'll get ready to go home really slowly. That should be enough to keep me from getting mocked.

I stretch again and scrub at my eyes with my palms. There are traces of eyeliner when I look at my hands. My makeup isn't quite rinsing off like I thought. I run my fingers under my lashes and they get covered in mascara flakes. Shoot, my towel's all the way on the other end of the pool—I can't even use it to get off the excess. Argh. Maybe this stuff will come off in this next lap.

Breath caught, at least temporarily, I manage to propel myself to the other end of the pool. All my muscles have turned to stone, and I feel like I'm breathing through a cocktail straw. This trip down, I use a kickboard, and it makes the whole process easier. I'm not sucking nearly as much wind when I get to the shallow end this time. While I'm catching my breath, I notice how many more people have gotten in the pool since I started, and the lanes are getting crowded.

The people here seem to take this whole lap business kind of seriously. Everyone's wearing a bathing cap—no, thank you—and goggles, and many are wearing special racing suits. All week long I've been calling this pool a hidden jewel, but maybe it's not so hidden after all?

On my third and, let's be honest, probably last trip down the lane, I decide to backstroke again. My pace is still kind of poky, so it comes as quite a surprise when I end up hitting the girl who started off half a length in front of me. "Oof!" she cries.

"Sorry! Sorry! I'm so sorry—I didn't think you were anywhere near me," I effuse with one hundred percent sincerity.

Well, almost a hundred percent, anyway. This is the same girl who made me feel dumb for asking about the kickboards.

I flip back over and begin to swim the crawl stroke again, and we both end up in the shallow end at the same time. "Again," I say, as we lean against the edge, "I'm so sorry.

This is my first time doing laps here, and I guess I have bad pool etiquette."

"Yeah," she replies.

"So," I say gamely, my stupid endorphins accidentally making me all happy and nice, "is it usually less crowded during the morning session?"

She looks me up and down before replying, taking in my cosmetically blackened eyes, moth-eaten swimsuit, and crazy pigtails. I am the only person here not in racing suit, cap, and goggles, and I notice her angling away from me. "I wouldn't know. My friend and I don't come here in the morning. We have jobs." And with a larger splash than is necessary, she's off toward the deep end.

On the one hand, this means I've lost enough weight for people to entertain the possibility that I could be homeless. But on the other, *you bitch*.

I look around the pool and notice that the lane next to us is less busy, so I slip under the divider and start another lap. My interaction has left me feeling somewhat energized, and I decide to see if I can't do another lap or two. I try to make conversation with a couple of other people, but I guess my capless, goggleless appearance is foreign and off-putting, and no one really answers me.

Forty-five minutes later, almost everyone else has quit, and I'm among the last to leave the pool when the final whistle blows. Save a quick rest at each end, I've managed to swim the entire time, putting in twenty more laps than I'd originally planned. Each time I'd complete a pass, I'd tell myself, *I can do one more*. And I did.

I round the end of the pool, and with all the chlorine I've gotten in my eyes, my vision is even hazier than usual. But as I approach my towel, I see a very thin person jackknifed over by the other table.

What the . . . ?

As I get closer, I see it's not a person bending over at an odd angle at all. Rather, it's a prosthetic leg, and it appears to belong to the sarcastic girl.

I guess that would explain why she was cranky, and I grudgingly forgive her.

And yet a very petty part of me can't help but think, *Maybe you've got a fancy swim cap and snappy goggles, but since you only have the one leg, I could certainly beat you in an ass-kicking contest.*

Session Twenty-eight

"Since appropriate headgear is apparently so important for fitting in at that pool, next time I'm totally wearing one of those big rubber-daisy caps with a chin strap and possibly a snorkel mask."

"Ha! I love it!" Barbie replies. "All right, that was the last of the pushes. We're going to move on to pulls."

Barbie has really turned my workout up today and forced me to do the worst thing I've ever done here. In pike position, I have to move these two little padded plastic discs all over the floor with my hands, propelling myself with my legs. The discs are almost exactly what I use to scoot my furniture around when I'm rearranging things, so I call this exercise "moving the couch." The problem is, with each set I've worked up too much momentum and I've fallen flat on my stomach at the end. This last time I actually knocked the wind out of myself, and now I'm trying desperately to not vomit grape energy drink. Barbie tries to make me feel better, saying how I'm showing terrific effort. When compliments fail to rally me, she points out how much better I must be at the furniture-mover than the mean girl at the pool.

Oh, yes, she's good.

Barbie picks up her clipboard to see which exercise we're going to do next and then begins to howl.

"What? Do you have more medieval torture moves for me? What's so funny?" I demand.

"Even better. Check out the name of the next move I'm having you do." She's shaking as she gestures with the set list she created after my last workout.

"Which one?"

"Here," she gasps. She points to the top of the list in the third column. "Can you read my writing?"

"Not really," I admit.

Barbie's laughing so hard that she's turned beet red by the time she reads it off to me.

"You won't believe this, but it's called . . . the one-legged swimmer."

I bought regular swim goggles.

So I'm a sheep.

Baa.

I wouldn't have given in to the pool's unofficial lap-swimmer dress code, except my eyes felt like hard-boiled eggs the whole night after I swam. My vision was so blurred, I had to pull the ottoman right next to the TV so I could watch *So You Think You Can Dance*, and even then it was a struggle. I'm still not wearing a bathing cap, though, even though the chlorine has made my hair distinctly more flammable. I keep asking Fletch to not smoke too close to me, fearing perfectly highlighted bonfires.

I'm turning into quite a regular at the pool, and each time I've come, I've been able to add an additional lap before the session ends. I'm still not fast, but I do have better endurance than many of the people here. I've yet to quit before the final whistle, and my breaks between laps are getting shorter and shorter. I'll probably never master the underwater-turnaround-and-keep-swimming dealie the show-offs do, but I'm more than satisfied with my progress. One guy here keeps a little plastic flipbook at the end of his lane to keep track of how many laps he's done. Oh, yeah? Well, I can count to twenty-five in my head, pal.

I'd forgotten what a Zen activity swimming is. With all the other exercise I do, I'm either talking to Barbie, or listening to music on my iPod, or reading a book. The laps give me a chance for reflection. Tonight in the pool I keep replaying the conversation Fletch and I had after my Weight Watchers meeting.

"I'm telling you, by the time I was done, I wanted to punch that smug leader in the throat," I said. *"Encouraging people*

to fear food is just swapping one set of neuroses for another, and it's wrong."

"Consider this, Jen—if you want people to stop a certain behavior, the easiest path to compliance is getting them to fear it," Fletch told me.

"How so?"

"Look at religion—the best way biblical scribes had to get people to not kill each other, steal their neighbors' stuff, or sleep with wives other than their own was to make these societal problems sinful. Think of the animal world—all the stuff I just mentioned, rampant breeding, jockeying for position, survival of the fittest—these instincts are hardwired into us to propagate the species. But then religion came along and got society to fight its natural instincts by overriding them with the fear of God."

I consider what he's said for a moment. *"I guess it worked. Fear is a powerful motivator."*

"Yeah, but look at society today—it's coming apart at the seams. Fear only works if people are afraid."

I'm looking up at the sky, and all I can hear is the gentle *swish-swish* as I slice through the water, yet Fletch's words keep running through my head. I keep thinking about my own fears.

As I paddle along, I slowly become aware that it's been fear keeping me out of this pool for so many years. I never came here before because I was afraid I'd make a fool of myself by not having the endurance to complete a lap. The swimming wasn't what scared me; failure was.

My fear locked me in a state of arrested development for

so many years. Fear kept me from tackling my weight, which I understand has simply been symptomatic of my greater fear, growing up.

I glide down the lane on my back and reflect on how good I feel right now.

It's not because I've lost more than thirty pounds.

I feel incredible because I've stopped being afraid.

TO: AjaXXX
FROM: jen@jenlancaster.com
SUBJECT: Thank you

Hi, AjaXXX,

Thank you for responding to my ad for a biweekly housekeeper on Craigslist. The thing is, we just want REGULAR cleaning service, and not, you know, a topless cleaning service.

I'm way more concerned about getting my shower tiles de-limed than seeing a *n-u-d-e* person trying to figure out how to operate the attachments on my Dyson.

Thank you anyway, and best of luck,

Jen

The N-a-k-e-d Truth

Session Thirty

"Where are you off to?" I'm standing in the living room across from Fletch, holding bottles of Smartwater and Ripped to the Max energy supplement,[163] and my hair's yanked back in a do-rag and ponytail. I've got on my black Gojira shorts and a pink T, and I'm wearing sneakers and thick socks.

"I'm going out to sell Girl Scout cookies. If I don't meet my Samoa quota, they're busting me back down to Brownie."

Nonplussed, he replies, "I meant that as a greeting," and he returns his attention to his laptop.

"Sho' nuff." I lean over to give him a kiss.

---

[163]Orange-death flavored!

He looks suspicious. "Why are you in such a good mood?"

"I have every reason to be happy. The humidity finally broke, it's a gorgeous day, and I feel terrific. I'm not even dreading going to my training session one iota. . . . I might *even* be looking forward to it. Progress, right? Remember when I first started and I'd celebrate every time I came home because it meant I didn't have to go back for two days?"

"No, and I don't remember you moaning and wailing. At all. For hours on end. For weeks."

"*Ha!* You're hilarious. Not." I notice that Fletch is firmly entrenched on the couch with work stuff spread from end to end. "Are you going to the office at all today?"

"Everyone's on vacation, so there's no reason for me to go downtown."

"Cool. Then I'm taking your car to the gym."

"Don't get it all sweaty."

"Saying it like that just makes me want to get it extra-sweaty."

"See you later."

I get into the car, crack the sunroof, roll down the windows, and crank Guns n' Roses. I cruise down the expressway looking and sounding completely cool . . . I mean, if it were twenty years ago or anyone gave a shit about *Appetite for Destruction* anymore. I'm broadcasting an old-Adam-Sandler-cranking-Billy-Squire-at-the-high-school-in-*Billy-Madison* vibe, but I don't care. Welcome to the jungle, fellow motorists! You can taste my *Bright Lights*, but you won't get them for free.[164] I'm barely two songs into the CD when I get to the gym. Oh, well; there's always the ride home.

I stash my stuff in a locker and wait by the front desk for Barbie. Mike, the West Loop Gym's manager and resident powerlifter, is standing with his back turned to me, watching a segment on *Jerry Springer*. Poor Jerry. I know he's making scads of money and has a really cushy life, but I wonder if he ever wants to shout at his assembled band of idiots, *I used to be the mayor, damn it!*[165]

While I ponder, Mike turns around and notices me. "Hey, you're here!"

"I'm here!" I reply heartily. "And so are you!"

Mike picks up a clipboard. "No, I mean, I'm training you today. Barbie's out of town. Didn't she tell you?"

I wait for my heart to stop dropping all the way to my feet before I answer. "No. I was . . . unaware." Had I been informed that Mike was training me, I'd have concocted an excuse to not come, like the couple of other times Barbie's been unavailable. Although he's friendly to the point of charming, Mike has trained Fletch before, and every single time, he pushed Fletch so hard he barfed. I want to exercise and feel good. I don't want to exercise and revisit my lunch. "It's probably too late for me to run away screaming like a little girl, isn't it?"

"Ah, come on. We'll have fun! It's good for you to swap up trainers every once in a while. We all do things differently,

---

[164]But you can get them at your favorite bookseller for $14 US.

[165]If Mayor Daley ever gets his own talk show, I'm totally watching it.

so we'll probably hit some muscles today you haven't hit in a while." He begins to walk back to the training room, while I stay firmly planted.

"You're going to hurt me."

"I won't *hurt* you. I *will* make sure you're working hard."

"Which equals deep hurting."

"My job is to push you outside of your comfort zone, and that's what we'll do today. Come on."

"If I barf in the car, Fletch is going to divorce me." Oh, no. I'm not moving from this spot.

"We won't go that far," he promises me. His expression is so sincere, I almost believe him.

"Please understand—part of my training process entails quite a bit of complaining."

"I hear you swear a lot, too."

"Yes, but not *at* you. About you, later, though. Count on that." He motions toward the training room with his clipboard, and, grudgingly, I fall in step behind him.

"Hey, what's the worst that could happen?" he asks.

Good thing I'm over that being-afraid business. If I weren't, those would be some scary final words.

"I didn't even hear you come in." Fletch is in the bedroom changing into his own gym clothes.

"That's because it took me ten minutes to get from the garage to the house."

"Why?"

"Turn around and take a look at me." There's not an inch

of my shirt that isn't soaked, and at some point in the last hour, I cried every bit of my eye makeup off. I tear off my sodden top and collapse on the bed. "Am dead now. Blerg."

"Whoa. Barbie have you do something new today? Usually you're so energized when you get home, I can't stand you." Fletch begins to pack his gym bag.

"Barbie wasn't there today. She had me train with Mike. And she didn't tell me beforehand because she knew I'd ditch. You know what it was like? It was like thinking I was heading to a surprise party and instead it was a surprise pap smear. Plus, right now, I'm a nine point five on the vomometer."

"The what?"

"The about-to-vomit thermometer."

Fletch looks stricken. "The car's OK, right?"

"The car is fine. I, on the other hand, have completely lost the use of my legs. That bastard had me step up on this really tall box eighty times. And then he had me do a sitting motion with a medicine ball another eighty times. Do you realize that's eighty lunges and eighty squats? I believe that's illegal in the continental U.S. My quadriceps are completely gone. I'm going to have to go on eBay to search for another pair. Don't even start me on how many crunches I did, either. And look at this." I hold up my almost-full bottle of Smartwater. "Normally I finish the whole thirty-three ounces in the course of a session, but Mike only let me take a break for about a second each time. When you get to the gym, I would like you to punch him right in the junk."

"Yeah, I'm not going to do that."

"Are you sure? It would mean a lot to me."

"You're not getting any sympathy here. If you didn't throw up working out with Mike, then he was holding back. He could have worked you harder."

"The second I can lift myself from this bed, I'm going right out to the garage to eat a sandwich in your car. And then I'm going to leave a bunch of sweaty ass-prints all over the hood."

"I'm going to finish up my project, and then I'm going to the gym." Fletch leaves the bedroom and trots down the stairs.

"You think you're so cool just because you can walk!" I shout. I lie on the bed for a few minutes before I realize I'm absolutely ravenous. I need to eat something right this second. I manage to lean on the dog and nightstand enough to elevate myself. I stagger over to the stairs and attempt to take a step down. My right thigh responds by telling me, *No fucking way.* I lift the other leg, and Lefty expresses the same sentiment. I try again on both sides and finally am forced to turn around and back down the stairs on my hands and shu-nu-nu-nu-nu-nu-nu knees, knees.

I'll tell you one thing—the next time I see Barbie, I'm giving her a present.

Maybe she'd like a nice Guns n' Roses CD?

Session Thirty-four
"Today we're doing a circuit!"

Barbie bounces out from behind the reception desk. This

is a troubling development. Barbie's enthusiasm is directly proportionate to my workout's level of difficulty.

"Explain 'circuit,'" I say.

"I'm going to have you work through a set of exercises, and once you're done, you're going to go through them again." Barbie doesn't make eye contact when she says this.

"Isn't that what we do every time?"

"Yeah . . . ," she hedges.

"What aren't you telling me?"

"You usually do a total of nine exercises . . . so today isn't *really* different."

I notice she's holding a stopwatch. "And what's that for? Have you got a burrito in the microwave?"

"Um, instead of doing three sets of three, we're going to do all nine in a row."

"You neatly avoided answering the question. The watch is for what?"

"I'm going to time you."

OK, having *strongs* is one thing. Having my *strongs* timed? Not so much. "*And*?"

"And we're going to see how many circuits you can do in an hour."

"How many of these do you anticipate my doing?"

"Um . . . why don't we start and we'll find out together?"

"I don't get a vote here, do I?" She gives me a huge grin and dances into the training room. Against my better judgment, I follow.

Four and a half.

I make it through four and a half circuits. It would have been more like five except we have to modify a couple of the lunging-jumping sets when my left knee begins to howl.

The whole time I'm doing my circuits, a couple of skinny girls work out with weights on the periphery of the training room. Every time I grunt or complain, I keep thinking they're giving each other a *look*. I recognize this look—it's a mixture of pity and contempt. I've gotten it many times over the past few years when I've put cake in my shopping cart or knocked over someone's wine with my butt. Why are women always giving anyone heavier than them the evil eye? Is it to ward off contagious fat? Whatever, it pisses me off.

I decide not to yell at them. Instead, I pledge to work harder. And I do.

"You did such a good job!" Barbie congratulates me at our conclusion.

"Thank you. I worked my ass off today." Did those girls just smirk at me? I pretend to ignore them but watch as they finish their strength training and hop on adjacent treadmills.

"See you Friday?" Barbie asks.

"Yeah, but . . . I'm not done yet. I feel a little tight, so I'm going to loosen up on the treadmill." Barbie squeals with delight and attempts to hug me. "Oh, honey, no. You don't want a piece of this right now." My shirt is soaked with sweat all the way down past my bra.

"All right! Keep it up!" She trots off to her desk in the office on the other side of the gym.

I mount the treadmill and begin at a slow pace. I haven't walked on it for a while because I've been so busy swimming and training. I input my usual speed and incline, and the conveyor belt begins to roll. Did I always move this slowly? It's like I'm keeping pace with someone's grandmother. Using a walker. Tipped with tennis balls.

OK, this is *way* too easy. This machine must be broken, because I was never this slow. I hop off and decide to grab a drink before I switch over. I can feel the two girls' eyes on my back as I walk to the water cooler. When I turn around, I smile beatifically at them. *Oh, no, bitches. I'm not quitting. I'm just getting on a different treadmill.*

I select the same numbers on the second machine, and it's still easy. How about *that*? My speed is not a fluke; it's *me*.

I coast along for a few minutes, realizing I can continue to go faster and higher. I peek at the numbers the two girls selected and reset my input accordingly. I have a ton of stuff to do today, but I rationalize that if I can do more at the gym, I should.

All right, that's a lie.

I want to outlast the smirking girls. I don't care how long they stay on their treadmills, because *I will be here longer.*

Fueled by contempt, I kick the digits up another notch and begin a slow jog. I pound the treadmill for thirty-six minutes until the two bitchy girls hop off their machines.

Winnah! Victory! I beat your asses, bitches!

I'm gloating when I notice the girls begin to walk over to me. Oh, great, I'm going to get into a fight here? What am I, forty?

"Excuse me," the first one says.

"What?" I bark.

"Are you . . . Jen Lancaster?"

I narrow my eyes. "Yeah. Why?"

"I told you it was her," the second one says. "We just wanted to tell you we saw you talk at Printer's Row and that you look really great. How much weight have you lost?"

"Um . . . quite a bit," I stammer.

"Well, keep it up!" says Number One.

Number Two adds, "We can't wait to read your next book!" They walk away toward the locker room.

Argh. I'm down forty pounds, but I've yet to lose what makes me a big ass.

Jen's Life Lesson #1985: If I stop looking for fights, I'll probably stop finding them.

I've logged three hours of sweat-inducing housework when I realize I don't have any cash to pay the lady from the cleaning service when she comes tomorrow morning.[166]

As an aside, I absolutely understand exactly how clichéd it is to sweep and scrub the night before the professionals arrive. I'm not doing this because I'm neurotic.[167] I want the cleaning lady to be able to actually get to the stuff that needs cleaning, rather than moving all our detritus around for two hours until she gets to a clear surface. I feel obligated to help,

---

[166]I'm starting to get busy writing and I can't keep up with the housework.

[167]In this particular instance.

since making this place sanitary is no easy task given the seven fur-losing, hairball-barfing, happily whizzing-on-the-floor mammals living in this house. (I'm counting Fletch in that sum.)

Maybe I *am* neurotic in not wanting the maid service to think we're completely vile, dirty people. Plus, Fletch engaged in his quarterly "manscaping" this week, and even though he says he cleaned up afterward, the master bath still looks like the floor of the barbershop on the first day of army boot camp. No one not married to him should have to deal with this. Or possibly I'm running around with a Swiffer mop and a can of Pledge because I'm cheap and don't want to pay for more than three hours of Magnificent Maids' time. Yes, sounds more like it. FYI? My pride costs exactly $20 per hour.

"How much money do you have?" I call down the stairs to Fletch, who's watching *Fargo* for the hundredth time and eating Wheat Thins. Another wild Friday night at our place. . . . Man, when did we get so lame? Shouldn't we be drunk or *b-u-s-y* at this point, possibly both? Barring that, at least I should be doing something other than vacuuming Fletch's shorn back hair off the faucets. Yet I'm content. Huh.

"Why?" he answers.

"Because I'm running off to join a cult, and I need to buy a track suit and some Nikes," I yell.

I can hear him munching on the Wheat Thins from the second floor. "OK. Eight dollars enough?"

"Nope, I'll never catch a ride on Hale-Bopp with less

than ten bucks in my pocket. I'm going out to get some cash. Come with me?"

"No, thanks. I'm just about to the point where William H. Macy has his meltdown when Marge comes to interview him." In his best Brainerd accent, he says, "*'I told ya! We haven't had any vehicles go missing!'* I'd rather stay here. And why are you venturing out now? It's midnight. Go tomorrow."

To assuage my bourgeois guilt over paying someone to do housework, I hired the cheapest possible provider.[168] When I researched companies, I couldn't believe how much some places charged. Shoot; I'll happily clean *your* apartment for seventy bucks an hour. Call me! I do windows! Then again, when I placed an ad for biweekly housekeeping services on Craigslist, the only folks who responded were offering erotic housekeeping, so my choices were limited.

Magnificent Maids, the place I finally settled on, does an efficient, fully clothed job, but the problem is, their concept of time is fluid. No matter when I schedule them, they show up at least half an hour early. If I plan on them being here at two, they're ringing my bell at one thirty. I keep telling them, if they need to be early, no problem, we'll just schedule them earlier, but please let me know in advance so I can make sure the dogs and cats are all squared away. (And also so I'm not still asleep when they arrive, because then I *really* feel guilty.) Tomorrow they're supposed to come at eleven, so I'm going to be up by nine thirty, just to be sure.

---

[168]See again *"$20: My Pride."*

"I don't want to be obligated to dash out of here in the morning to get money. And if I don't go now, I'll probably forget anyway. No big deal." I grab my purse and keys and open the door. "If I'm not back in seven minutes, avenge my death."

From his horizontal position on the couch, he says, "Sure; you betcha."

I close the heavy oak door behind me and double-lock it. The second I enter the yard, our security lights flash on, flooding the whole neighborhood with light. It's so bright, we could perform surgery out here. Or at least play a televised major league baseball night game.

I cut through the yard and notice that at some point this evening, a ginormous spider web cropped up in front of the door to the garage. I smile and recall that old Far Side cartoon where a couple of industrious spiders build a web at the bottom of a playground slide and one says to the other *"If we pull this off, we'll eat like kings."* I gently nudge the web aside with the end of a pooper-scooper—better luck next time, little guys—and I'm on my way.

I could go to the Amoco right down the block and use their ATM, but it's after midnight and my defenses are down. Their food shop stocks every variety of Dolly Madison and Hostess product, and I don't want to be left alone with them and a handful of twenties, still warm from the machine. I have willpower now, but there's no reason to force myself to confront temptation.

Also, the gas station is skeevy.

I drive down Elston Ave to the Harris Bank branch by

Kohl's. A new building is coming in between the store and the bank, and it's wrapped in a giant green construction canvas. Completely innocuous in the daylight, after midnight it looks cavernous and foreboding. The entrance to the bank is temporarily altered due to the construction, and to get to the ATMs, I have to drive down a narrow path and circle back in the darkened parking lot.

As I slowly swing around, out of the corner of my eye I see something out of place in the shadows just on the other side of the ATMs. I look closer and see two women sitting huddled together with their sweatshirt hoods pulled up, faces tense, clutching backpacks to their sides.

Back when I worked retail, it wasn't all selling prom dresses, swiping ice cream, and spitting out brownies. I learned an awful lot about how shoplifters behave. A normal shopper comes into the store and looks at the merchandise. Shoppers pay attention to sale signs and fancy displays of banana clips and artfully stacked sweater pyramids they insist on pawing through, even though *all of them are exactly the same size and color, and please stop unfolding every single freaking crewneck, for the love of God!*[169]

Even if shoppers acknowledge the clerk with a "just looking, thanks," the one thing they don't do is make eye contact, because there's no reason to—why look at the clerk when there are *three* racks of bathing suits to inspect? And sundresses on the clearance rack? Plus, accidentally make eye contact with the clerk, and he or she will go into sales mode.

---

[169] A rant for another day.

Suddenly you can't get away because you're trying to be polite and there's a likelihood you'll find yourself talked into a pair of stirrup pants or an acid-washed denim vest.[170] Shoplifters, on the other hand, watch the clerk's eyes and avert their own when the clerk looks back.

The two women in the hooded sweatshirts are doing exactly this.

In the four seconds it takes me to drive past them and up to the ATM, thoughts race through my head. *Why are they in this parking lot? Why are they sitting in the dark? What's in their backpacks? Why are they clutching them like that instead of wearing them on their backs? How come they look nervous? And, since it's still almost eighty degrees outside with a zillion percent humidity, what the fuck is up with the hoods?*

I pull directly through the ATM, and when I pass the support post the hooded two were hiding behind, they're both on their feet and are lingering an arm's length from my window, right on the other side of the pole.

Our eyes meet again and I give them both a jaunty single-fingered wave. I step on the gas and the car explodes out of the ATM lane like a shot. I drive away like I'm making an escape, even though they didn't actually threaten me.

Then again, I wasn't about to give them the chance.

As I head to a different ATM in a more well-lit area, I dial 911.

"Chicago Police. What's your emergency?"

"Hi. I'm at the corner of Webster and Elston and I'm just

---

[170]That is, if you walked into Ups 'N Downs. In 1987.

leaving the Harris Bank branch. I'm calling to report suspicious behavior."

"Suspicious behavior? What kind?"

"Um, technically this isn't an emergency and I don't want to waste your time on a call." Shouldn't there be 611 for stuff that's important but not life threatening? "I just encountered something odd and I wanted to make you aware of the situation." I briefly explain my experience to the highly disinterested dispatcher.

"Did anything transgress?"

"Well, no. But it seemed suspicious, and I thought you'd want to know before it turns into a problem."

"Can you describe the people you saw?"

"Yes, there were two kids—"

"Kids? How old?"

"I'm sorry, not *children* kids, but young, maybe late teens or early twenties." The older I get, the more likely I am to call anyone younger than me "kids," but I feel the dispatcher will not be enlightened with this angst-ridden ode to my fleeting thirties, so I spare her. "One Caucasian female with a dirty blond ponytail hanging out the side of her hood and one girl with dark, curly hair. I can't tell ethnicity on the second gal. Actually, I couldn't see much of their faces because they were obscured by the hoods they're wearing."

I do not add "on this sweltering-hot evening" because it's patently obvious.

"They're *women*?" The dispatcher sounds incredulous.

"Right."

"So you want to report . . . what?"

I'm sorry, do chicks never break the law? If that's true, then why do they have women's prisons? Just to add sexy scenes to B movies? And how do you explain Bonnie Parker? And that woman Charlize Theron got all ugly to play?

Even if these girls are completely guileless, sitting in the dark right where a speeding car could swerve and run over their feet seems like a terrible idea. Maybe my call won't prevent a robbery or carjacking. Maybe I'm just keeping two stupid girls from walking with a limp for the next three months. Or maybe I'm paranoid. I readily admit that the camera on my cell phone is completely full of photos I take of bad drivers' license plates.

Further, I understand the police have a whole bunch of real crimes to pursue, and I don't want to give the dispatcher a hard time, because she works one of the most stressful jobs in the world. I'll guarantee you she has better things to do than deal with a highly strung yuppie tooling around in a snappy car she probably doesn't deserve.

Yet the fact remains, there were more than thirty-two thousand robberies and aggravated assaults in the city of Chicago last year.[171]

Stunned, I reply, "I guess I thought two homeless-looking teenagers crouching in the dark by an isolated ATM, masking their identities with sweatshirts on a hot summer night, *might just be cause for concern*."

"Oh." There's a long pause. "We'll send a cruiser by. Elston and Webster?"

---

[171]According to FBI.gov. Hey! Look at this! A real footnote. I rule!

"Yep. Thank you." I snap my phone shut and shove it back in my purse. I get to the light at Webster and Ashland, and there are two cars idling in front of me side by side, having a conversation through their open windows. Even though the light's green and there's plenty of room to pull over, the drivers chat with each other well into the next red light. I honk and shout and seethe and am completely ignored. I may or may not shake my fists, and it's possible I point angry fingers at them in a threatening manner.

After I get cash, I'm driving down Clybourn, and a bunch of drunk girls stagger into the street, waving their arms like crazy and yelling "Taxi!" I look around to make sure I'm not in the way of a speeding cab and realize I'm the only car for a couple of blocks. They're yelling "Taxi!" at me.

Did I just get *hailed*?

And as I round the bend to get home, I see an old-school VW bus stuffed full of people and weaving all over the road in front of me, almost clipping off the side mirrors of three separate autos on Fullerton. I slow down to ten miles an hour and give them a wide berth. I flip open my phone again, trying to decide whether I should call the police or take a photo. I wonder whether it wouldn't have been useful just to stay on the line with the 911 dispatcher so I could narrate my entire trip to the cash machine.

As I pull down the alley and click to open the garage door, a thought strikes me like a van full of hipsters hopped up on Fat Tire Ale and self-loathing. . . .

I don't belong in the city anymore.

Don't misunderstand me—I believe Chicago is the greatest

place in the world. For the rest of my life and no matter where on the globe I might find myself living, I'll proudly tell anyone who asks that I'm from the Windy City, damn it. When Fletch and I were unemployed, the reason I struggled so hard to stay afloat was because I couldn't bear the idea of being away from here. I was so afraid that if we left, even temporarily, we'd never find our way back. After ten full years, I still can't look at the skyline without losing my breath for a minute. Stand in the bar on the ninety-sixth floor of the Hancock building and soak in Chicago's majesty, and I guarantee you'll go weak in the knees. Carl Sandburg was right—this City of the Big Shoulders, my city, is proud to be alive, and it's strong and coarse and brutal.

But everything I love about this city, everything that makes it so unique and exciting, is also *causing me to be a raving bitch.*

I think if I'm going to finally embrace this whole being-a-grown-up business, I have to give up my hackneyed notion of being a hip urbanite. I've always enjoyed my smug sense of superiority when telling people, no, I don't live in the *Chicago area*, I live in *Chicago*. But who cares if I sound cool to some asshole on a plane I'm never going to see again? At this point in my life, I'd rather be uncool and have a lawn requiring more than a set of household scissors to trim.

Come to think of it, I want to go to a grocery store where the meat isn't either brown or $34 per pound.

I want to open a window without burglar bars on it because it doesn't *need* burglar bars.

I'd like to have a barbecue and not have to tell guests to

tuck their pant legs into their socks due to the nightly Running of the Rats.

I want to drive five miles and have it take five minutes.

I want to stop flushing thousands of dollars down the toilet every year in rent and own a home.

I've been so frustrated because I want Chicago to be all these things. If it were, then it would be Mayberry, not Chicago. Maybe part of my process of growing up is realizing the futility of trying to force everyone in the city to change to suit my needs. I can't make cashiers be polite. I can't force the homeless to stop trying to wash my windshield with spit and old newspaper. I can't keep sending anonymous letters to my neighbors hoping my clever words will finally make them care enough to replace their garbage-bag-covered windows with panes of glass. What's that definition of insanity? When you keep doing the exact same thing and expect different results? Because that's the hamster wheel I've been on for the past few years.

The only change I can control—the only difference I can make that isn't insane—is to modify my own circumstances. If garbage in the street makes me crazy and it won't go away no matter how many times I pick it up, I need to live somewhere clean. If I get apoplectic when there's noise, I should be somewhere quiet.

The solution is so simple.

I pull into my garage. Waiting 'til everything's locked and lit, I get out of the car and walk into the house.

"Hey, dere!" Fletch greets me with a mouthful of crackers. Little particles fly out, which means I'm going to have to vacuum the living room again tonight, too. "Where were you? You were gone a while. Anything exciting happen?"

"Sure, you could say so. I was almost carjacked. . . . I practically got into a fistfight at a stoplight. . . . I nearly ran over some stupid girls who thought I was a taxi. . . . Oh, and I didn't get killed by a VW bus full of drunk hipsters, but only because I was paying attention."

Swallowing hard, Fletch looks at me, dumbfounded. "The heckya mean?"

"I mean maybe next time you should come with me." I begin to walk up the stairs to grab the vacuum, but when I reach the landing, I remember the most important point. "By the way? You win. I give in. Uncle. We move to the suburbs next spring."

There's a pregnant pause, and right before I get to the bedroom, I hear Fletch say, "Real good, then."

Bang! Bang! Bang!

I wake up to some sort of strange noise outside. I squint at the clock to see what time it is. It's 8:48 a.m., which means I've been asleep for only four hours.

Bang! Bang! Bang!

Fletch and I went to bed really late because we were busy making plans for next year. The more we talk about moving out of Chicago, the more sense it makes. We won't go far; we want to be close enough to take advantage of everything the city offers without feeling like we're missing out but far enough that the rats can't follow us.

Bang! Bang! Bang!

What the hell *is* that?

Bang! Bang! Bang!

Groggily, I peek out the window and see a woman in a babushka with a bucket pounding on our front door. Huh. Apparently the cleaning service is two hours and twelve minutes early, a new record.

Suddenly I'm way less bothered by the idea of a topless maid. As long as she's wearing a watch, I'll be happy.

Session Thirty-five

Deep in the throes of a summer cold, I'm coughing and sniffling all over the place. And I spent the morning sneezing on my computer monitor, so now I need Kleenex *and* Windex.

I had to miss a couple of training sessions earlier this week because I was too under the weather. I used the time to work on my manuscript, marveling about having gotten to the point where I'd rather work out than write. I'm really excited to be back in the training room right now and am trying to keep my nose-blowing breaks to a minimum.

We're catching up on our week when Barbie says, "Everyone's been kind of out of it. I've had half a dozen cancellations. One of my clients came in this morning, and he was so tired and sore, he asked if we could just spend the hour doing some stretching."

I'm on a stability ball, hands hooked behind my ears, in the middle of doing what I call "Captain Crunches." "Whoa.

Stop right there. You're telling me a client asked you to take it easy on him *and you did?* Are you kidding me? What the fuck? I've asked—no, begged and pleaded—for you ten thousand times to take it easier on me, and you never, ever have. Why did this guy get a free pass and I never did?"

"He's one of my older clients and he legitimately needed a break." Barbie smiles and shrugs. "With you? Never. Because I knew you could do it."

Who'd have guessed she was right?

After my session, I'm home and showered. When I dress, I choose the khaki shorts I've practically worn out this summer. They're a couple of sizes too big, but I like them and they look cute. The interior plastic button popped the first time I wore them because they were too tight, so now each time I put them on, it feels like a huge victory. I zip them and do up the two metal snaps. Nice and roomy!

I'm supposed to be working on my manuscript, but I keep procrastinating. I decide I can't *possibly* start writing until Angie and I have chatted. We talk for about an hour, and then I realize I can't *possibly* do any work until I have a venti iced latte[172] running through my system. I grab my purse[173] and head to the Starbucks in Target. Besides, I need more Kleenex and maybe some throat lozenges, so it's not a wasted trip.

I place my drink order at the counter and am waiting for the baristas to make it when an old Mexican grandmother

---

[172] Made with two-percent milk, it's only four Weight Watchers points.

[173] The same one—I *told* you I'd carry it forever.

begins to cry, "*Mira! Mira!* Look!" She bends over and picks up a praying mantis that's somehow found its way into the store. Everyone watches as she holds the bug up and shows her granddaughter, and then the security guard. I'm not grossed out because I find praying mantises fascinating and I wonder how he ended up here. I don't think Target is their natural habitat.

I scan my internal database, trying to remember what other information I have on praying mantises. I know they eat roaches and gnats, and as I take in the overflowing garbage cans in the food court area, I suspect that's the answer to my *Why here?* question. I once read that they hiss, pinch, and bite when pissed off, which is probably why I like them. We're kindred spirits.

Aren't they a protected species, too? I vaguely recall a story once about a family keeping one as an exotic pet somewhere Asia-y. Aren't they supposed to be good luck? Or, like, a good sign? One time I was visiting my brother and sister-in-law and their kids and I spotted a praying mantis on their front porch. I warned my niece and nephews to leave it alone because it was a "good" kind of bug. Then I tried to nudge a soccer ball out of the way so one of the kids didn't inadvertently kick it into the mantis and I accidentally did just that. The sickening crunch could be heard all the way to the mailbox, and I felt so bad. Not long after, I got laid off.

While I ponder the coincidence of the gruesome mantis death and the end of my career in corporate communications, my sinuses and throat begin to tingle and I can feel a massive sneeze coming on, and . . . *a-choo*! The force of my sneeze causes me to bend over so quickly, the paltry little snaps on my shorts give out and the zipper flies open.

It takes me a second to realize why there's a breeze where thick cotton khaki should be. Or once was.

Apparently my pants, without the benefit of the excess rolls of fat, and due to the laws of gravity, have fallen down.

Me.

Pants.

Off.

In the middle of goddamned Target.

Daytime talk shows often feature these grizzled old topless dancers telling their stories about having fallen into a life of stripping accidentally. I figured they were full of shit, not ever realizing, until this moment, that it's possible to unintentionally strip. Good thing I don't have on that stupid racer-back bra or impossible-to-keep-buttoned madras-plaid shirt, or I'd really be in trouble. I mean, one minute I'd be all queued up for a latte, and one sneeze later, I'd be guilty of public indecency. Me, the person who has trouble even saying *n-a-k-e-d*. The gal who locks the bathroom door even when she's home alone. The chick who never once skinny-dipped in her pool in the twenty-seven years her parents owned that home.

So here I am, standing with my shorts about midthigh and my baggy striped underwear waving hello to all the fellow coffee lovers.

And not a single person notices.

Thank God everyone's attention is focused on Abuela Entomology and no one sees me with my pants down, nor do they see me yanking my shorts back up. One knobby green bug just saved me from never being able to walk into that Target again.

Two things to note here: (1) from now on, I'm definitely counting the praying mantis as a good-luck charm, and (2) it's time to buy smaller pants.

I'm speed walking to the park in order to arrive before lap swim begins. When I got in my car a few minutes ago, I noticed our street was blocked with construction. Fletch isn't home and I don't want to miss or delay my workout, especially since I'm going to Stacey's house later. The park isn't far, so the easiest thing to do is walk.

The streets are still so smoldering from the day that my Crocs go a bit soft, almost like they're melting into it. That water's going to feel extranice tonight. Because it's so warm, I've forgone my usual T-shirt over my bathing suit. This is the first time I've left my house sans sleeves since the nineties. What liberation! I have abdicated wearing shirts! (At least for the next hour.) I've also got on a pair of mesh gym shorts, I'm wearing goggles around my neck, and my towel is looped around my shoulders, so you can't really see my naked shoulders, but they are indeed bare.

I cut through the playground and I'm getting close to the field house at the pool when I hear someone behind me. "Hey! Hey! Hey, lady!" I stop in my tracks, spin around, and come face-to-top-of-the-head with a small woman dressed in a dirty-tennis-ball yellow tank top.

"I'm sorry, were you talking to me?" I ask, an eye toward the pool. The lifeguards are going to open it up for lap swim any minute now, and I want to make sure I'm ready to go when they do. Last night I made it up to twenty-nine laps in the allotted time, and I'm dying to see if I can do thirty tonight.

"Yes, lady. I want to tell you I . . . like your towel." I peer at this woman, taking in her wild eyes, filthy hair, and the tiny red bull's-eyes all over her spindly arms, shoulders, and legs. She's heroin chic, minus the chic.

"You like my towel? You stopped me because you were desperate to tell me you like *this*?" I hold up the battered piece of terrycloth. My mom bought this towel in South Carolina ten years ago. White and now almost threadbare, the towel sports a faded blue dolphin and the words MYRTLE BEACH stitched onto the end. The only reason I'm using it is that all my other beach towels are dirty because I've been swimming so often. I had to dig it out of the top of my closet and fend off Fletch's attempt to turn it into a car-polishing rag.

"Yeah . . . it's nice." Although it's broiling out here, the woman is shivering and clutching her elbows.[174]

"Quick question—is there any chance you might be moving to Wheaton in the next year or two?"

She looks confused. "Um . . . no?"

"How about Saint Charles?"

"Where?"

....

[174]Comin' down, man.

"Geneva? Batavia? North Aurora, home of the new mall that features a Kate Spade outlet store?"[175]

Now she's shivering and confused. "Kate who?"

"Tell me, do you have family out in the western suburbs you might visit, say, in downtown Naperville or one of the surrounding lower-cost subdivisions? Maybe whichever one is filled with starter homes?"

"What?"

"Glen Ellyn? Downers Grove? Lisle?" She shakes her head in response to my rapid-fire line of questioning. "All right then; sounds like you're not going to be my neighbor anytime soon, so let's cut to the chase here."

"OK?"

I take a deep breath and begin my assault, pointing a still-somewhat-plump finger. "You didn't stop me because you like my towel. You stopped me because you want me to give you something for no other reason than the fact you're standing there. Number one, I'm not giving you a dime so you can continue slowly killing yourself, and number two, even if I were to take pity on you—which I'm not—I'm wearing a bathing suit and running shorts. Where exactly do you think I'd be storing my Money for Junkies fund? In the coin purse up my ass?"

"No, I . . . I . . . ," she stammers.

A bead of sweat rolls off my forehead, down the side of my face, and into my cleavage. Yuck. "Listen, you: I'm

---

[175] I did not buy a new purse there, but it's nice to know there's a discount option.

hot, I want to swim, and if there's no chance you're going to be living next door, I'm not obligated to try and be nice to you. This newfound-maturity thing? Even I have my limits. This conversation is going to end with me giving you exactly nothing except for the advice that you grow up and start taking care of yourself. OK? Bye!" I hear the whistle blow, and I sprint to the locker room in the field house.

I throw my old glasses and shorts into a locker and dash out to the pool. When I get there, I see a small tennis-ball-colored blob on the other side of the fence. "Hey, lady!" the blob calls. "Lady! Hey! You're a . . . you're a fat bitch!"

I study my reflection in the clear blue water beneath me. Despite all this dieting and working out, I'm not yet thin. As a matter of fact, many parts of me are still pretty thick. My arms could be smaller, my legs more toned, and my stomach less bloat-y. There's no longer an ass-teau behind me, yet I'm not even close to having a shapely little melon butt. My cheeks are round, and my wrists are far from dainty.

But I can carry laundry up two flights of stairs, and I can run for the phone or on a treadmill.

I don't sweat when I eat anymore, and when I do eat, it's not cookies for dinner.

My blood pressure is now normal, my cholesterol is out of the danger zone, and I don't even have to take Ambien, because obesity no longer causes my insomnia. And my doctor doesn't hand me a death sentence when I walk in her door anymore.

I laugh in the direction of the fence and adjust my swim goggles before replying, "No, honey. I'm a *fit* bitch. You don't know it, but there's an ocean of difference."

And then I dive in.

By the Numbers

Pairs of Crocs purchased:
5 (shut up, Angie)

Magazines that recognized Angie's brilliance and hired her to write for them:
1

Atkins diet attempts:
8

Atkins diet failures:
8 (awful)

Flying squirrels caught by University Pest Control:
0

Rats mistaken for flying squirrels caught by University Pest Control:
6

Episodes of Top Chef, Top Design, *and* Project Runway
watched with Stacey:
>>> All but one (I think)

Total times Vanilla Ice played on iPod at gym:
>>> 32 (shameful)

Total personal training sessions:
>>> 40 (and counting!)

Murderous thoughts had toward personal trainer:
>>> Too many to count (but not now!)

Sizes dropped:
>>> 4 (and counting!)

Total times dialed 911:
>>> Far too many to ever run for public office

Television interviews prepared for:
>>> Thousands

Television interviews conducted:
>>> 2 (v. impressive!)

Barbies accidentally ordered while high on Ambien:
>>> 11

Barbies given to friends' children:
>>> 10 (am keeping the head)

Friends who will brave our dogs and come to our house:
>>> 2 (my good buddy Shayla moved to
>>> Minneapolis)

Barky neighbor dogs who disappeared under mysterious circumstances:
>1 (I had nothing to do with it, I promise)

Author friends mentioned in book:
>4

Mentions of own books available from fine, fine booksellers everywhere:
>Countless

Total book proposals sold:
>1

Total book titles changed because original title idea linked to a fat-girl fetish site:
>1 *(y-i-k-e-s)*

Total blatant Bridget Jones–*style final chapter rip-offs:*
>1

Total pounds gained while writing this book:
>0 (that's right, bitches!)

Total pounds gained while editing *this book and being too busy to get to the gym and train:*
>12 (oh, dear)

E·P·I·L·O·G·U·E

TO: angie_at_home
FROM: jen@jenlancaster.com
SUBJECT: Uh-oh
DATE: October 17, 2007

Ang,

I accidentally turned Barbie on to the show *The Biggest Loser*, and she's totally been inspired by bad-ass trainer Jillian's policy of "beatings, beatings, beatings, and more beatings."

Now that I'm finally done editing this book, Barbie says it's time to get serious. She's making me come to the gym and train five days a week until we get these twelve pounds off. I just got an e-mail from her, and her closing line was, "Bitch Barbie is back on the shelf."

Am afraid.

Am *deeply* afraid.

Jen

A·C·K·N·O·W·L·E·D·G·M·E·N·T·S

As always, my biggest thanks have to go to Fletch. You spent six months wandering around without a clue what you were allowed to eat while I worked on this project. To show the extent of my gratitude, I pledge to never consume French fries in your car. (I'd say more nice stuff here about how awesome you are, except you don't actually read my books and therefore won't see my promises; thus I've nicely afforded myself some wiggle room if I ever need to hit a McDonald's while on a solo road trip.)

(What? You can't eat a *salad* while you're driving, right?)

As always, heartfelt thanks go to my agent, Kate Garrick. I would say, "Who'd have imagined we'd ever get here?" but apparently *you* did. You're the reason I'm living my dream. You rock, as do Lauren "Roller Girl" Gilchrist and Brian DeFiore.

A million thanks go to Kara Cesare of NAL, my most

favoritest editor. (Ha! Correct this line; I dare you!) Seriously, you pushed me really far out of my comfort zone on this one, and I'm so proud of what we've accomplished together. I pink-puffy-heart adore you.

To Mary Ann Zissimos and Craig Burke in publicity, I can't express enough gratitude for keeping me both on message and in media. Thanks for making sure people hear it when this particular tree falls in the forest. (Most likely after a night of cocktails.)

Many, many thanks to Kara Welsh and Claire Zion for absolutely betting on my ability to not inhale my own weight in Ding Dongs. (I suspect there's an oddsmaker in Vegas who's pretty unhappy with you both right about now.) And for Lindsay Nouis, the art department, the sales team, production, and everyone else at Penguin who came together on my behalf, thank you so much.

(I know, I know, I already hear the orchestra cueing up. But writing a book takes a lot more than one person, and I need to recognize all of them.)

Endless thanks to my muses, Angie, Stacey Ballis, and Jennifer Coburn, for not only the inspiration but for living this with me. And much love goes to the girls, Carol, Wendy, and Jen.

Big thanks to my parents—I'm sorry for spilling the beans about your culinary skills, but, seriously, I still have nightmares about those hamburgers.

For everyone at the West Loop Gym, particularly Barbie, Tim, Mike, and Julie, who bore the brunt of this experience almost as much as Fletch did, um . . . sorry about all the yelling and swearing. More important, thanks for help-ing me find a way to get healthy. There's special place in heaven for all of you, and there's no wait for the treadmill up there, either.

As promised, here's the super-shout-out to my Postcard Posse—Brooke Kukay Lorenz (and her students), Candice Kakerbeck, Kristin Kaminski, Aimee Harris (and Chance), Chelsey Lentini, Ashley Sandvi, Nicole Voges, Carolyn Purver (nice to finally meet!), Pattie Mangone, Valerie Dixon, Amy Brewer (creator of the Big Asstini), and Kate Anable.

Big hugs and thanks to all the book clubs who hosted me over the summer—next time, I promise there will be more drinking. And thank you for everyone who came to my live events, where there was possibly too much drinking. (See? I told you I wasn't exaggerating about the sweating and spitting.)

Finally, thanks *so* much to the fans and the booksellers. You guys make it all possible.

About the Author

Jen Lancaster is the author of three bestselling memoirs. She's appeared on NPR's *All Things Considered,* written for *Women's Health* and *Cosmopolitan UK,* and she resides in Chicago. When not busy writing, she's vacuuming because she has two shedding dogs, four shedding cats, and one shedding husband. She plans to have them all shaved later this year. Visit her popular blog at www.jennsylvania.com.

Read on for a sneak peek of *New York Times* bestselling author Jen Lancaster's hardcover debut, *Pretty in Plaid*, in which Jen Lancaster reveals how she developed the hubris that perpetually gets her into trouble. Using fashion icons of her youth to tell her hilarious and insightful stories, we'll meet the girl she used to be. . . .

Available from New American Library in May 2009

1996—Navy Suit

"**Y**ou look very stylish," my mother assures me as I gaze warily at myself from every angle in the three-way mirror.

I glower, saying nothing.

She continues, growing more and more excited as she picks and pulls at me, tugging on cuffs and straightening seams. "Very professional but also quite chic. I think this is it! I think this is the one!"

I knit my brows and purse my lips into a straight line. I am NOT buying what she's selling.

Perhaps I'd be quicker to believe my mother's sartorial assessment were she not currently clad in a peasant blouse circa 1981 and Birkenstocks paired with reinforced-toe panty hose. Mind you, this is the same person who refuses to drop off my old clothes at Goodwill, insisting they're still good and she can use them.

Do you know how disconcerting it is to see an almost sixty-year-old woman running around the grocery store wearing a Sig Ep barn dance favor?

Or a neon green T-shirt that reads *I Stand on My Head for Surf Fetish*?[1]

Don't get me wrong, I love my mom, but all her fashion tips come from *Prevention* magazine. Anna Wintour, she's not.

At the moment I'm modeling a double-breasted navy blue suit with silver dollar–sized brass buttons embossed with anchors. The suit is too long in the sleeves, and the skirt ends at the exact spot midcalf that ensures maximum stumpy-ness. An ancient powder puff–haired salesclerk has paired said suit with a short-sleeve white blouse trimmed in gold piping. I look less like I'm getting ready for my first professional job interview, and more like I'm about to welcome a foreign dignitary onto the bridge of my aircraft carrier.

"Lovely!" the salesclerk coos in agreement. When she exhales in this close little room, I can smell the menthol of her lozenge.

I spin around again, noting how the jacket completely belies the fact I have an hourglass figure. I'm cut off at the hips, and I look far wider than I am. The skirt is too tight around my midriff, and the waistband bisects my stomach

---

[1] Granted, she looks really good for her age. But come on—seeing your mom in terry cloth *Three's Company*-type booty shorts is just *wrong*.

into two separate rolls. The skirt has some pleats at the top, and it flattens my butt completely.

No, that's not true.

I do still have a butt—but thanks to poor tailoring, it's simply been moved to the front, giving me ass-belly. What I'm wearing right now is the mom-jeans equivalent of a skirt. The blouse is just that—blousy—and tents, rather than drapes, over my torso.

Yeah, *lovely*.

I continue to scowl, saying nothing.

"Wait!" The clerk snaps her brittle fingers. "I have the perfect touch!" She dashes out of the fitting area and returns moments later with a long scrap of fabric. Given her advanced years, I'm surprised at how quickly she moves. Before I can even blink, she's grabbed me and tied a giant plaid bow around my neck like a big, horrible birthday present.

I see the now-complete outfit, bathed in the sickly green glow of the overhead fluorescent lights.

Oh, the humanity.

"Do you love it?" my mother asks.

I'm speechless. Seriously? If this is how I have to dress to get a real job, maybe I'd rather waitress once I move to Chicago. That way, if I have to put on an ugly outfit for work, people will understand I didn't pick it out myself.

"You look so elegant!" the clerk agrees.

"Why don't we ask Fletch what he thinks?" I finally suggest after a long moment of stunned silence. I exit the fitting room and find Fletch on a rigid ladder-back chair at the side of the store, reading a magazine.

Fletch was sweet to tag along on this shopping expedition, coming all the way over to Fort Wayne for the day, especially given his work schedule. He graduated in December and got his first real job in February, and he's been living up in the Chicago suburbs since then. The plan is for me to move in with him next month, provided I can get a job after graduation. But I'm not so sure I'll ace my interview with the HMO dressed like Admiral Halsey.

"What do you think? Should this outfit be burned or buried?"

Fletch opens his mouth, and gasps fishlike for a couple of seconds. Finally he replies, "Does Captain Steubing know you're not on the Lido Deck right now?"

"It really *is* that bad, isn't it?" I ask flatly. What's unfortunate is I've been shopping all day, and this suit is the closest I've come to finding anything that fits. Size-wise, I'm somewhere in between regular and plus, and nothing is cut for my shape. I need to either lose or gain twenty pounds.[2]

As soon as we're done here at the mall, Fletch and I are supposed to take off for Chicago. I want to be up there tonight so I can do a practice run into the city tomorrow before my interview. But if I don't find something appropriate to wear, I'm not going anywhere. Tears begin to well in the corner of my eyes.

Fletch jumps up and gently puts his arm around me. "No, no, we can work with this. Blue suits are classic, neutral. That's why they're a staple of men's wardrobes. Hmm . . ."

....

[2]Guess which one I eventually choose.

He assesses me again. "Lose the bow. Tell the saleslady to return it to nineteen eighty-two, where it belongs. Maybe you can put on some nice jewelry with the outfit to make it look more . . . *you*." He kisses me on the forehead.

For the first time today, I smile. He really does understand how to make everything better. As I sail back to the fitting room, he calls, "Please tell Isaac I'd like a piña colada."

Aarrgh.

I return to find my mother and the clerk beaming in anticipation. I sigh. "Fine. Wrap it up. I'll take it. But we're going to swap out this stupid bow for some fake pearls."